Research Methods for Educational Dialogue

BLOOMSBURY RESEARCH METHODS FOR EDUCATION SERIES

Edited by Melanie Nind, University of Southampton, UK

The Bloomsbury Research Methods for Education series p overviews of the range of sometimes interconnected and methodological possibilities for researching aspects of ed such as education contexts, sectors, problems or phenomen: volume discusses prevailing, less obvious and more inn methods and approaches for the particular area of educ research.

More targeted than general methods textbooks, authoritative yet accessible books are invaluable resour students and researchers planning their research design and w to explore methodological possibilities to make well-in decisions regarding their choice of methods.

Also available in the series

Research Methods for Classroom Discourse, Jenni Ingram and Elliott

Research Methods for Education in the Digital Age, M: Baden and Gemma Tombs

Research Methods for Social Justice and Equity in E Atkins and Vicky Duckworth

Research Methods for Pedagogy, Melanie Nind, Alicia Kathy Hall

Research Methods for Understanding Professional Learn Hall and Kate Wall

Place-Based Methods for Researching Schools, Pat Tho Christine Hall

Forthcoming

Research Methods for Early Childhood Education, Rosie l Lynn Ang

Research Methods for Educational Dialogue

**RUTH KERSHNER,
SARA HENNESSY,
RUPERT WEGERIF
AND AYESHA AHMED**

BLOOMSBURY ACADEMIC
LONDON • NEW YORK • OXFORD • NEW DELHI • SYDNEY

BLOOMSBURY ACADEMIC
Bloomsbury Publishing Plc
50 Bedford Square, London, WC1B 3DP, UK
1385 Broadway, New York, NY 10018, USA

BLOOMSBURY, BLOOMSBURY ACADEMIC and the Diana logo are trademarks
of Bloomsbury Publishing Plc

First published in Great Britain 2020

ISBN: HB: 978-1-3500-6007-4
PB: 978-1-3500-6008-1
ePDF: 978-1-3500-6010-4
eBook: 978-1-3500-6009-8

Series: Bloomsbury Research Methods for Education

Typeset by Newgen KnowledgeWorks Pvt. Ltd., Chennai, India
Printed and bound in Great Britain

To find out more about our authors and books visit www.bloomsbury.com
and sign up for our newsletters.

CONTENTS

List of Figures vii
List of Tables viii
List of Boxes ix
About the Authors xi
About the Commentators xiii
Series Editor's Foreword xv
Acknowledgements xvii

1 Introduction *Ruth Kershner, Ayesha Ahmed, Sara Hennessy and Rupert Wegerif* 1

2 Foundations for Research on Educational Dialogue *Rupert Wegerif, Ruth Kershner, Sara Hennessy and Ayesha Ahmed* 9

3 Orientations and Ground Rules: A Framework for Researching Educational Dialogue *Rupert Wegerif, with commentary by Antonia Larrain* 27

4 Methodological Developments in Research on Educational Dialogue: Mapping the Field *Ruth Kershner, Sara Hennessy, Rupert Wegerif and Ayesha Ahmed* 47

5 Dialogic Participation and Outcomes: Evaluation and Assessment   *Ayesha Ahmed, with commentary by Gordon Stobart* 75

6 Analytical Coding Schemes for Classroom Dialogue   *Sara Hennessy, with commentary by Adam Lefstein and Matan Barak* 95

7 Methods for Researching Technology-Mediated Dialogue   *Sara Hennessy, with commentary by Manoli Pifarré Turmo* 135

8 Researching Online Dialogues: Introducing the 'Chiasm' Methodology   *Rupert Wegerif, with commentary by M. Beatrice Ligorio* 173

9 Dialogue, Participation and Social Relationships   *Ruth Kershner, with commentary by Antti Rajala* 197

10 Researching Dialogue in Educational Decision-Making   *Ruth Kershner, with commentary by Sherice Clarke* 223

11 Conclusion   *Rupert Wegerif, Ruth Kershner, Sara Hennessy and Ayesha Ahmed* 247

Glossary of Research Methods and Terminology 251
Bibliography 261
Index 289

FIGURES

3.1 Example of similar problem to the one the 9-year-olds are working on together 32

5.1 Group work rating scale 86

6.1 Chart of coded teacher turns over the course of a lesson 107

6.2 Academically productive talk moves 122

7.1 Storyboard to dramatize a war poem in a secondary history class 137

7.2 Brainstorm exploring feelings of character in poem: Secondary English lesson 142

7.3 Collective drawing of trench in secondary history lesson 143

7.4 Using an IWB in thinking about primary and secondary light sources 144

7.5 Example of discussion map co-constructed using Metafora 160

7.6 Concept map annotated by learners in a science lesson 162

7.7 Food chain created in a primary science class 163

7.8 Portrait of Queen Elizabeth I discussed in a secondary history class 164

7.9 Spotlight feature of IWB used to zoom in on portrait of Elizabeth 164

7.10 Multimodal video transcript using a timeline layout 166

8.1 Dynamic-Inverted-Pyramid (DIP) methodology 182

9.1 Some examples of research starting points 206

9.2 Focusing a research project on social and relational aspects of educational dialogue 210

TABLES

3.1 Types of talk 41

4.1 Methodological questions and developments in researching educational dialogue 66

6.1 Strengths and weaknesses of coding dialogue 98

6.2 Coded excerpt from a primary science lesson on the water cycle 111

6.3 Cam-UNAM Scheme for Educational Dialogue Analysis (SEDA) 120

6.4 Coverage of the excerpt by the three schemes 126

7.1 Example of a multimodal analysis table 154

8.1 Difference in the post-blog reflection for 'how' question 189

8.2 Change in pronoun use from pre- to post-reflection for 'how' question 190

9.1 Starting points for developing research on social and relational aspects of educational dialogue, with possible aims and outcomes 203

9.2 Common empirical methods used in, and across, three core strands of research interest in social relationships and dialogue 211

9.3 Some distinctive purposes of common methods for researching dialogic participation and social relationships and generating data for analysis 216

10.1 Self-audit for identifying an initial 'grasp of the issues' (Robson & McCartan, 2016) when researching dialogue and decision-making 232

BOXES

1.1 'Hot topics' in educational dialogue research 4
3.1 Transcript extract 1: A transition in talk 33
4.1 Who is participating in classroom talk? 54
4.2 What is known about teacher collaboration? 60
4.3 A case study of research for inclusive dialogic participation in education: Enhancing community involvement 63
4.4 Investigating a collaborative approach to literature review 71
5.1 Accountability to Knowledge rating scale 87
6.1 Epistemic network analysis – the nitty-gritty of how it works 101
6.2 Selected follow-up moves in Wells's (2001) coding framework 103
6.3 Levels of analysis of dialogue 104
6.4 Water cycle lesson activities 110
6.5 Transacts and orientations 123
7.1 How technology can enhance classroom dialogue 136
7.2 Phases of video review in T-MEDIA project 146
7.3 Common affordances of technology for dialogue 151
9.1 Observing cultural patterns of collaboration and communication 212
9.2 Understanding participants' social and relational experience of dialogue 213
9.3 Investigating wider social and relational contexts of dialogue 214
10.1 Example 1: From didactic to dialogue: Assessing the use of an innovative classroom resource to support decision-making about cannabis use 224
10.2 Example 2: Students' views of factors affecting their bystander behaviours in response to school bullying: A cross-collaborative conceptual qualitative analysis 225

10.3 Example 3: Authenticity and the relevance of discourse and figured worlds in secondary students' discussions of socioscientific issues 226

10.4 Example 4: A sociocultural understanding of children's 'voice' 234

10.5 Example 5: Experiential learning to develop voice 236

10.6 Example 6: Use of digital media to amplify voice 236

10.7 Example 7: Institutional structures, values and commitments 237

10.8 Example 8: Sharing expertise in interprofessional collaboration 239

ABOUT THE
AUTHORS

Ayesha Ahmed is Senior Teaching Associate at the Faculty of Education at the University of Cambridge. Her research focuses on the assessment of dialogue, particularly in small-group discussions, and on validity issues in the design of assessments. She works closely with assessment practitioners and policymakers on research-informed approaches to assessment design. She is a member of both the Psychology, Education and Learning Studies (PELS) research group and the Cambridge Educational Dialogue Research group (CEDiR). She is also a member of the management team of Oracy Cambridge: the Hughes Hall Centre for Effective Spoken Communication and is a Fellow of the Association for Educational Assessment – Europe.

Sara Hennessy is Reader in Teacher Development and Pedagogical Innovation in the Faculty of Education at the University of Cambridge. She is co-founder of the interdisciplinary Cambridge Educational Dialogue Research (CEDiR) group (http://bit.ly/cedirgroup). Her research focuses on technology-mediated classroom dialogue, especially on the use of interactive display screens and mobile devices; teacher professional development; and analytic schemes for looking at the quality of dialogue. She co-led with Christine Howe and Neil Mercer a large-scale ESRC-funded project exploring the relationship between dialogic teaching in schools and pupil attainment, reasoning and attitudes to school (http://tinyurl.com/ESRCdialogue). Sara has also worked with teachers as co-researchers, bridging research and practice through developing and refining theory together.

Ruth Kershner is Lecturer in Psychology of Education and Primary Education in the Faculty of Education at the University of Cambridge. She has particular research interests in inclusive pedagogy and children's classroom learning; collaborative learning; social and emotional relationships in classrooms; teachers' professional learning in school-based inquiry and in the development of dialogic research methods. She is a steering-group member of the Cambridge Educational Dialogue Research Group (CEDiR) and co-leads the classroom dialogue research strand with Sara Hennessy. Recent projects include the development, with CEDiR colleagues, of the Teacher Scheme for Educational Dialogue Analysis (T-SEDA: http://bit.ly/T-SEDA) involving practitioners in reflective inquiry using systematic observation of classroom dialogue and participation.

Rupert Wegerif is Professor of Education in the Faculty of Education at the University of Cambridge. His research focuses on education for dialogue in the context of the Internet Age. He has been working on a general dialogic theory of education as well as conducting research on ways of teaching through dialogue and teaching for dialogue in classrooms and teaching the complex competence of 'learning to learn together' online. He has worked on some substantial funded projects developing internet-based technology supports for dialogic education. He is co-lead with Sara Hennessy of the Cambridge Educational Dialogue Research group (CEDiR) and is currently co-convenor of the Argumentation, Reasoning and Dialogue Special Interest Group (SIG) of the European Association of Research on Learning and Instruction (EARLI).

ABOUT THE COMMENTATORS

Matan Barak is a doctoral candidate in the Department of Education at Ben-Gurion University of the Negev, Israel. His research investigates the social and cultural contexts of classroom discourse as potential levers for educational improvement.

Sherice Clarke is Assistant Professor of Education in the Department of Education Studies at University of California San Diego, United States. Her research focuses on teaching and learning through dialogic pedagogy, with a goal of designing learning environments that promote educational equity for learners of the greatest need.

Antonia Larrain is Associate Professor in the Faculty of Psychology at Universidad Alberto Hurtado, Chile. Her research focuses on the relationship between human speech and cognition, both from a theoretical and empirical perspective, and she has a special interest in processes of thought development and the role that discourse and social situations play in it.

Adam Lefstein is Associate Professor and Chair of the Department of Education at Ben-Gurion University of the Negev, Israel. He employs linguistic ethnographic methods to study classroom discourse and interaction, dialogic pedagogy, teacher learning and educational change.

Maria Beatrice Ligorio is Full Professor in the Department of Educational Sciences, Psychology and Communication at the University of Bari Aldo Moro, Italy. Her main research interests are in blended learning, innovation in higher education, communities, identity, intersubjectivity, dialogical approach, virtual environments, knowledge building, social networks and web-forum in education.

Antti Rajala is a postdoctoral researcher in the Faculty of Educational Sciences at University of Helsinki, Finland. His research focuses on dialogic pedagogy, educational change, and agency in education and he is currently working on the project Constituting Cultures of Compassion in Early Childhood Education.

Gordon Stobart is an honorary research fellow at the Oxford University Centre for Educational Assessment and Emeritus Professor of Education at the Institute of Education, University College London, UK. He has worked for over twenty years on developing Assessment for Learning and his current focus is on how expertise develops and the implications for classroom teaching and learning.

Manoli Pifarré Turmo is Assistant Professor in Educational Psychology at University of Lleida, Spain. Her main research interests are based on how Information and Communication Technologies may influence the development of cognitive, metacognitive and social processes.

SERIES EDITOR'S FOREWORD

The idea of the *Bloomsbury Research Methods for Education* series is to provide books that are useful to researchers wanting to think about research methods in the context of their research area, research problem or research aims. While researchers may use any methods textbook for ideas and inspiration, the onus falls on them to apply something from social science research methods to education in particular, or from education to a particular dimension of education (pedagogy, schools, the digital dimension, practitioner learning, to name some examples). This application of ideas is not beyond us and has led to some great research and also to methodological development. In this series though, the books are more targeted, making them a good place to start for the student, researcher or person wanting to craft a research proposal. Each book brings together in one place the range of sometimes interconnected and often diverse methodological possibilities for researching one aspect or sector of education, one research problem or phenomenon. Thus, readers will quickly find a discussion of the methods they associate with that bit of education research they are interested in, but in addition they will find less obvious and more innovative methods and approaches. A quick look at the glossary will give you an idea of the methods you will find included within each book. You can expect a discussion of those methods that is critical, authoritative *and* situated. In each text the authors use powerful examples of the methods in use in the arena with which you are concerned.

There are other features that make this series distinctive. In each of the books the authors draw on their own research and on the research of others making alternative methodological choices. In this way they address the affordances of the methods in terms of real studies; they illustrate the potential with real data. The authors also discuss the rationale behind the choice of methods and behind how researchers put them together in research designs. As readers you will get behind the scenes of published research and into the kind of methodological decision-making that you are grappling with. In each of the books you will find yourself moving between methods, theory and data; you will find theoretical concepts to think with and with which you might be able to enhance your methods. You will find that the authors develop arguments about methods rather than just describing them.

Research Methods for Educational Dialogue explores methods for researching a dynamic field of education research with eclectic roots. The authors are internationally renowned figures in the development of the field of educational dialogue and they are at the cutting edge of methodological and theoretical developments. Their commitment to dialogue is evident in the way they have put together chapters in dialogue with each other and, unusually for the series, with commentators upon the chapters. You will find within this book a passion for exploring how different methods can evidence the role of dialogue in education and in learning in particular. You will find that it is packed with examples and with detail. Yet the authors succeed in standing back to help us to see what is most critical as we weigh up methodological options for specific purposes. However knowledgeable about educational dialogue you were when you picked up this book, you will find it brings you much to learn and think about, and you will want to read on.

This book (as with any in the series) cannot be the only book you need to read to formulate, justify and implement your research methods. Other books may cover a different range or methods or more operational detail. The aim for this series though, is to provide books that take you to the heart of the methods thinking you will want and need to do. They are books by authors who are equally passionate about their substantive topic and about research methods and they are books that will be invaluable for inspiring deep and informed methods thinking.

Melanie Nind

ACKNOWLEDGEMENTS

A huge thank you to our esteemed colleagues from seven countries who provided independent commentaries on each of the substantive chapters of the book; these have widened the dialogic space in more ways than one. We are also very grateful to our colleagues in the Cambridge Educational Dialogue Research (CEDiR) group (http:// bit.ly/cedirgroup), who kindly gave constructive feedback on earlier drafts of our chapters, especially Farah Ahmed, Elisa Calcagni, Pete Dudley, Riikka Hofmann, Fiona Maine and Louis Major. It is impossible to list everyone whose work has influenced us over the years but other key collaborators whose ideas we have drawn on in various ways in this book include CEDiR group co-founders Rupert Higham, Christine Howe, Neil Mercer, Sylvia Rojas-Drummond and Paul Warwick.

We are grateful to series editor, Melanie Nind, and our anonymous reviewers for their helpful comments and suggestions. We also wish to thank Catherine Ridler who expertly helped us prepare our manuscript for publication. Finally, we acknowledge all of the participants and practitioner co-researchers in our research studies, without whom this book would not have been possible. Sponsors of the work are acknowledged in individual chapters. The images derive from our classroom research studies unless indicated otherwise; originators and participants gave consent for them to be shared.

ACKNOWLEDGMENTS

CHAPTER ONE

Introduction

Ruth Kershner, Ayesha Ahmed, Sara Hennessy and Rupert Wegerif

This book is about research methods for educational dialogue. It includes many examples of different research approaches, methods and projects, and it is written to be accessible. We hope that researchers of all kinds, practitioner-researchers and academic colleagues, will find it useful, especially those new to the area.

The field of educational dialogue is emerging as a distinctive area of interest among researchers and practitioners. It is gaining strength as a meaningful idea to colleagues across the world and many ideas are being shared, so now is not the time to delineate its boundaries or fix its content. Educational dialogue is a broad and dynamic field that currently encompasses different research traditions, interests and methods. In this book we refer to a wide variety of international research studies with children and adults in different educational contexts. We are sure that methodologies will continue to develop in interesting and useful ways as people continue to discuss their research approaches and findings. There are many associated publications and lively debates about its nature, origins, theoretical foundations and methods, as discussed in this book and elsewhere, including in the international handbook on dialogic education edited by Mercer, Wegerif and Major (forthcoming), which contains fifty chapters reporting work undertaken in twenty countries.

A recent working paper of the Cambridge Educational Dialogue Research Group (CEDiR Group, 2018) presented extended online discussions about educational dialogue. Contributors were asked to warrant their perspectives through referencing relevant research. Several 'lines of inquiry' arose in these conversations, focusing on the meaning of educational dialogue, the relationship between educational dialogue and learning, and the means by which dialogue may be supported and constrained. Some key questions are given below, each leading to wide-ranging theoretical and methodological discussions that raised further questions for research:

1. Should we define educational dialogue as that which *does* occur or that which *should* occur in educational settings?
2. How can dialogue be defined in relation to other processes, such as communication, talk, non-verbal interaction, and particular sets of discourse features?
3. Is there a potential conflict between dialogue understood philosophically as an ethical form of relating authentically to others, and dialogue seen as a pedagogical tool?
4. Which aspects of dialogic encounters make dialogue a natural medium for learning?
5. What are the conditions, attitudes or orientations that are required for genuine educational dialogue to take place?
6. How might certain methods and outcomes evidence the role of dialogue in learning?

The last question is particularly relevant to thinking about research methods for educational dialogue when supporting learning is the main concern. Similar questions could be asked about evidencing the role of dialogue in decision-making, conflict resolution and so on. As people added their views to the working paper and compared ideas about the investigation of dialogue and learning, it became evident that the answers are far from simple, yet all agreed on the importance of establishing a firm research base as a priority. In the working paper it was noted that several contributors had drawn attention to

the sheer diversity of research objectives and approaches that have resulted in the development of a substantial but highly fragmented evidence base ... There are both massive constraints and opportunities in the accumulation of evidence, much of which stem from the open system within which educational research takes place. (CEDiR Group, 2018, p. 27)

This reference to the educational research context gives a useful perspective. Educational research is indeed diverse, but it has a common core of educational purpose even while acknowledging that educational aims may differ. Similarly, the contributors to the CEDiR working paper had educational relevance and value in mind while recognizing considerable challenges in strengthening the evidence base in a diverse field of study. The paper ends on an optimistic note in outlining how current work is moving forward in many innovative ways. Entering into dialogue about research is a process that itself brings to mind all sorts of interesting research ideas, knowledge and personal memories. This is something we have found in the writing of this book and would want to extend to readers.

What is educational dialogue?

Current 'hot topics' in researching educational dialogue range from classroom dialogue and learning to large-scale interventions for intercultural understanding and conflict resolution. From our own research, wider reading and discussion we would propose the following list. Some of these topics are covered individually in Chapters 5–10 while others represent cross-cutting themes and emerging areas of research interest. General methodological approaches and developments in the field as a whole are outlined in Chapter 4.

All of these 'hot topics' have a case for inclusion in the field of educational dialogue research. There are several overlaps between them, such as the application of technology-mediated dialogue in both research on classroom dialogue and learning (see Chapter 6) and for intercultural dialogue (see Chapter 8). Another book in this series, *Research Methods for Classroom Discourse* (Ingram & Elliott, 2019), deals in more detail with conversation analysis, discursive psychology and positioning theory, all of which approaches are very relevant for studying educational dialogues. There are also connections with neighbouring fields of study that

Box 1.1 'Hot topics' in educational dialogue research

1. classroom dialogue, learning and knowledge construction in different domains and activities
2. technology-mediated dialogue
3. social and relational conditions for, and of, participation in dialogue
4. dialogue, evaluation and assessment
5. educational decision-making, dialogue and stakeholder involvement (including student voice)
6. professional inquiry, dialogic collaboration and learning
7. intercultural dialogue
8. dialogue and conflict resolution
9. multimodal dialogue
10. silence in dialogue

have their own identities and discourses, such as oracy (e.g. Mercer, Warwick & Ahmed, 2017), argumentation (e.g. Schwarz & Baker, 2017), culturally responsive pedagogy (e.g. Gay, 2010; Richards & Robertson, 2016), multimodal literacy (e.g. Jewitt, 2006), student voice (e.g. Flutter & Rudduck, 2004), teacher collaboration (e.g. Vangrieken,, Dochy, Raes, & Kyndt, 2015), community involvement (e.g. Flecha & Soler, 2013), inclusion (e.g. Kershner, 2016) and peace education (e.g. Cremin & Bevington, 2017; Gill & Niens, 2014). Different terminology is used by researchers in these various areas; for instance, many analysts now talk about multimodal interaction rather than 'non-verbal' interaction in order to acknowledge the multiplicity and equal importance of interlinked modes of communication.

We see this diversity and interconnectedness as a strength: it seems reasonable to expect researchers who locate themselves in the field of educational dialogue to be open to new ideas and eager to construct new ways of thinking about education in collaboration with others. This is one of the reasons that we have invited international colleagues to comment on certain chapters in this book, from their own perspectives and with reference to their own research. The four authors of this book also have their own interests and voices, as will be seen in different chapters. A familiar field of study can sometimes be viewed in a blinkered way, so we would argue that it is worth actively seeking out alternative approaches and views in order to clarify and extend one's own thinking. Engaging in this sort of dialogue is intended to give due attention to the diverse research approaches and methods that are both close enough, and different enough, to prompt productive methodological conversation.

The structure of this book

Chapters 2–4 are introductory chapters in which we lay the foundations for the rest of the book. In Chapters 5–10 we address specific approaches to research methods in educational dialogue. Each of these latter chapters is followed by a commentary from an international expert in the field.

In Chapter 2 we discuss the theoretical underpinnings of the field of educational dialogue research. In particular, we outline dialogic theory and the concept of shared dialogic space. Education is seen as a complex adaptive system, requiring caution in making simple causal assumptions. Innovative approaches to theory testing such as simulations and design-based research are discussed. The chapter concludes with a discussion of the chiasm: the dialogue between an inside perspective and an outside perspective which is essential to dialogic research approaches.

Chapter 3 builds on the theories described in Chapter 2 and outlines a framework for researching educational dialogue. A case is made for embedding theory in research methodology, prompting the active questioning of culturally default assumptions throughout the research process. Three familiar types of talk – disputational, cumulative and exploratory (Mercer, 1995) – are revisited and developed to include playful talk. There follows a commentary that extends the discussion of playful talk, imagination and creative thinking.

Chapter 4 provides an overview of methodological developments in the field of educational dialogue. Translation between research and practice is problematized, and four key methodological questions are discussed: how we consider dialogic principles in designing research, how we investigate outcomes of dialogic participation, the impact of technology, and the importance of engaging with practitioners and other stakeholders. The chapter concludes with a discussion of literature review as a dialogue research method.

Chapter 5 focuses on the assessment and evaluation of educational dialogue, asking why and how we might want to do this. The chapter presents three examples of assessment of different forms of dialogue: small group dialogue, whole class dialogue and second-language paired dialogue. Finally, the role of dialogue in Assessment for Learning is discussed. The commentary picks up on the importance of being open to the many methodological possibilities and to consider the fitness-for-purpose of the instruments that we use.

Chapter 6 concentrates on analytic coding schemes for classroom dialogue at the level of conversational turns or utterances. The chapter includes a transcript of a dialogue which the author has coded using three schemes in order to illustrate how these schemes differ and overlap. Methodological issues such as granularity and reliability are aired and illustrated. The commentators add to this discussion by bringing in a range of non-cognitive dimensions of dialogue from their own linguistic, ethnographic and pedagogic perspectives.

Chapter 7 explores how technology can mediate dialogue and what the implications are for research methods. Issues and challenges of capturing and analysing multimodal dialogue are discussed, and examples are given to illustrate how technology can support learners and teachers thinking together in educational settings. The commentary adds further weight to this discussion, including the notion of a multi-voiced analysis, which resonates with discussion in several other chapters.

Chapter 8 discusses online dialogues. The argument is made that removing dialogues from their face-to-face context enables us to see what is most essential in educational dialogues. The idea of the 'chiasm' methodology introduced in Chapter 2 is revisited and expanded with an example from recent research on a programme of dialogue between students in different countries intended to build understanding in contexts of violent extremism. The commentary expands on this dialogic theoretical framework with reference to other research projects on online learning.

In Chapter 9 the focus changes towards research on the social and relationship aspects of participation in educational dialogue. Cultural and ethical issues are explored and starting points for designing research studies in this area are suggested. The importance of combining different research methods is argued. The commentary on this chapter draws on further research, highlighting the importance of organizational culture, compassion and community relations in dialogic interactions, suggesting that fostering care is a challenge for education itself.

Chapter 10 explores how dialogue interacts with decision-making by building shared understandings. Cultural and ethical issues are seen as important here, as is the need to investigate equitable participation in dialogue. Several research examples of engagement in 'real-life' decision-making are discussed and compared. The commentary expands on the notion of who has a legitimate 'voice' in these decisions and how research must attend to the coordinated processes at different levels that result in decisions being made.

We end the book in Chapter 11 with some concluding remarks, looking to the future of the field and encouraging further engagement in dialogic research.

CHAPTER TWO

Foundations for Research on Educational Dialogue

Rupert Wegerif, Ruth Kershner, Sara Hennessy and Ayesha Ahmed

Defining educational dialogue

In everyday language the term 'dialogue' is often used quite loosely to refer to almost any kind of social interaction. Bakhtin, a Russian philosopher referred to as a major source for recent approaches to dialogic education, defined dialogue indirectly when he claimed that 'if an answer does not give rise to a new question from itself, it falls out of the dialogue' (Bakhtin, 1986, p. 168). Robin Alexander quotes this sentence from Bakhtin in outlining his Dialogic Teaching approach. This approach aims to engage students in sustained stretches of talk, enabling speakers and listeners to explore and build on their own and others' ideas (Alexander, 2008).

It is sometimes assumed that educational dialogue is solely about talk in classrooms, but this can be a limited view. Discussions about the meaning of educational dialogue have ranged from its connections to classroom talk towards wider consideration of the intrinsically human disposition to engage with other people and develop mutual understanding (CEDiR Group, 2018), indeed to be more 'open to learning' (Phillipson & Wegerif, 2017). The definition of dialogue by Bakhtin given above does not necessarily limit itself to explicit spoken language or even to any form of explicit language. Since personality and tone of voice are part of dialogues for Bakhtin, it is clear that some forms of music, jazz for example, and some forms of improvised dance can be dialogic. Bakhtin was interested in the way in which holding different ideas or perspectives together in the tension of a dialogue leads to new insights. For Bakhtin, dialogue is not just about talk or texts but includes the more general idea that the inter-animation of different perspectives can lead to mutual illumination (Bakhtin, 1984).

Dialogue as a way of making meaning

There are not many contemporary approaches to education that do not imply at least some use of dialogue. But a specific focus on educational dialogue tends to bring with it the view that dialogue is essential to meaning-making. This focus on how we gain knowledge suggests that education should be understood as engaging students in an ongoing process of shared enquiry taking the form of a dialogue (Linell, 2009; Wells, 1999). Dialogic teaching, for example, developed by Alexander, mentioned above, is **epistemological** in focus, drawing students into the process of the shared construction of knowledge. A similar epistemological focus can often be found in the community of enquiry approach in Philosophy for Children (Lipman, 2003), in the promotion of Exploratory Talk (Littleton & Mercer, 2013) and in the promotion of Accountable Talk (Michaels, O'Connor & Resnick, 2008).

The theory that meaning requires dialogue between two or more perspectives is often referred to using the technical term 'dialogism' or simply 'dialogic'. At its simplest, dialogic theory makes the claim that the meaning of any utterance is not given by a dictionary but always depends upon how it is being used within a dialogue. Someone saying the word 'sick' to me, for example, does not mean anything on its own. To interpret meaning you need to know the context, what it is a response to, what it is trying to achieve and how it is actually taken up (Linell, 2009; Rommetveit, 1992). Put this way, dialogism looks like common sense. But this apparent common sense has implications for how we understand education, and research on education, that many find quite challenging. The term 'dialogic' used in this more technical way is a contrast to the term 'monologic' which expresses the idea that everything has one correct meaning in one true perspective on the world. For 'dialogic', by contrast, knowledge is never direct knowledge of an external world but always emerges only within dialogue as an aspect of dialogue. This is simply because knowledge has to take the form of an answer to a question, and questions arise in the context of dialogue – both dialogue between human voices and dialogue with the larger context or the world around. Since the dialogue is never closed, the questions we ask will change, and so what counts as knowledge is never final. The dialogue is never closed because when you think it is over and reflect back on it, your understanding of the dialogue inevitably takes the form of 'answering words' even if these are not spoken or written down or even explicitly recognized as such. Since your reflection is itself a new utterance in the dialogue, the dialogue is not yet finished.

Dialogue as a way of being

Epistemology is about how we know things, so any purely epistemological approach in education tends to assume that there is a knowing self and an external reality that is known about. Some claim that taking dialogic seriously as a theory of meaning implies that it is not just a means to knowledge construction mediating between selves and reality, but that how we understand the nature of selves and reality is also part of the dialogue. Applied to education this **ontological** interpretation of dialogic suggests that dialogue is not just a means or tool to be used to help construct content knowledge, but, more than that, engagement in dialogue is a way to change ourselves and to change our reality.

Different versions of ontologic dialogic education focus in different ways on understanding and transforming (a) the self, or (b) reality as a whole, or (c) social reality. Understanding the self as a kind of dialogic author, and education as developing both the freedom and the responsibility of this authorial self defines one strand of ontologic dialogic educational theory (Matusov, 2009; Sidorkin, 1999). Another strand puts more focus on the transformation of reality, seeing education as about learning to participate more fully in a kind of universal dialogue (Kennedy, 2014; Wegerif, 2007). A more apparently political interpretation of dialogic education can be seen in the vision of Freire (1971) – and those influenced by Freire (e.g. Flecha, 2000) – of dialogic education as a way to empower the oppressed such that they can learn to 'name' their own reality. For this approach, dialogic education implies both an expansion of consciousness ('conscientization') and, at the same time, a transformation of social reality. Where a particular concept of what counts as social justice is established in advance of dialogue then this Freirean vision may be accused of being instrumental and manipulative rather than genuinely dialogic (Matusov, 2009). However, if the focus is on empowering all students to be able to participate as fully as possible in dialogues that shape a shared social reality, then this is a truly dialogic educational goal, albeit one with political implications.

Discussion of the definition of educational dialogue

The theory of educational dialogue has a variety of strands and there are significant differences in focus across these strands. Nonetheless, some shared themes emerge. The first of these is the dialogic form. Dialogic approaches to education tend to involve interaction that looks like dialogue, usually in the form of face-to-face talk including questioning and exploration of ideas of a kind that might have been familiar to Socrates. However, what makes this talk educational dialogue or 'dialogic education' is not the external form alone, but also the internal or lived experience of a shared space which Buber called 'the in-between' ([1923] 1958) and which, more recently, is often referred to as 'dialogic space' (e.g. Mercer, Warwick, Kershner & Kleine Staarman, 2010). The idea behind dialogic space is summed up by Merleau-Ponty, who wrote that when dialogue works it is no longer possible to say who is thinking (Merleau-Ponty, 1968) because we find ourselves thinking together. This connects with the sociocultural notion of 'interthinking', which involves people in combining their intellectual resources to achieve more that an individual could on their own.

In teaching through the opening of a shared dialogic space, educational dialogue draws students into participation in the processes through which shared knowledge is constructed and validated. In other words, educational dialogue or a 'dialogic education' often promotes dialogue as an end in itself, usually alongside other educational goals such as acquiring content knowledge. The phrase 'dialogue as an end in itself' means that, as a result of participation in educational dialogue or in 'dialogic education', students are expected to become better skilled at dialogue, which means getting better at learning things together with others.

There are three levels of definition of educational dialogue.

- At level one, educational dialogue can be defined through its form, that is, it looks like a dialogue with different voices participating roughly equally and all being listened to with respect. Contributions are chained, that is, they respond to each other.

- At level two, educational dialogue can be defined by its epistemology: new meaning emerges out of the opening of a dialogic space in which there is uncertainty and a multiplicity of perspectives.

- At a third, ontological, level, the dialogue itself is a real thing and not just a 'relation' between prior real things such as people. The dialogic space that opens out of the gap between voices in a dialogue can have impact and that needs to be expanded within education. Dialogue now is not just about knowledge construction but also about changing people and society or perhaps about changing how people understand themselves. For this ontological level it is important that people change to become more dialogic as a result of educational dialogues.

Although they can be found separately, in practice all three levels of educational dialogue can coexist. Programmes based upon educational dialogue often combine, first, a dialogic form, second, opening a shared dialogic space and third, the aim of teaching for better quality dialogue.

The sociocultural research tradition

Much research on educational dialogue aligns itself with sociocultural theory and cites the Russian psychologist Vygotsky as a key influence. But 'sociocultural' is a broad term. Perhaps the easiest way to understand it is as a reaction to the decontextualized and overly mathematical or logical nature of much psychological theory related to education in the 1950s and 1960s. Sociocultural researchers questioned the assumption that cognition is an individual property and a logical process like a computer operation such that it is the same everywhere regardless of context. For sociocultural theory meaning is situated and it depends upon the context (Scribner & Cole, 1978). Cognition, for example, is always found bound up with achieving culturally desired ends in a context where the thinking is done with cultural artefacts and also usually with other people. Dialogism, with its stress on the contextual nature of meaning within dialogues, fits well within this broad sociocultural theory.

The foundations of sociocultural theory in education tend to be attributed to the work of Vygotsky ([1934] 1987; 1978) writing in the Soviet Union in the 1920s and early 1930s who argued that thinking cannot be separated from culture and particularly from the acquisition and use of language as mediated by teachers. He described language as both a cultural tool (for the development and sharing of knowledge among members of a community or society) and as a psychological tool (for structuring the processes and content of individual thought). He also proposed that there is a close relationship between social thinking, exchanging words in dialogues, for example, and individual thinking which could be understood as a form of internal dialogue or 'talking to yourself' (Fernyhough, 1996). All the 'higher mental functions', Vygotsky claimed, are an internalization of processes that are to be found originally in social interaction.

Mercer (2002) argues that one of the cultural tools that children need to learn how to use in order to think well is what he calls 'language as a tool for thinking'. This includes an educationally effective type of interaction named 'Exploratory Talk' and often characterized by features that include explicit reasoning. Studies of the impact of Exploratory Talk suggest that it is effective in improving children's reasoning and problem solving (e.g. Mercer & Sams, 2006; Monaghan, 2005). Mercer proposes that applying sociocultural ideas in analysing classroom discourse leads to a distinctive method which he calls **sociocultural discourse analysis.** This kind of (mixed methods) analysis focuses on the use of language as a social mode of thinking, a tool for teaching-and-learning, constructing knowledge, creating joint understanding and tackling problems collaboratively (Mercer, 2004). Mercer (2013) summarizes the causal processes that might be behind the link between Exploratory Talk and problem-solving as 'appropriation, co-construction and transformation'. *Appropriation* is where one child shows another how to solve a problem, so it is about transmitting knowledge. *Co-construction* is about generating new knowledge together. Mercer's third causal process, *transformation*, refers to the idea that through engaging in dialogue with others children learn to engage more effectively in 'intra-mental' dialogue.

Vygotsky (1978) proposed that education takes place in a *zone of proximal development* (ZPD) where learners are drawn beyond their current individual level of understanding and ability by working with a teacher, adult or more competent peer. In the ZPD the spontaneous concepts of the child are taken up by the teacher and grafted onto the scientific concepts that pre-exist in the culture and are represented by tools such as mathematical procedures and concept words (Vygotsky, [1934] 1987). A key concept that emerged from applying Vygotsky's ZPD notion is that of 'scaffolding', referring to the way a teacher will simplify a task initially to make it easier for a learner and then gradually remove the scaffold until the learner can manage alone (Wood, Bruner & Ross, 1976). There are various issues with relating the concept of scaffolding to teaching dialogue. In a way dialogue is a kind of scaffold for individual thinking whereby complex ideas can be distributed around a group and sustained with prompts and recall moves, but it is not the sort of scaffold that we intend to remove (Fernández et al., 2001). In educational dialogue the focus is usually as much, if not more, on the quality of group thinking than on the quality of individual thinking. Some argue that thinking in a dialogue is very different from the kind of thinking you get through scaffolding (Bakker, Smit & Wegerif, 2015). Nonetheless, scaffolding has a role in dialogic education or education for dialogue (e.g. Rojas-Drummond, Torreblanca, Pedraza, Vélez & Guzmán, 2013). One way to think of this role is as scaffolding for dialogue (Kazak, Wegerif & Fujita, 2015). Even a simple prompt like asking an open 'why?' question and pausing for a bit, can be seen as part of how a teacher or peer can scaffold for dialogue.

Implicature and culture change

Conversational implicature (Grice, 1975) concerns the assumptions that people make, and often have to make, to interpret what others say in a dialogue. For example, we normally assume that what another person says is relevant, so if I ask 'where are the keys?' and my son says 'on the table' then I can just assume that he means the car keys I am looking for as I am about to leave the house and that he means that they are on the nearest and most obvious table to both of us. Of course, there are lots of misunderstandings but that is why we know that the rules of implicature apply, because we can see the assumptions being made that generate the misunderstandings. 'They are not on the table!', 'Yes they are – I didn't mean the big table, I meant the small table in the hall' and so on.

Implicature in dialogue is interesting because it suggests that explicit meaning rests upon a larger background of shared implicit assumptions. It is only because we have a shared 'form of life' as Wittgenstein (2009) put it that people can make sense of what others are saying. Grice (1975) proposed a universal set of criteria for making meaning, including the relevance assumption that whatever is said is relevant to the matter at hand. However, work in linguistic anthropology suggests that the implicit assumptions that make up implicature vary across cultures and change over time (Blimes, 1993). They depend on who we think we are and what we think we are doing. Moreover, if we do not question them and take conscious responsibility for them, they determine who we think we are and what we think we are doing. Foucault (1972) has suggested, for example, that it is not so much that subjects (us) speak the discourse as we tend to assume, it is the other way around: the subjects – us – are spoken by the discourse.

Implicature features in research on educational dialogue in the idea of 'ground rules' (Mercer, 2004). Ground rules need to be shared. If one person had a set of implicit assumptions that she used to interpret the meaning of utterances and no one else shared those then they would not be ground rules. While ground rules might be found reflected in neural activity in individual brains, their primary nature is to be shared and social. Ground rules are invisible features of dialogic space. Dialogic space is that meaning space shared between people in dialogue together. When ground rules are made explicit, written down on cards and discussed together, then they are part of the contents of dialogic space. Anything that enters into dialogic space can be seen from multiple perspectives. It becomes a sign in an ongoing dialogue with a meaning that evolves as the dialogue moves on. However, before they are made into objects of shared attention, before they are written down, they are hidden in the background. Ground rules originate as part of the invisible architecture of dialogic space. Although, as Wegerif (2007) has argued, dialogic space always has an infinite potential for generating new meaning, in practice any given dialogue has a hidden architecture that shapes what is likely to be said and what is likely to be thought.

Ground rules are part of what Merleau-Ponty (1968) called, in a striking phrase, 'the invisibles of this world'. They lie just beneath the audible and visible surface of dialogues structuring them from below. But the exciting thing is that we can make them visible and we can alter them and send them back underground again, as it were, to become invisible again behind behaviour. This is exactly what we do when we teach ground rules for effective dialogue. By teaching ground rules for talk in classrooms we can consciously take charge of some of the implicit shared assumptions that shape us and re-design them so that we can collectively think together better, learn together better and live together better.

Monologic and dialogic

One important often unacknowledged source for dialogic theory is Martin Buber's distinction between the 'I–it' orientation and the 'I–thou' orientation (Buber, [1923] 1958). Buber pointed out that there are two fundamentally different ways to relate to other people and, indeed, to the whole world and to any and every thing within the world. One way is to objectify others such that they can be measured, analysed and compared. With the 'I–it' orientation one can claim that one understands another person and form theories about them, but without needing to engage with them, feel any empathy for them or be able to see things from their point of view. While research based on taking the 'I–it' orientation claims to understand others it offers only a partial understanding based on taking an external view. Another kind of understanding of others and perhaps also, according to Buber, of otherness in general, can be provided by engaging in dialogue with others in order to understand what it might be like to be them; to see, as far as possible, through their eyes and to walk, as far as possible, in their shoes. This other kind of understanding or knowledge implies taking what Buber refers to as the 'I–thou' orientation. This is about listening to others as if what they say matters. This form of understanding means entering into a shared space. Buber refers to this as 'das Zwischen' or the space of the In-Between. In more recent dialogic theory in education Buber's 'in-between' has been linked to the 'dialogic space' discussed earlier. In dialogic space 'the researcher' has to be open to being questioned and understood as much as the other or object of the research. To understand what is going on in a dialogue one has to be a participant in that dialogue. To be a participant means to be open to learning from others. For a researcher to understand meaning in a dialogue, even a recording of a dialogue after the event, is not possible without entering, however vicariously, into a form of participant–observer mode. The 'outside' of the dialogue, the words and other signs recorded and transcribed, do not give us access to the 'inside' of the dialogue or its meaning unless we enter that dialogue as a participant (Habermas, 1979, p. 29).

Much research that claims to be 'scientific' adopts a monologic world view. Monologism is the idea (delusion) that there is only one correct perspective on the world. This worldview was rightly satirized by Foucault (1972) as the idea that everything relevant to understanding the world can be laid out in front of you on the surface of a table. While monologism as an approach has been quite effective in some areas of knowledge, its fatal flaw is that any map of reality that we draw has to come from an embodied perspective. While this problem might not be too obvious in studies of rock formations, it becomes very obvious in studies of classroom discourse. The problem is that we only ever really understand what is going on in the talk that we record and analyse because we are vicarious participants in the dialogue. Dialogic assumes there are always multiple voices in play and so, to interpret the meaning of a dialogue, we need to enter into dialogue with it as one voice amongst others. This theoretical understanding is a challenge to the field of education research to develop research methods that can acknowledge the situated perspective of researchers whilst also producing shared knowledge that is of general value.

Design-based research as a way to do living dialogic modelling

Monologic science tends to understand by explaining in terms of causal models. If we code and count classroom talk and relate this to outcomes, the implication can be that certain kinds of language use are causing results on tests in much the same sort of way that, for example, taking a certain drug treatment might lower blood pressure. Yet the influences on students' test results are many and complicated. So does taking a dialogic stance imply that we have to abandon this sort of 'scientific' research and all hope of a scientific explanation?

Complexity theory in mathematics offers a serious challenge to the traditional monologic and linear approach to causal modelling. In complex systems, small differences in inputs can lead to large difference in outputs in an unpredictable and apparently irregular way. Monologic causal models assume that input A is going to lead to output B in a consistent way. The technique of causal modelling arose in the study of relatively closed and relatively simple systems where it works well. However learning in a classroom is perhaps one of the most complex adaptive systems available to study. It is said of weather systems that a small change made by a butterfly flapping its wings over the Amazon might lead, in theory, to a major change such as a storm over New York. However the complexity in classrooms is even greater as, unlike the weather, in classrooms conscious agents adapt to each other's behaviour. It is entirely plausible that small changes in input such as a smile from a teacher or the wrong word said at the wrong time could have large impacts on learning outcomes. The simple monologic assumptions of linear causation applied in most quantitative research on classroom learning seem inappropriate once complexity is taken seriously.

An alternative approach to modelling in the light of complexity is to produce simulations with many agents following rules and then to run the simulation and empirically observe what happens (Casti, 1997; Edmonds & Meyer, 2015; Preiser et al., 2018). Computer simulations of complex adaptive systems are based on a computer implementation of the complex feedback loops that characterize dialogues and dialogicality. Casti (1997) argues that such simulations represent a new scientific method distinct from methods of experiment and linear mathematical modelling. A complex adaptive system is any system in which several agents reciprocally adapt to each other. Once agents reciprocally adapt to each other the circular feedback loops involved produce a level of complexity that makes reduction to a monological model impossible. One solution adopted to studying complex adaptive systems is to simulate them with programmes in which multiple agents are each given a set of rules of behaviour and possibly also rules on how to adapt those rules and then set loose to interact. Such studies have found that the interaction of many agents each following simple rules can result in the 'emergence' of new self-organizing systems that cannot be predicted or explained by the rules that the agents are following. The classic often quoted example is the simulation of flocking behaviour which was achieved by giving virtual birds three simple rules to guide their flight: keep a minimum distance from neighbours, fly at about the same speed as neighbours and always fly towards the perceived centre of the mass of birds. Understanding flocking had been seen as a hard problem until this simulation clarified how it might work (Waldrop, 1992). An illustration of 'emergence' in complex adaptive systems closer to dialogues is provided by Axelrod's (1997) various demonstrations of the emergence of apparently co-operative behaviour in simulations of social interaction.

While it might be interesting to study learning systems through computer simulations that incorporate dialogic complexity (e.g. see Watson & Szathmáry, 2016) that is not an approach yet taken by the authors of this book. Instead we discuss a related approach to be implemented live in classrooms. For instance, Chapter 3 describes a dialogical model of reason or social cognition that includes intersubjective orientations and a description of the social ground rules followed by agents in an interaction. Teaching these orientations and ground rules to students and then empirically observing what happens represents research using a living dialogical model. This research methodology is a specific application of **design-based research** (Bakker, 2018). Design-based research is perfect for this kind of living dialogic modelling experiment. Related to **action research** in its focus on understanding and developing practice, it puts the focus on testing and developing theory by implementing it in teaching, often in collaboration with practitioners, and evaluating the results insofar as they impact on theory and lead to confirmation or revision of the theory.

Influential approaches to teaching educational dialogue have emerged from close-to-practice educational design-based research (EDBR). The Exploratory Talk approach described in Chapter 3 was refined and developed through many iterations of observing talk in classrooms, intervening to teach for talk in certain ways, observing the consequences of the intervention, revising the intervention and then trying again until the way of teaching achieved the results desired. Although this process was recorded (Wegerif & Scrimshaw, 1997), it was not fully understood as an example of EDBR at the time perhaps because the literature on EDBR was still emerging (Bakker, 2018). Hilliard (2013) offers a more recent account of EDBR applied to research educational dialogue as a PhD research project. Seeking to improve the quality of argumentation in A Level History essays, Hilliard tried introducing educational dialogue into her teaching. Many small teaching experiments were used changing factors such as the 'ground rules' that were taught by the teacher, the timing of the talk sessions within the overall teaching and learning process and also the way in which the students were told to introduce and refer to historical evidence. In this way, over multiple iterations, a way of integrating dialogic talk in small groups was developed that was effective in improving the quality of written history essays.

The role of technology

The default assumption carried by the word dialogue still tends to be face-to-face dialogue mediated by talk in the form of sound waves in the air modulated by the vocal cords of participants. The dominance of this single context can blind people to the need to take the cognitive **affordances** of the medium into account in studies of dialogue. The notion of affordances relates to how technologies might *potentially* be used, the 'enabling conditions' (Linell, 2009) and how their functional properties are *perceived* to support learning (Gibson, 1982). As Ong (2013) points out in his seminal comparison of oracy and literacy, face-to-face talk has an effervescence problem: the meaning tends to vanish almost as soon as it is heard. Therefore people use various strategies to keep what was said in play. Technology is often involved in providing the continuity between talk episodes needed for educational progress. Literacy can also mediate dialogue but this offers a very different set of affordances. Writing enables the seeing of words and so the analysis of meaning (Wegerif, 2013). It supports the possibility of a very different kind of thinking from that afforded by oracy, a thinking in terms of abstract classifications that remain fixed over a range of contexts and the whole idea of truth as a representation rather than of truth as a kind of relationship (Goody & Goody, 1977). Writing has an extraordinary power to transcend space and time. Contemporary education systems globally are based on the affordance of writing to represent knowledge as if it was a kind of thing that can be held in a store (books in a library for example) and transmitted across generations. The monological delusion of a knowledge that exists outside of dialogue is probably a product of this educational affordance of writing, especially in print. This does not mean that writing cannot also be used to carry very dialogic dialogues. Indeed Bakhtin's analysis of dialogicity is based on written texts (Bakhtin, 1986). The methodology of literature review can itself be dialogic in purpose and form (as discussed in Chapter 4).

There is no simple technological determinism in the impact of mediating technologies on the qualities and cognitive consequences of dialogues. However there is an influence that comes from an affordance that perhaps is best expressed as a probability gradient: different media make different kinds of thinking more or less easy. New media provide new ways of engaging in dialogue that carry new affordances. We explore this in subsequent chapters. Some of these affordances are of new forms of dialogue altogether.

The chiasm

Much empirical research on educational dialogue treats it as if it was a thing in the world that can be located and measured. But this is to assume a monologic ontology. In taking a monological stance perhaps researchers were seduced by the apparent obviousness and graspableness of face-to-face dialogues. The more evasive and intangible nature of new technologically mediated forms of dialogue, especially online dialogue, might help us develop a dialogic form of analysis more appropriate to the nature of what it is that we are studying.

While research often seems to be motivated by the fantasy of reducing everything to a single formula within a closed system, it is not really how we understand. Ethnographers have long struggled with the tension between 'emic' knowledge that is all about understanding the point of view of the group being studied and 'etic' knowledge that is interpreting the same group from the outside, applying a more universal scheme, labelling their means of production as 'hunter-gatherer' for example or their religious word-view as 'animist' (Holbraad & Pedersen, 2017). The kind of knowledge produced by Social Anthropology always implies a combination of the emic and the etic. We can only become aware of and try to make sense of indigenous ways of thinking because we see them from an outside perspective. We can only take an emic or external perspective on the basis of some insider knowledge which we translate and interpret into our outsider scheme (Pelto & Pelto, 1978).

If we look at a dialogue from the outside we might say there are many voices in play. We might analyse transcripts and break down those different voices. But this is potentially already to fall into the illusion of objectification, as if the dialogue was over there in front of our gaze. In reality we are always already involved in the dialogue. There is always a first-person perspective as well as a third-person perspective. The essential structure of a dialogue is not just two or more voices but an inside and an outside. I label you and contain you within my universe when I pretend or claim to understand you and, if I am dialogically engaged with you, I am also aware that you are doing the same to me. In other words you are not just the person I have an image of – you are the transcendent consciousness that can locate me and define me within your gaze (Wegerif, 2013, p. 31). Clearly these two perspectives in any dialogue are incommensurate in the way in which Kuhn ([1962] 2012) claims that different research paradigms are incommensurate. The inside and the outside perspectives cannot be reduced to a single measure or a single gaze. Yet it is the tension between them that is generative of meaning and of understanding.

If most research on dialogues is conducted in a monologic framework then a more dialogic framework would begin with the awareness that all research involves a living dialogue between two incommensurate or irreducibly different perspectives; the perspective of the lived experience of the subjects of the research moving from the inside out and the view that is trying to define and locate that experience moving from the outside in. This combination of an inside view looking out and an outside view looking in corresponds to Merleau-Ponty's concept of the 'chiasm'. Chiasm is a term Merleau-Ponty borrowed from rhetoric where it refers to the reversibility of a subject and object in a sentence. The sentence 'I see the world: the world sees me' is an example of a chiasm. Merleau-Ponty applied this to his understanding of the nature of perceptual events.

In proposing a chiasm methodology for research on educational dialogues we are not just proposing mixed methods. As Shaffer (2017) brings out in his work on **quantitative ethnography,** we can use numbers and statistics to explore the unique significance of events taking an inside 'qualitative' or interpretive perspective. The difference between an inside and an outside approach is not in the method used but in the stance. The outside view objectifies and compares, taking what Buber referred to as an I–It stance. The inside view subjectifies and understands empathetically from within, taking what Buber referred to as an I–thou stance. The idea of the chiasm suggests a principled way to bring these two research approaches together in one whole. This is to inter-react and inter-animate the inside view and the outside view systematically at each level and type of analysis to gain insights and make meaning without ever fully integrating them into a single vision. If we are comparing classes in terms of test results we should try through videos – if they are group tests, or perhaps stimulated recall interviews (see Chapter 8) – to also find out what it feels like to perform on this test and what was going on for the student from the inside point of view. If we are trying to understand teaching practices, we really need the teacher's perspective as an authentic voice in the analytic process (as exemplified in Chapter 7). Another way to think about chiasm is as figure-ground reversal. In a video or transcript we are as much concerned to understand unique learning incidents as to find general patterns. Our interest is in the way in which patterns flow from incidents and how incidents may illustrate patterns but in a way in which the two points of view are dialogically inter-illuminated rather than, as in the nomothetic (monologic) approach, one side is reduced to or subsumed within the other. How this might work in practice is illustrated in Chapter 3 in which we find patterns of language associated with learning incidents but not defining them. These patterns can be counted to compare classrooms statistically but understanding their meaning comes from interrelating such statistics with a detailed interpretation of how learning occurs in practice in unique incidents. The generalizable patterns are only ever indicators of possible learning and not the event of learning itself.

Concluding remarks

Theory is essential for research on educational dialogues. Sometimes people write about methods of 'data collection' like interviews, or 'data analysis' like coding, as if these were quite independent of theory. This is to assume a 'monologic' theory of meaning. The assumption of monologism is that concepts like 'data' refer unproblematically to things in the world that can be collected and analysed. Dialogic or dialogism is the alternative view that all meaning requires and implies the inter-animation of more than one voice. Determining what is and what is not to count as data in a dialogue, for example, already necessarily requires a participant point of view which is one voice among other voices. In this chapter we have offered several strategies to suggest how this dialogic theory can be consistent with conducting effective research.

Our main conclusion is that dialogic research involves a chiasm which is a dialogue between an inside perspective and an outside perspective. An example of this applied in the context of online research is worked out in Chapter 8 where an interpretation of the meaning of individual blog posts is combined with a statistical analysis of patterns of language use in the educational intervention as a whole. Other examples of chiasm as a methodology can be found in the other chapters of the book. In Chapter 7 we describe how coding can be combined with critical-event recall interviews to unpack their meaning. Chapter 4 explores the tension between personal perspectives and the aspiration to universalism in literature reviews.

The chiasm approach does not mean that we dismiss the objectifying outside voice of more traditional monologism or positivism. We interpret this voice as an aspiration to see things clearly as others would see them. Not just the specific others around us but even others in the future taking the form, perhaps, of the future community of scientists (Pierce, 1974, 5.565). However, for useful understanding in a context, we always need to combine this externalizing would-be 'objective' voice with one or more inside voices. Ultimately understanding in research arises out of the tension of juxtaposing together an attempt to take an outside point of view with an attempt to take an inside point of view. While on the one hand this meaning is always inevitably situated and partial, because we as researchers are inevitably situated and partial, on the other hand it is always aspiring to be of more general relevance. This is just another way of saying what Bakhtin (1986) said already, that the truth is to be found in the dialogue as a whole, in this case educational research understood as a long-term and global shared inquiry, but that the final perspective of the dialogue as a whole is not available to us because in reality we participate as best we can in an ongoing open-ended dialogue, always seeking the truth, always knowing that our perspective is partial and fallible. We do not, however, see this as a reason to abandon research effort! It is, rather, an exciting and invigorating challenge to employ research methods that are dialogic in principle and practice, as discussed throughout this book.

CHAPTER THREE

Orientations and Ground Rules: A Framework for Researching Educational Dialogue

Rupert Wegerif

Background and introduction

In a book about practical research methods it might seem odd that this chapter focuses so much on theory. The chapter is partly an argument for the importance of theory as a research method – perhaps the first and most fundamental of all research methods. My claim is that unless we are able to employ theory as a method we are unable to question the assumptions that are given to us with any area of research. For example, what is 'dialogue'? What is 'thinking'? Who exactly is it who speaks in any area of discourse? The assumptions behind research methods always have a history and imply theories of their own. I will return to this argument about the importance of theory at the end of chapter. So please read the chapter and see if I can manage to persuade you.

'Thinking Together', a practical approach to dialogic education, depends upon applying the notion of 'Exploratory Talk'. Although the idea of Exploratory Talk originated in the work of Douglas Barnes (1976), the version of Exploratory Talk behind Thinking Together was developed mostly by Neil Mercer as part of a triad of 'types of talk' (Fisher, 1993; Mercer, 1995). I was working closely with Neil Mercer at the time (Mercer & Wegerif, 1999; Wegerif & Mercer, 1997a). In this article I revisit our original analysis of types of talk to consider what kind of research method is implied. This is worth doing because 'types of talk', unlike most methods in the area of classroom talk research, are not simply monologic but try to be, at least in part, dialogic.

The three types of talk proposed by Neil Mercer emerged originally from analyses of small groups of children from a range of age groups working together at computer-based educational tasks (Fisher, 1993; Mercer, 1994, 1995; Wegerif & Scrimshaw, 1997). Mercer elaborated on the definitions of the three types of talk, and discussed their nature as, in his phrase, 'social modes of thinking'. The following characterization of the three types and variations on this can be found in several books, articles and websites:

- Disputational Talk, which is characterized by disagreement and individualized decision-making. There are few attempts to pool resources, to offer constructive criticism or make suggestions. Disputational Talk also has some characteristic discourse features – short exchanges consisting of assertions and challenges or counter assertions

- Cumulative Talk, in which speakers build positively but uncritically on what the others have said. Partners use talk to construct 'common knowledge' by accumulation. Cumulative discourse is characterized by repetitions, confirmations and elaborations.

- Exploratory Talk, in which partners engage critically but constructively with each other's ideas. Statements and suggestions are offered for joint consideration. These may be challenged and counter-challenged, but challenges are justified and alternative hypotheses are offered. Partners all actively participate, and opinions are sought and considered before decisions are jointly made. Compared with the other two types, in Exploratory Talk knowledge is made more publicly accountable, and reasoning is more visible in the talk (Mercer & Wegerif, 2004, p. 72).

Each time that these types of talk were presented in print it was made clear that this was not meant to be a new coding scheme. However, types of talk were nonetheless presented as 'analytic categories' drawn from the way in which children work together. In this way the analysis of types of talk was claiming to engage more directly with the meaning of the talk, based on the belief that we participate in the meaning of relationships first before we step back to observe and collect talk as data. When you see a child smile do you have to measure that smile in order to feel the happiness? (Wittgenstein, 2009).

If a teacher listens in on a group of children talking in their class, they do not usually have time to apply a coding scheme in order to analyse that talk but they might be able to recognize the type of talk that it is even just from body language and from tone of voice. If they hear challenges being given in the absence of any feeling that the children are being constructive then it is probably 'Disputational Talk'. If they hear reasons being given for claims and they see body language and expressions that show engagement in the task then it is probably 'Exploratory Talk'. This way of analysing talk in action in a busy classroom depends on the teacher's ability to be a participant in the dialogues of the children in her class, to put herself in their place and understand what is really going on in the talk, grasping relationships between the children that are not always immediately reflected in the words being used.

In the past, questions such as what exactly is a 'type of talk' have mostly been answered with reference to data of children talking. Extracts of transcripts of children talking together have been used extensively not only in writing about Exploratory Talk but also in continuing professional development activities with teachers. Those who look at these extracts tend to agree that it is possible to see that these different ways of talking together are also different ways of thinking together that are likely to have different educational consequences. Disputational Talk is represented by extracts that boil down to the kind of exchange where one person says 'Yes it is' and the other says 'No it isn't' and there is no explanation, engagement with the views of the other or movement towards a resolution of differences. Cumulative talk is represented by extracts in which a small group agrees with each other and builds on from each other's ideas but without any criticism or challenge. Exploratory Talk is represented by extracts with explicit reasoning, asking questions, challenging, elaborating and so on (examples of extracts of types of talk used in professional development activities can be found online[1]).

Exploratory Talk is really key to this analysis as a kind of dialogic or talk-based model of 'reason'. Types of talk are not just a neutral analysis of talk as if we were linguists just interested in the patterns of talk for their own sake; we are educationalists and our analysis stems from a desire to teach the most effective kind of talk for thinking together and learning together. Exploratory Talk is essentially that kind of talk which we want to teach more of as it helps learners of any age to think and learn together. In order to teach Exploratory Talk we need to understand it, or at least that might help us to teach it better.

Barnes originally contrasted Exploratory Talk with 'Presentational Talk'. He wrote that often when children talk in classrooms it is simply in order to show what they know to the teachers or to the class. With many convincing examples Barnes argued for the value of a different kind of talk, Exploratory Talk, as a more provisional, hesitant, constructivist alternative to presentation in which thinking was actually developing in the talking process itself. He referred to this at times as entering into 'hypothetical mode'. At one point, looking at talk around a poem, he pointed out that the Exploratory Talk being used was characterized by the frequent use of hypothetical expressions such as 'you'd think', 'she might have thought', 'perhaps it was' and so on (Barnes, 1976, p. 28). This is not the case in Presentational Talk because this type of talk simply presents the results of prior thinking. Barnes's account of Exploratory Talk is similar to Mercer's in many ways, but the big contrast that Barnes is making is not between Exploratory Talk and a range of other kinds of talk but a simple dichotomy: the difference between thinking talk – talk where you can 'see' the thinking taking place – and unthinking talk, talk which is intended to display and impress but without any new thinking being present.

---

[1] https://thinkingtogether.educ.cam.ac.uk/resources/5_examples_of_talk_in_groups.pdf.

The idea of finding thinking in the talk of children is a very good idea but whenever Barnes and Mercer refer to examples of thinking they do so in terms of explicit reasoning, hypotheses, claims, counterclaims with elaborations and justifications and so on. This reflects a view of thinking that has been in the culture for a long time but that is increasingly being found to not really correspond to how most of us think most of the time. The issue here of how we recognize thinking in talk illustrates the need for theory in research methods. The objects we deal with in research on dialogue depend upon theory. To look at thinking in talk we need a theory of thinking. If we do not explicitly examine theory here we end up with the default assumptions about thinking that are embedded in the culture.

In the rest of this chapter I will argue that the distinction drawn by Barnes between thinking talk and unthinking talk is a useful one that can be unpacked further into a combination of orientations and ground rules. I will then argue that just as there are different ways of not thinking in talk, disputational and cumulative being the two examples brought out by Mercer, so there are also different ways of thinking well in talk. The model of thinking put forward by Barnes and Mercer focussed on explicit reasoning. This can be useful. But then so can other kinds of thinking. I will argue with some illustrative examples that a more creative kind of 'thinking by resonance' can also be found in talk. This is found particularly in playful talk. But if we have a new kind of playful or creative talk that is not characterized by explicit reasoning then how is that to be distinguished from Mercer's 'cumulative talk'? Understanding how playful talk can lead to shared creative thinking suggests that we need to expand the original definition of Exploratory Talk.

Transitions as a way of getting at the ontological reality behind types of talk

Are types of talk real? If so, then what kind of reality do they have? Coding in terms of words or utterances tends to assume that words and utterances are real. You can see when a word begins and ends

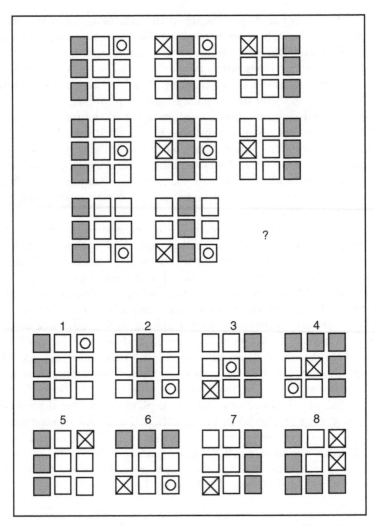

FIGURE 3.1 *Example of similar problem to the one the 9-year-olds are working on together.*

in a transcript so it seems real enough. The turns at talk by different speakers are usually quite easy to distinguish, so segmenting talk analysis by utterances understood as turns at talk seems to be rooted in an ontologically real distinction. But what then is the ontology behind types of talk? Is there really a boundary separating Exploratory Talk from Disputational Talk?

One way to explore the reality of types of talk could be to look for sudden transitions in talk reflecting depth shifts in the way in which participants relate together. In Wegerif and Mercer's (1997a) 'A Dialogic Framework for Researching Peer Talk' we gave an example of a sudden transition in the talk of a small group of primary students as a kind of proof of concept that types of talk are real and impact on group work. In the example taken from our recordings of classroom talk a girl was working well in an 'Exploratory Talk' manner with two partners. When their response to her suggestion, backed up by the researcher who was present, was interpreted by her as a lack of respect, this led her to pull away, physically leaving the table. This episode offered a relatively clear shift from 'Exploratory Talk' to 'Disputational Talk'.

It is worth re-visiting this example briefly to illustrate the way in which a types-of-talk analysis proceeds. First the type of talk is intuited preferably by being part of it or if not by reconstructing it

Box 3.1 Transcript extract 1: A transition in talk

Jane: Yeah but there's three of them and there's 3 of them and that and that makes that.

Natalie: No look you get three and 1 and 3 and 1 and ...

Jane: Mr Wegerif does that and that make that?

(*Jane appeals to the researcher who comes over but doesn't intervene.*)

Natalie: I just disagree.

Researcher: You must give a reason. You must explain why Natalie.

Natalie: No, because look. (*Points to the page with the graphical puzzle but does not explain.*)

George: You have to have a reason Natalie.

(*Natalie leaves the group table and goes over to another group.*)

George: Natalie you're supposed to be working with us not with Sujatta.

from videos of the event or, failing videos, transcripts of the talk. In the next short sequence, three 9-year-old pupils are working on a series of graphical puzzles taken from a reasoning test (Raven's progressive matrices: Raven, Raven & Court, 2003). Figure 3.1 illustrates the type of problem. They have been given only one answer sheet for these puzzles and asked to cooperate to reach agreement on each answer.

Commentary on extract

Up to this point the children have apparently reached a reasoned agreement on the right answer to each puzzle. Towards the end of the task, however, Natalie begins to propose answers more strongly than before, and shows exasperation with her partners through her raised voice and sharp manner. When George uses the same words as the researcher in order to criticize her, she perhaps feels that everyone is against her and decides to leave. This sequence shows a fairly abrupt breakdown of the cooperative framework, as the talk moves from exploratory to disputational.

Through the commentary above I am interpreting what is going on in the talk in a way that depends upon a kind of vicarious participation in the dialogue. I could be wrong. The researcher has no special privileged position.

In the example above the shift in orientation was very obvious from observing the physical action of leaving the group. However, sometimes this sort of breakdown of trust and sudden shift in orientation is not so easy to see reflected in the actual words chosen and spoken. We can reconstruct an understanding of this kind of abrupt transition from the intuitions of all those who engage in dialogue.

I witnessed one example quite recently. I was walking with a couple who are friends of mine, let us call them Jane and Tom, and we met another couple whom I also knew, Agathe and Simeon. I introduced the two couples. Everyone was very friendly and seemed genuinely pleased to meet. Soon they were sharing stories about their children. Jane described a recent birthday party at Pizza Hut which was their son's favourite place in all the world. Agathe shared that her children's favourite was 'Pizza Express'. Perhaps she was sharing that their children all liked pizza but

I saw a slight frown of anxiety from Jane and wondered if she felt that perhaps Pizza Hut was a little too common. Tom mentioned the struggle he had getting their son to read proper books but that they had discovered some amazing cartoons which combined good stories with pictures. Simeon shared that their son, Tristan, about the same age, was enjoying reading the Illiad by Homer. He did not bother to qualify this in anyway. This revelation about the Illiad led to a sudden transition in the talk. On the surface everything was the same. The expressions were accompanied by the same smiles and positive affect terms, 'wonderful', 'delightful', 'great', 'of course we must meet up again' and so on, but the eyes of Jane and Tom had become reserved and watchful. I could sense that they were now uncomfortable and being careful about what they revealed. They had shifted from an open friendly attitude of all talking together in a shared space to a defensive attitude. They felt that Agathe and Simeon were not being open with them really but were talking in a way designed to enhance their sense of superiority by locating Jane and Tom as their inferiors in matters of taste and education.

I hope that you agree that this kind of shift in 'intersubjective orientation' is something that we are all familiar with as participants in dialogue. It is not about the surface of the talk which might remain almost the same. It is therefore not always easy to code. Recognizing this kind of transition involves an interpretation of the depth structure of the talk. This depth structure is about relationships. It is what is really going on despite what people might claim about it.

This analysis of transitions in talk at a depth rather than a surface level suggests that 'types of talk' should be characterized by their distinctive intersubjective orientations. In Exploratory Talk people are open to each other, willing to learn from each other, identifying with the shared project of the dialogue and not with individual egos. In Disputational Talk, on the other hand, the only identification is with the ego and talk is engaged in as a kind of game to advance the ego. This distinction between two fundamental intersubjective attitudes or orientations in talk can be related to the distinction Habermas draws between a communicative attitude, oriented to understanding and a strategic attitude oriented towards success (Habermas, 1984). Perhaps this distinction also relates, more indirectly, to the distinction drawn between an 'I–it' or objectifying attitude towards the other and an 'I–thou' or responsive and open attitude to the other by Buber (see Chapter 2).

'Ground rules' or social norms

As already mentioned, we are only really interested in researching types of talk because we want to teach Exploratory Talk and this is because it is a way of teaching reasoning. Being 'open to the other', which means open to the possibility of learning something new from the other, is, essential for shared thinking, but it is not enough, on its own, to provide us with a dialogic characterization of reason. Two children who were open to learning from each other while playing in a sandpit could not really be described as reasoning together. A more culturally specific level of description is required if we are to understand how reason emerges in social contexts and how reason can be taught.

Mercer and his research team moved on to this second level when they specified Exploratory Talk in terms of specific ground rules:[2]

- everyone in the group is encouraged to contribute
- contributions are treated with respect
- reasons are asked for
- everyone is prepared to accept challenges
- alternatives are discussed before a decision is taken
- all relevant information is shared
- the group seeks to reach agreement.

Ground rules are essentially social norms (Hoffman & Ruthven, 2018). They are not meant to be explicit rules but implicit guides to actions. We sometimes make them explicit to teach them but this is so that they can become implicit again through practice. For example, in a 'Philosophy for Children' class I once observed that the teacher taught very young children to say 'I think' before they gave an opinion (Wegerif, 2002). This is because they do not always

---

[2]http://thinkingtogether.educ.cam.ac.uk/resources/Ground_rules_for_Exploratory_Talk.pdf.

talk in a way that acknowledges that what they are saying is only one possible point of view that could be questioned and that is open to challenge and to possible change. But after a bit of practice with dialogue, the 'I think' in front of utterances becomes implicit. In a real dialogue we know, as educated adults, that everything put forward is put forward provisionally as an opinion which can be challenged and can be changed, so we no longer need to spell this assumption out explicitly.

One way to think about teaching ground rules for effective dialogue is as a form of culture change. Any culture has implicit assumptions or expectations that shape explicit behaviour. These assumptions tend to be unconscious because you only become aware of them when they are challenged. If the culture of a classroom is individualistic and competitive, for example, then inviting a child to tell the class what she thinks about an issue might be interpreted either as an opportunity to perform or as an invitation to be judged and found wanting or, indeed, as both. If the culture of the classroom is 'dialogic' and collaborative then exactly the same invitation might be interpreted simply as a chance to participate in shared thinking with the goal of shared understanding in which case provisional or 'half-baked' thoughts are welcome and mistakes are understood as valuable learning opportunities.

Playful talk

So far I have argued that types of talk consist of a combination of intersubjective orientations and social ground rules. Exploratory Talk can be seen as a type of talk that is a social model of reason appropriate for classrooms in the UK. By teaching Exploratory Talk using the programme 'Thinking Together' (Dawes, Mercer & Wegerif, 2000) and evaluating the impact of this on a range of measures including learning gains and reasoning tests we have demonstrated the value of this model. However, the question can and should be asked: is this the only model of reason available or is the way in which we have characterized it influenced by cultural biases? (Lambirth, 2009).

One day, many years ago now, I was visiting a classroom in a school in Milton Keynes, and I arrived a bit early. There was no supervising teacher and the children, aged about 8, seemed quite excited. Several rushed to the window and looked out at my car which was a rather run-down green Vauxhall Chevette. 'Is that your car Mr Wegerif?' one asked. Another started rhyming, 'Mr Wegerif's car ... won't get you very far.' A third continued, 'it is yucky and green' and a fourth, 'it's a mean machine.' They carried on like this with some quite surreal links to my car, often using words that they made up and did not obviously mean anything like 'a zoomy beam'. I was impressed with this spontaneous collaborative creativity.

I mentioned this to my colleagues and found that many researchers observing and recording children's talk in classrooms are aware that there is a great deal of apparently off-task nonsense talk or banter which displays some creative skill. When the 'Thinking Together' research team discussed the three types of talk we realized that this off-task banter was possibly itself a type of talk that could be characterized in terms of a fundamental intersubjective orientation, one of playfulness, with a concomitant set of ground rules. In Mexico, working with Sylvia Rojas-Drummond and her team of researchers, we even ran a workshop with students in which we found that it was possible to produce a convincing set of ground rules for playful talk including 'do not take anything said too seriously' and 'make images as strange and apparently inconsequential as possible'. Although 'Playful Talk' was discussed by research teams in the UK and in Mexico, it was not included in presentations of the types of talk idea. The reason for this is probably that it mostly concerned off-task talk and did not seem very relevant to educators. Whenever a member of the research team introduced the three types of talk, we did so with the qualification that this was not an exhaustive description of all types of talk but only of some types of talk: those types of talk that we thought were most 'relevant to educational goals'.

It is interesting that the research team, of which I was a part, acknowledged the existence of 'playful talk' but dismissed it as marginal to educational objectives whereas we saw Exploratory Talk, defined through the presence of explicit reasoning, as central to educational objectives. It seemed to me, from research on children talking in 'Philosophy for Children' contexts, that resonances between ideas were often important to their reasoning together (Wegerif, 2005). Playful talk makes use of a kind of spontaneous metaphoricity in dialogues that can perhaps contribute to creative thinking. In science there are many anecdotes about problems being solved through analogies and metaphors that just pop into the mind without there being any explicit process. The classic case is how the chemist Kekule realized that the structure of the benzine molecule was in the form of a ring after falling asleep in front of a fire and dreaming of salamander-like serpents eating their own tails (Dunbar, 1997). That might be an extreme example but research on talk in science labs has confirmed the importance of analogical or metaphorical reasoning for breakthroughs, even suggesting that it is important to have a variety of specialists as the pressure of having to explain ideas to those who lack the same technical language leads to analogies and so, sometimes, to creative new ways to look at things (Dunbar, 1997).

I have not found many good examples of how playful talk leads to understanding new concepts in classrooms. I am convinced that it happens though. This would be a good topic for further classroom talk research if any readers were interested.

Questioning the centrality of explicit reasoning to Exploratory Talk

In Mexico, Sylvia Rojas-Drummond led an interesting experimental study that tested the importance of explicit reasoning to the effectiveness of Exploratory Talk. Students who had been taught Exploratory Talk over three months using the Thinking Together approach were given two different kinds of test. One was a version of the kind of reasoning test that has already been widely used. The other was a more creative task in which groups of students had to collaborate together to write a short text. The students did better on the reasoning task than they had in a pre-test and this improved result went together with more explicit reasoning. However, the students also did better on the more creative task, using established ways of judging the creative quality of the writing, but this improvement did not go together with explicit reasoning (Rojas-Drummond, Mazón, Fernández & Wegerif, 2006).

We do not have recordings of the talk of the groups doing the more creative task, but it is possible that their lack of explicit reasoning was compensated for by more of the kind of thinking by resonance that characterizes playful talk. Derrida has found a lot of this kind of thinking by metaphorical resonance shaping what was claimed to be rational thought, and I have found it also in researching the talk of children engaged in Philosophy for Children (Derrida, 1982; Wegerif, 2005).

Perhaps the focus on explicit reasoning found in Barnes and in Mercer represents a particular 'modernist' or 'Enlightenment' understanding of reason that can be augmented by a more creative understanding of how the free competition between metaphorical ways of thinking leads to new ways of seeing things some of which prove to be useful.

Continua in types of talk

Creative talk requires analogies and metaphors to solve problems. Books on creativity are full of examples of new connections that have been made between contexts in a way that solves a problem. In 'Mind Expanding' I give the example of how a business technique to generate creative thinking, 'Synectics', discovered that the way that a horse's backside works, with two separate openings, was perfect for dispensing creams in a way that keeps them from going dry (Wegerif, 2010, pp. 47–8). This might seem a long way from the playful talk I described when children made up silly names for my car. But both kinds of talk use metaphors in a way that explicit reasoning talk does not. There is a continuum between more silly 'playful talk' and more serious 'creative talk'. In a similar way Rojas-Drummond, Perez, Velez, Gomez and Mendoza (2003) found a continuum between full-bodied reasoning talk or Exploratory Talk and what she called 'incipient' Exploratory Talk which offered a single reason without articulating or elaborating fully.

A new dialogic framework for researching peer talk

Intersubjective orientations

As Buber and Habermas have argued, the deepest level is that of the intersubjective orientation or attitude of being open to the other or closed to the other. The implication from their work is that this is a human universal. Habermas argues convincingly that the natural state of children growing up within a community is to be open and willing to learn from the other, what he calls a communicative attitude but that we might here be calling a dialogic orientation. Habermas argues that strategic thinking including profit maximizing thinking is something we learn later.

If we take Exploratory Talk in the spirit of Barnes as that kind of talk in which children can work out their thinking together, then we need to expand our understanding of this type of talk to include creative talk which builds understanding through resonances between ideas even if no explicit critical thinking is present.

This kind of thinking together through resonances and recollections might fit cumulative talk if this is defined simply by an absence of explicit reasoning. However, it is most useful to reserve the term cumulative talk for that kind of closed talk which preserves the image of the harmony of the group. I am sure we have all been in meetings where it was clear that criticism of any kind was not welcome; we can add on to what has been said, we can agree with the others but we are not allowed to challenge.

This discussion leads us to the types of talk listed in Table 3.1.

Thinking includes creative thinking by resonance and metaphor. I therefore think we need to expand the definition of Exploratory Talk given earlier to recognize that explicit reasoning is only present for some tasks in some contexts and that for other tasks in other contexts more creative and even playful forms of talk are also exploratory.

Social norms

Each 'type of talk' will be characterized by a set of appropriate social norms, which vary greatly across history, culture and activity context. The social norms that best support Exploratory Talk in

Table 3.1 Types of talk

Closed (defensive or presentational)	Disputational	Cumulative
Open (Exploratory)	Reasoning talk	Playful or creative talk

mathematics might not be the same as those in an art class, but the exploratory orientation might be the same. The social norms we should teach for Exploratory Talk in China might not be same as those we should teach in Mexico.

Levels of depth of analysis

The surface of dialogue is anything that can be measured. The number of words used. The length of utterances. The exact words used and how many times. Even the tone of voice used. The greatest depth of dialogue is the level of intersubjective orientation. Above orientations we have ground rules that instantiate types of talk in different social cultural and historical contexts. In between ground rules and the surface level we have interaction patterns and communicative acts.

This framework for analysing educational dialogue can itself be called dialogic as it begins with the most fundamental insight of dialogic theory, that there is a difference between living words and dead words. Exploratory Talk is the idea of living thinking speech that is not yet fixed but involves a play of multiple voices and is open as to possibilities. We cannot adequately research living dialogue by remaining outside of it and merely coding and counting the surface features that are left in its wake. We need to participate, to recognize and to feel the types of talk from within.

Concluding remarks

It is not possible to understand what is going on in a dialogue by standing outside of it. You have to dive in. You have to participate as fully as possible in order to understand depth meanings that might not be apparent on the surface. But once you are swimming in dialogue you might feel that you have lost the privileged position of researcher and just become another voice. The framework outlined in this chapter is designed to help by offering a flexible set of tools and questions to reflect upon and reconstruct some of the causal drivers and structures behind what is experienced in dialogue.

This particular framework focuses on unpacking Exploratory Talk because it is designed not only to help understand what is going on in educational dialogues, but more importantly, it is intended also as a guide to how to change them. Exploratory Talk has, from the beginning, been an educational ideal that was found in classroom dialogues mainly because it was taught. The better we understand the real nature of Exploratory Talk the better we can teach it. Perhaps the best evidence that can be offered confirming the value of this framework is the consequences of the teaching that is designed according to it (a point raised in Chapter 2 with reference to design-based research). This kind of educational research then has to be understood as a kind of virtuous circle uniting reflective understanding about how educational dialogues work to the practice of teaching in a way that promotes dialogues.

The flexible framework of levels and types of dialogue offered in this chapter is not meant to be a replacement for thinking but a support for thinking. Purely empirical research is dangerous because it leaves assumptions unquestioned. Theoretical research involves questioning assumptions and reconceptualizing them in the light of empirical experience. Theory should not really be treated as an optional extra in educational research because it determines what we can see. One of the findings of the types-of-talk analysis outlined in this chapter, for example, is that the kind of thinking that occurs in different contexts depends upon ground rules that are often not visible or apparent to participants. Something as basic as whether or not you are able to speak or to think for yourself at all will be determined by these ground rules. In Disputational Talk speakers find themselves narrowly defined in opposition to others. In Exploratory Talk speakers may forget themselves at times and flow into participating in a more general shared self of an inquiry that is not individually owned or controlled. Where empirical research alone might assume that there is a clear distinction between talk and individual speakers, a more theoretically self-reflective inquiry can be open to exploring the complex way in which different kinds of talk allow for and even bring into being different kinds of subjectivity.

In the short commentary on this chapter that follows, Chilean researcher Antonia Larrain focuses particularly on the idea of playful talk as a type of dialogic talk. She argues, bringing in her own research on imagination, that we need to do detailed follow-up research linking specific ways of talking to specific psychological effects such as imagination.

Many questions remain to be explored. How useful is this framework? Can it really be applied? What insights does it offer? What aspects of educational dialogue does it obscure or make harder to see? Can we find empirical evidence for the distinction made between cumulative talk and creative talk? Can playful talk lead to valued educational outcomes? If so what kind of pedagogy promotes this?

Expert commentary

Classroom talk and imagination: The importance of a theory of language for understanding the relationship between dialogue and thinking

Antonia Larrain, Universidad Alberto Hurtado, Chile

Rupert Wegerif raises the interesting idea of playful talk as a fourth type of educational dialogue. It is not the identification of a new analytical code that he argues for, but rather a new way of conceptualizing educational dialogue. In this new way, the salient aspect would be that dialogue is more than an object of analysis, but it is assumed as a flow of communicative process in which analysts are necessarily immersed, acting and reacting as a way of participating in meaning-making. This is an interesting case of how and why theorization is a relevant part of the practice of researching in education. Wegerif's proposal is relevant because the way we conceptualize classroom talk, that is, the way we think about it in a generalized way, impacts decisively on the pragmatic and concrete research decisions that we make, which, in turn, determine what can be thought of the relationship between dialogue and thinking. For instance, the statement that playful talk is relevant for reasoning and thinking sheds light on something that, although recognized by classical authors such as Vico ([1744] 1948), Vygotsky ([1930] 2004) and Peirce (1955), has been overlooked by the research on educational dialogue: the role of imagination in knowledge construction and thinking. Coherently, Wegerif argues for playful talk as a type of classroom dialogue that can contribute to creative thinking and conceptual understanding. The question, which I found very interesting, is how playful talk would prompt thinking development (in both its creative and conceptual aspects). Of course, this may become an empirical question; however, in order to design an empirical study to answer the question, once again we need theory.

As researchers in the field of education, we are commonly unaware of the existence and influence of various theories of language with different, often tensioned, assumptions regarding human communication and cognition. For instance, if Wegerif were talking from an *expressivist view of language* (see Locke, 1689), in which language is conceived of as expressing ideas that are already formed in the mind through non-linguistic mental processes, playful talk would be relevant not because it prompts creative thinking but because it expresses the already formed creative idea, allowing students to share their creative thinking and reasoning, and teachers to have evidence of it. On the contrary, if playful talk were seen from a *romantic theory of language* (see Bertau, 2011), it would have not an expressive but rather a *formative function* (Bertau, 2011), in which the specific forms of language give form to thinking and verbal thinking is a process unfolding through specific linguistic forms (also see Vygotsky [1934] 1987). However, if playful talk were seen from a more *hermeneutic approach*, which I believe is the case, it would be a sort of general way in which thinking and imagination co-participate from the more general flow of discursive life. More than identifying it as occurring at some specific points, it would be a sort of background of understanding of every interaction.

More than trying to account for the broader theory of language Wegerif is thinking from, let's illustrate with Wegerif's proposal regarding the relationship between playful talk and thinking, how theory is absolutely crucial to educational empirical work. Were Wegerif drawing on an expressivist theory of language, attending to specific linguistic moves within playful talk would only be useful in terms of knowing how students think creatively and conceptualize. Moreover, from this point of view, it would be hard to conceive of concepts and playful talk as related at all. Were Wegerif drawing on a hermeneutic notion of language and stating playful talk as a general overtone of every discursive interaction, playful talk and imagination are closely intertwined through the imaginative aspect of every stream of thinking (see Peirce, 1955), and its focus or identification would implicate the intimate participation as a co-author in this meaning-making flow. In terms of educational analysis, more than identifying one or another utterance or episode, the thing is how to empathize with the emotional and creative tone of meaning-making at a given point, to make it salient and relevant to analysis. On the contrary, if Wegerif were drawing on a romantic theory of language (which probably is the case), focusing on playful talk might be a medium for fostering creative thinking and concept development.

Whatever is the case, in order to develop a clear account of this type of talk we need to develop two additional steps. First, we need to elaborate further the relationship between playful talk, imagination and creative thinking and/or concept development. For instance, what is imagination from this approach to dialogue and meaning-making? Is it a condition of any experience and understanding, or a particular sphere of psychological activity with no connection or value to practical and material life (i.e. *phantasia*)? Are imagination and thinking different but interdependent psychological processes? Do they always develop intertwinedly, or do they emerge independently? What is their relation to dialogue? Is dialogue a prerequisite or are different sides of the same coin? What is the role played in imagination and concept development? What is the role in education? Is it just emotional, or also intellectual? Among many others. Second, identifying playful talk as a general type of talk (or speech genre? see Bakhtin, 1986) is not enough: it would be necessary to account for which discursive conditions should be present to identify it as a relevant way of organizing educational activity.

To advance the research on educational dialogue and its relevance to learning we need a clearer theory of language, and Wegerif poses us that challenge clearly. But we also need a clearer theory of thinking and learning. We cannot rely on the wide agreement between the community of educational researchers on the importance of dialogue in school learning, because that agreement does not imply agreement on the psychological processes involved. Empirical research interested in classroom dialogue should pay careful attention to theoretical constructs and assumptions that orient its practice.

CHAPTER FOUR

Methodological Developments in Research on Educational Dialogue: Mapping the Field

Ruth Kershner, Sara Hennessy, Rupert Wegerif and Ayesha Ahmed

Introduction

Research on educational dialogue has expanded hugely in the last two decades. This is evident not just in the publication of numerous academic research papers, books, blogs and other writings, but also in the growing number of conferences, school-based inquiries, classroom intervention programmes and professional development (PD) initiatives. This chapter provides an overview of current research interests and methods in this area, aiming to position our choice of topics for this book and look to the future. In addition to the areas of inquiry covered in different chapters, there are certain key aspects or themes of educational dialogue that are discussed at different points. One example is small group work by students.

This is considered from different perspectives, including 'types of talk' in Chapter 3, quality of participation in Chapter 5 and social and relational processes in Chapter 9. Another example is cultural aspects of dialogue. This theme extends throughout the book in terms of the cultural contexts of activities and the uses of cultural tools and resources (e.g. Chapters 3, 6, 7, 10), and more specifically in relation to the nature and purposes of intercultural dialogue (e.g. Chapters 8 and 9). Such interconnections between topics and themes are intrinsic to the research field of educational dialogue.

Engaging with published research: Research and practice in translation

Creating knowledge and understanding of educational dialogue is a central aim of the research process. Dialogic principles suggest that engaging with others to question, exchange knowledge and reason together about research evidence is likely to be productive. As research findings are published over time the body of knowledge accumulates, allowing deeper understanding to be developed within and between individual investigations. Yet there are some barriers to participation in this process. While writing (and reading) is a central professional responsibility for academic researchers, published research findings are not always accessible or even visible to educational practitioners and others who may also be interested. Many academic publishers require payment for journal access, and academic libraries can be inaccessible. 'Open-access' material is available, but it is not highly publicized outside the academic world. Blogs, newspapers and other media often refer to research, but without securing full access to the original data and findings.

Concerns may also arise in relation to the commissioning and use of research by policy makers, and associated assumptions about the meaning of 'research impact'. To take one example, Cain and Allan (2017) conducted a content analysis of a sample of highly graded impact case studies submitted by UK universities for the regular assessment of 'research excellence' that is the basis of UK government research funding. They conclude that 'there is evidence that research impacts on educational structures and arrangements but very few indications ... of practitioners engaging with research, interrogating and discussing it, bringing it into relationship with other forms of knowledge, and reviewing their practice in its light' (p. 728). While this may admittedly be a particular feature, and failure, of the given UK research-grading system, it is well known that a process of 'knowledge translation' is required when reading other people's scholarly or professional writing. This is because much educational research is dependent on the specific context of inquiry. Practitioners and researchers in other contexts therefore have to 'translate' what they read in the light of their own knowledge and interests, recontextualizing and reformulating research findings in their own contexts. In practice contexts, this process in turn adds informed and professional rigour to the often loosely understood process of reflective practice (Schwimmer, 2017). Significant gains are made when understandings are informed by what happens in different authentic educational contexts, suggesting that practitioner involvement in research is essential. While it can be undoubtedly difficult for researchers and practitioners to cross conceptual, linguistic and professional boundaries, communication can be successful when carefully planned and research partnerships are given sufficient time to develop. This is central to the uptake of new developments, such as **'Close-to-practice' research** that involves researchers working in partnership with practitioners addressing problems in practice (BERA, 2018b).

Cumulative knowledge building through research depends on how researchers initially locate themselves in relation to their own and others' previous work. This mirrors the dialogic ways in which people may draw on their existing knowledge when coming to debate a knotty issue from different perspectives. Positioning oneself is usually an explicit part of the literature review of a published paper, when authors write about a selection of existing work that has informed their thinking. It may also occur reflexively when one's own understanding develops in response to hearing a conference paper, participating in a PD course, being a research participant or simply by reading research discussions in newspapers, blogs and other social media.

Reflexivity paves the way for understanding the type of reasoning that may be embedded in methodological processes and conventions: is the thinking generally **deductive** in that conclusions are judged to be sound if already existing research frameworks and procedures are followed (e.g. using an established language-coding scheme), **inductive** in that conclusions are seen as provisional until contradicted (e.g. identifying emerging patterns of interaction in an open way) or **abductive** in that conclusions are evaluated in terms of their plausibility in the light of the best knowledge available from both research and practice? These three forms of reasoning may all appear at different stages of any inquiry and they each contribute to iterative processes of analysis in which we return to data for checking and new insights. They differ, however, in terms of the weight given to uses of existing theory, empirical data and everyday practical knowledge (Patakorpi, 2009), which may initially create divides between researchers interested in the same topic from different perspectives.

Conferences and other meetings are central to the creation or consolidation of research identities by providing practical opportunities to meet others with similar research interests. One influential text on dialogic learning and teaching emerged from a conference that gave a new opportunity to 'talk about talk', as Resnick, Asterhan and Clarke (2015, pp. 1–3) explain:

> In September 2011, the American Educational Research Association sponsored a research conference in Pittsburgh that brought together leading scholars from across the world in education, learning sciences, cognitive psychology, educational psychology, linguistics, and computer science. ... [W]e came together in Pittsburgh to talk about talk—specifically, the role of academic dialogue in learning. Working from different theoretical perspectives and research traditions, the scholars who attended the conference have generated new inquiries and approaches to the study of talk and produced some surprisingly powerful evidence.... Prior to the Pittsburgh meeting, the work took the form of 'islands of evidence', unconnected to a whole. We organized the conference as a working meeting to interrogate the boundaries of our respective islands. Its primary goal was to place these varied bodies of research and evidence in conversation with one another.

Resnick et al.'s image of 'islands of evidence' reflects the concerns mentioned in Chapter 1 about the need to bring together fragmentary research evidence in a diverse field of study. Research development in any complex and interdisciplinary field of study calls for dialogic strategies like questioning, elaboration, reflecting and offering new perspectives on what has already been written and understood about the given topic. When fully developed, it is essentially a process of learning for everyone involved. We see from the Pittsburgh example above that coming together in person is an exciting experience that can shift the ground considerably. It resulted in the seminal edited collection of Resnick et al. (2015) as well as ongoing international research collaborations. Active engagement with other researchers and practitioners, together with new forms of communication through social media, support the 'virtual' dialogues that develop when reading and responding to published articles and books. Any type of dialogic engagement in research potentially makes a valuable contribution to the field.

Established and emerging methods in educational dialogue research

Research projects in this area vary from small-scale classroom studies to large-scale international online discussions, with participants of different ages and roles as well as different designs, methods and approaches to data analysis. Research studies inevitably vary in their purposes, foci, contexts and scale, generally driven by interests in one or more of the following: developing theoretical understanding, generating empirical evidence, foregrounding stakeholder engagement, capitalizing on new technologies and solving problems in practice (as discussed further in Chapter 9).

Most research methods for educational dialogue would be recognizable to any educational researcher, but the underlying research stance is more distinctive and fundamental, that is, dialogic rather than monologic. Just as an ethical stance will lead the way in deciding about what *should* be done in research, a dialogic research stance is intrinsically part of research thinking and decision-making. This is evident at different levels, from making individual interviews more dialogic (e.g. Harvey, 2015) to the dialogic involvement of whole communities (e.g. Flecha & Soler, 2013).

In preparing this chapter we traced research published over several decades into the last century with the aim of mapping out some central methodological approaches and trends. We drew on a range of published evidence in books and papers, including existing reviews and commentaries (e.g. Besley & Peters, 2012; Howe & Abedin, 2013; Resnick et al., 2015; Schwarz & Baker, 2017; Skidmore & Murakami, 2016). These were supplemented by further systematic searches of journal databases using key terms such as 'dialog/ic', 'method/ology', 'review' and so on, in various combinations. After considering different options for making sense of all this material, we identified three (very) broad lines of inquiry that seem to cover the ground in the most coherent and inclusive way. These focus on dialogic interaction in relation to:

- classroom learning and teaching
- processes of participation and collaboration
- social and intercultural understanding

Research participants include students of all ages, teachers and other adults in school, family and community members, friends, other peers and colleagues.

Research developments in classroom dialogue, learning and teaching: The interplay of theory, empirical evidence and technology

Research methods for classroom dialogue, learning and teaching have responded to changes in thinking, and in turn prompted new questions and lines of inquiry. Howe and Abedin (2013) systematically reviewed 225 international studies of classroom dialogue published between 1972 and 2011. They noted methodological changes in the sampling of participants and classrooms, curriculum contexts and research procedures. Most studies involved teacher–student dialogue over the whole time period, while interest in student–student dialogue grew notably in the 1990s with a particular focus on science learning in small groups. Methods in use virtually all involved analysing samples of dialogue that were recorded during lessons, but there were noticeable methodological shifts over the four decades. For instance, the field coding of classroom activities and interactions was very popular in the 1970s and 1980s, commonly using existing observation frameworks with fixed categories to select from (e.g. Brophy & Good, 1970; see also Chapter 6). This approach was strongly associated with quantitative data analysis using frequencies and more complex inferential statistics. Audio recording peaked in the 1980s and 1990s, while the use of video increased considerably since 1992 and is now the most favoured approach. There has been an increasing tendency to supplement observation and recording with reflective interviews with the people involved, especially in more recent studies in the 2000s. The growing tendency to combine methods and procedures has been accompanied by an increasing use of qualitative data analysis, reflecting increasing efforts to attend to the context and flow of conversation over time.

Some of the most important early work on classroom talk took the form of detailed observational studies of conversation between teachers and students. Research on the structures of classroom discourse has built on this work from the 1970s, when a typical triadic pattern was observed in teacher–student interaction: 'initiation-response-feedback (IRF)' (Sinclair & Coulthard, 1975). More recently, attention has been given to the ways in which longer sequences of interaction work between teachers and students. This includes how apparently similar IRF discourse structures can foster different orientations to learning (Molinari, Mameli & Gnisci, 2013), and the development of extended 'spiral' and 'loop' IRF sequences when teachers scaffold students' learning through dialogic interaction (Rojas-Drummond, Perez, Velez, Gomez & Mendoza, 2013). Research methodology in this area has also developed in response to critical reflection and questioning about what is both shown and omitted in systematic observation, such as increasing attention to equity and cultural inclusion in talk (see Box 4.1).

Recent methodological developments for researching classroom dialogue have been prompted by different concerns, purposes and opportunities. Some of these are conceptual, such as the explicitly sociocultural location of classroom talk in the context of social interaction and communication over time. The methodological implications of this development have been extensively discussed by Mercer (2004, 2008, 2010; see also Chapter 2). Mercer suggests that many researchers in the area of sociocultural studies are oriented

Box 4.1 Who is participating in classroom talk?

Mehan and Cazden (2015) reflect on their pioneering 1970s study of one elementary classroom over the course of a year. At that time they observed the typical chain of conversational turns that occurs when teachers initiate an exchange, students respond and the teacher replies with a simple evaluation (IRE). Prompted by their concerns to increase the participation of underrepresented minority students, they considered the cultural limitations of teacher-centred IRE sequences and asked about the steps that could be taken to establish more equitable dialogic communication. Mehan and Cazden turned to the wealth of cross-cultural research conducted during the 1980s that clearly demonstrated the need to 'build on the strengths of home language and culture' (p. 18) in order to increase the active participation of certain minority student groups. They explain their move 'from recitation to reasoning' in class, that is, engaging all students in contributing their own ideas and responding carefully to what others may say. This shift of thinking towards more dialogic communication has methodological implications, some of which may appear to be quite simple, but carry considerable significance, such as developing more appropriate modes of transcrption.

towards applied work for educational improvement, raising typical research questions such as the following:

- How does dialogue promote learning and the development of understanding?
- What types of talk are associated with the best learning outcomes?
- Does collaborative activity help children to learn, or assist their conceptual development?

Mercer advocates mixed-methods approaches to such questions, such as **sociocultural discourse analysis (SDA)** (see Chapter 2).

Common research designs may be observational, or interventional and/or **quasi-experimental**, but it should be noted that the extensive use of intervention designs with pre- and post-testing of students' learning can be problematic due to the sheer number of potentially **confounding variables** in educational practice. There is also a need to examine factors like the **fidelity** of implementing interventions in practice and the extent to which participants 'buy in' to the programme. In awareness of these problems, a recent study of classroom dialogue developed a non-interventional **correlational design**, taking natural variation in teachers' dialogic practice as the starting point for analysis (Howe, Hennessy, Mercer, Vrikki & Wheatley, 2019).

There are also new conceptual understandings of what knowledge itself is understood to be. Knight and Littleton (2017) discuss the methodological implications of changing views of 'epistemic cognition' from the 'classic' cognitive emphasis on individual learners' beliefs about knowledge towards a social and value-driven view of how 'knowing' is constructed in classroom talk. The former employs individually focused methods such as interview schedules, **think-aloud protocols, systematic observation** and survey questionnaires, depending typically on self-report data and/or laboratory studies; the latter, in contrast, shifts the focus to analysing collective discourse, social relations and activities in the authentic setting where discussion is taking place. This shift to greater contextualization of classroom talk is also central to investigations of how classroom talk may vary across different subject disciplines and activities (e.g. Nassaji & Wells, 2000). In addition to observational approaches, networked systems such as Knowledge Forum for collaborative knowledge building and 'meta-discourse' (Scardamalia & Bereiter, 2006; and see Chapter 7 of this book) are now adding new methodological opportunities for analysing extended online communication in detail.

A further development highlights increasing attention to the prosodic features of talk, such as tone of voice. Skidmore and Murakami (2016) discuss emerging interest in the functions of prosody in pedagogic talk, explaining that prosody refers to 'the parameters of the speaking voice which vary dynamically during face-to-face interaction. Chief features include: intonation; loudness; and temporal phenomena such as rhythm, tempo, and pauses' (p. 6). These features are significant in conveying what speakers mean. Sensitivity to the nuances of expression help conversations to flow, and it becomes very obvious when this is not working successfully in formal and informal interactions. In their collection, Skidmore and Murakami give empirical examples of the workings of prosody, showing how teachers and students may signal intentions of evaluation, authority, reflection, playfulness and so on in ways that go beyond their words (see also Chapter 3 in this book). Methods for investigating prosody draw on the established field of **conversation analysis**, including systematic transcription conventions that indicate accents, pauses, pace, intonation and so on (Jefferson, 1984). This approach is considered in detail in another book in this series: *Research Methods for Classroom Discourse* (Ingram & Elliott, 2019).

Recent methodological interest focuses on new means of researching classroom talk at scale, capitalizing on technological developments. Mercer (2010) hails the 'revolutionary' development of software packages for analysing large databases of written or transcribed spoken language in his discussion of sociocultural discourse analysis. Software 'concordancers' can scan files for all instances of particular target words, thus allowing the researcher to trace occurrences of language use. This can be used either to target certain interactions and episodes of talk for further qualitative exploration, or to compare the relative incidence of certain keywords or types of interaction in quantitative terms. The latter includes new sophisticated ways of exploring how ideas are connected in talk, such as **epistemic network analysis (ENA)** (Shaffer, 2017; and see Chapter 6).

The strengths and weaknesses of the concordance approach require the researcher to weigh up the value of efficiency and statistical analysis against the potential loss and decontextualization of relevant data. There are trade-offs between focusing on the specific and the general. For instance, Rosé and Tovares (2015) describe their use of **machine learning** in the analysis of group discussions over time, notably in computer-supported collaborative learning. Machine learning involves the application of algorithms to text in order to find stable patterns of language in the text and identify characteristics that exemplify each category in a distinctive way. Interest may lie in word choices, such as the dialogic meaning of phrases like 'she claimed' or 'it demonstrated'. Rosé and Tovares comment that 'thorny questions' arise which machine learning in itself cannot answer, such as, 'As classroom cultures change over time, is it just the distribution of categories of behavior that change, or does the repertoire of categories change? Furthermore, does that manifestation of the same categories change?' (p. 293). It is clear that theoretical and empirical questions may arise in the use of new methodological approaches using new technologies, which in turn prompt further lines of inquiry.

Researching processes of dialogic participation and collaboration: Enhancing stakeholder engagement, problem-solving and educational action

Research on dialogic processes of participation and collaboration for students, teachers and others connected with education focuses not only on gaining better understandings of how participants talk, think and learn together, but also on the social and relational conditions for productive dialogue. It is commonly prompted by perceived needs for increasing educational and social justice.

From the student perspective, it has become almost taken for granted that students should have a 'voice', but active steps must be taken to make this a dialogic process (Cook-Sather, 2017; Flutter & Rudduck, 2004; and see Chapter 10). Approaches for eliciting students' views generally rely on familiar methods for engaging students in talk, together with other forms of expression such as drawings, writing, photography, film-making, drama and so on. Much of this research has focused on students' experiences of school, but it originally tended to focus on the school environment and routines rather than being fully embedded in the curriculum itself. There have been some recent developments in that direction, however. Laux's (2018) systematic review of research on student voice in the science curriculum is directed towards understanding how students can be helped to find value and meaning in science learning by expressing their voices in the classroom and linking to their out-of-school knowledge and interests. She turns to the perspectives of critical theory and constructivism to help in understanding both the power dynamics of classrooms and the construction of meaning in social interaction. Conclusions are drawn about the potential for empowerment, meaningful science learning, engagement and achievement, and motivation. Yet Laux comments: 'While many studies emphasized the importance of student voice, few described ways to realistically implement student voice in the classroom' (p. 126). Methods for finding out what students think are familiar (e.g. interview, questionnaire, observation, written work and drawings, to name a few), but there is a need to research their implementation in practice. In this case, aims to enhance stakeholder engagement and take educational action come to the fore to lead methodological development. One example is Djohari and Higham's (submitted) use of video analysis to evaluate the emerging use of peer-led focus groups in the context of a large-scale international network of schools investigating staff and students' adoption of guiding moral values in preparation for their prospects as future global citizens and leaders.

In some circumstances standard research methods may need re-thinking in order to engage with particular individuals and groups of students. For instance, in their systematic review of research methods for eliciting the views of young people identified with autism spectrum disorder (ASD) about their educational experiences, Fayette and Bond (2018) identify certain barriers to communication. Students identified with ASD differ widely from each other, but there are some typical patterns in uses of language, ways of thinking and willingness to initiate interaction. Fayette and Bond found that research methods predominantly include semi-structured interviews in home and school contexts, sometimes supplemented with classroom observation, drawings, symbols, gestures, photographs and videos. On the whole, participants were not actively involved in the research process, and there was little consultation with relevant professionals about the research instruments. They suggest that young people identified with ASD should be more actively involved in developing and evaluating ways in which their views should be elicited regarding important matters in their lives, so enhancing stakeholder engagement and educational action are again closely entwined with the research process. The active and inclusive involvement of all participants is an important area of critical discussion that has received extensive coverage in journals like the *International Journal of Research and Method in Education* and other contexts. A central point lies in understanding the dialogic principle of shared meaning-making that recognizes all children's capacities as thinkers in their own right (e.g. Cassidy, Conrad & José de Figueiroa-Rego, 2019) and similarly for participants of all ages. From a dialogic perspective, we might also wonder about a challenge to theory here: do different ways of communicating potentially change what dialogue is understood to be?

Another key methodological development relates to the need for improved and theoretically sound evaluation and assessment of the quality of participation in dialogue. Wegerif et al. (2017) discuss this from the perspective of (often) implicit assumptions about taking educational action on the basis of what 'good dialogue' should look like. Testing to a model means specifying criteria of what counts as effective talk and then evaluating the extent to which the observed and recorded talk in a classroom changes as a result of an intervention in the direction of meeting these criteria. Yet this approach may only achieve the circular effect of making a claim about success on the basis of what is already built into practice. An empirical focus on learning outcomes in response to intervention offers only limited prospects of understanding the causal processes linking dialogue and learning. Inductive methods using close observation of group work have been more promising in this respect, but these can also be criticized for focusing on what is easy to see, record and analyse, that is, the talk that is already assumed to be key to learning rather than other more 'invisible' communicative processes. With this conundrum in mind, researchers have turned to direct measurement of group thinking, which assesses the thinking of the whole group, not each individual. For instance, Wegerif, Mercer and Dawes (1999) used a standard **Raven's progressive matrices** test, giving some items to groups to solve working together and other items, separately, to the individuals who made up the groups. They found that the group cognitive ability did not correlate closely with the cognitive ability of the individuals making up the group. This has since been developed into the group-thinking test, which is now in use more widely (Wegerif et al., 2017). This new way of thinking could significantly affect educational action: if classroom learning occurs in social groups, then would educational assessment and intervention focus most productively on students in interaction with others, rather than on more traditional judgements about students' abilities in comparison to others? In research terms it suggests that the limitations of different approaches to assessing the quality of group thinking could be mitigated by a combination of direct quantitative measures of research-based signs of effective group work together with qualitative analysis of the processes involved.

In terms of adult collaboration, research reviews have provided evidence for the need to develop mutual understanding of what this means since many terms are in use internationally, see Box 4.2. Vangrieken, Dochy, Raes and Kyndt (2015) point to the value of investigating the importance of discussion in teacher collaboration within educational systems that support this. Links between dialogic

Box 4.2 What is known about teacher collaboration?

Vangrieken et al. (2015) analysed eighty-two studies published between 2000 and 2012, focusing on conceptual understandings of the central ideas rather than on methods. They found a range of terminology in use, which they suggest reflects conceptual confusion between 'teamwork', 'collaboration', 'learning communities' and so on. The possible benefits and consequences of teachers' collaboration appear at different levels: individual teacher, group and organization. Several criteria for effective collaboration emerged such as the application of effort, the use of everyone's knowledge and expertize, role-taking and flexible strategies appropriate to task and organizational setting. Vangrieken et al. noted that levels of collaboration can be superficial or deep, and they comment: 'Critical reflection on and discussion of teaching practice seems to be rare which hampers the possibilities for teachers' collaborative learning' (p. 35). Research suggested that most facilitating factors related to the collaborative process, but a key hindering factor appeared to lie in mindsets and cultures of individualism and autonomy: 'There is thus a need for a change in mentality in the case of teachers and education in general. Without an essential amount of openness to collaborate, every effort pushing teachers towards collaboration may become lost in a culture of contrived collegiality' (p. 36).

collaboration, learning and professional practice are seen in the cyclical processes of professional inquiry and action occurring both between teachers in schools and between teachers and research teams. The latter collaborations are now receiving much attention as means of trialling interventions systematically and building knowledge through **design-based research** (see Chapter 2).

Direct investigation of dialogue can show how practitioner collaborations actually work, or not. Havnes (2009), for instance, identifies different patterns and functions of 'team-talk' in Norwegian interdisciplinary secondary school teacher teams, using detailed video analysis of discussions. More recently, certain structures for professional learning have been investigated in dialogic terms, such as lesson study, which involves teachers in collaborative lesson planning, targeted observation and reflective discussion focusing on pupils' learning. Dudley (2013) analysed teacher talk in lesson study, coding post-lesson discussions in relation to existing frameworks of 'types of talk'. He found that the functions of teachers' spoken contributions, and the use of their different sources of knowledge, resonated with 'cumulative', 'disputational' and 'exploratory talk' (see Chapter 3) occurring at different points of the discussion. The dialogues and knowledge-sharing created the conditions for teacher learning, motivated powerfully by the will to improve pupils' learning. This analysis of teachers' discourse at the level of interaction is distinctive in not only giving access to how teachers use their tacit knowledge but also holding them to professional account within the increasingly popular lesson-study model. So research and practice are closely linked.

Researching social and intercultural understanding: Highlighting stakeholder engagement in research activity, capitalizing on new technologies

The third broad line of inquiry relates to social and intercultural dialogue, including projects directed at enhancing community involvement and conflict resolution that move beyond the investigation of dialogic learning and teaching within schools and colleges. Intercultural dialogue has emerged since the 1980s as a 'distinct form of communication practice ... increasingly associated with a liberal theory of modernity and internationalism that presupposes "freedom", "democracy", "human rights" and "tolerance"' (Besley & Peters, 2012, p. 5). This may cover a range of issues connected to multilingualism, anti-racist education, minority rights, cultural identity, and more. All of these are underpinned politically with assumptions about equity in human value and attitudes of openness to other cultures that lead to dialogue. Besley and Peters suggest, 'Pedagogically, interculturalism assumes in general that exposure to and engagement with a different culture will encourage a greater understanding of the world's people in all their ethnic and cultural diversity and thereby also provide the basis for intercultural understanding and the appropriate conditions for dialogue' (p. 6).

Besley and Peters highlight the social relations inherent in dialogue, entailing certain virtues and emotions: concern, trust, respect, appreciation, affection and hope (Burbules, 1993, p. 19). We can see how these can connect closely with the essential ethical considerations that should guide any research project. These are underpinned by the principle that 'all educational research should be conducted within *an ethic of respect* for: the person; knowledge; democratic values; the quality of educational research; and academic freedom' (BERA, 2018a, p. 5). The contemporary perspective on ethical decision-making is one of actively deliberating, through an ongoing and iterative process of assessing and reassessing the situation and issues as they arise (BERA, 2018a, p. 2); this is itself a dialogic process between researcher and co-researchers, participants, gatekeepers, sponsors and the research context itself.

Methodological implications of interculturalism range between studies *about* intercultural dialogic engagement and studies that *are dialogic* in themselves, for example, surveys of 'intercultural competence' (Luka, 2012), **ethnography** (Gobbo, 2012) and social activism (Zehra, 2012). Online discussions have also added much here, as discussed in Chapter 8. It is sometimes hard to separate research designs and educational activity. For example, in his discussion of an African perspective on intercultural dialogue, education and transformation, Rule (2012) draws attention to the combined uses of action research, experiential learning, and community of practice frameworks in a South African peace education program. This was developed through participatory workshop activities, including sharing stories. Dialogic stakeholder involvement in educational research activity is also seen in methodological approaches driven by principles of inclusion and educational transformation; see Box 4.3 for a **case study.**

> ### Box 4.3 A case study of research for inclusive dialogic participation in education: Enhancing community involvement
>
> Flecha and Soler (2013) write about 'turning difficulties into possibilities' in their account of including Roma families and students in school through dialogic learning in Spain. They were concerned to develop 'successful educational actions' to enhance children's engagement and academic success. They based their work on a dialogic learning approach that highlights the many interactions that support children's learning within and beyond school, such as social learning in groups and parental involvement in learning. They describe this work as entailing the transformation of the learners' social context through multiplying learning interactions in the different spaces in which children act (i.e. classroom, school, after school, home). It also considers the importance of dialogue based on egalitarian relationships, based on the validity of the arguments provided or based on the intentions to reach understanding and agreements, rather than power claims, or imposition (Habermas, 1984, pp. 453–4). In a longitudinal case study, qualitative and quantitative data were collected over four years. Data included communicative life stories with family members, one communicative focus group with professionals working in the school, five communicative observations and thirteen open-ended interviews. They also gathered quantitative performance data from standardized national tests, and a questionnaire soliciting pupil perceptions of these learning improvements. This is a highly integrated example of how multiple methods may be employed, with a contextual perspective, to intertwine stakeholder engagement in research activity and education with an intercultural and transformative aim.

Specific obstacles to intercultural (and any) dialogue must be considered, particularly in the uncritical use of language. Rule (2012) comments that languages are 'symbolic codes which represent their dominant speakers, and bear the weight of their culture and ideology' (p. 336). It has been shown in many studies that close analysis of language can provide distinctive insight into cultural practices of communication. For instance, Larry (2018) conducted a detailed study of language use in multiprofessional case discussions in a special school in an Arabic-speaking Gulf-Arabian country. She found clear evidence of communicative practices distinctive to this cultural and linguistic context, adding considerably to the understanding of assessment practices that have largely been researched in Western countries. **Linguistic ethnography** is relevant here as an approach that involves the investigation of the mutual influences between language and social practices, so language and culture become a single unit of analysis as people negotiate their identities and power relationships. Linguistic ethnographers focus closely on data, with close analysis of language in social use (Copland & Creese, 2015). This commonly involves methodological approaches using interviews, observational fieldwork, analysis of recorded interactions and textual analysis of existing documents. These approaches can be applied for different purposes, often in combination, bearing in mind the intercultural implications of fundamental ethical principles such as respect for participant autonomy, enhancing of participant benefits ('beneficence'), avoiding harm ('non-maleficence') and justice in equitable and fair treatment. As Copland and Creese point out (pp. 185–6), cultural expectations and practices may vary in relation to apparently straightforward processes like signing consent forms. There is, therefore, a need to discuss ethical issues with stakeholders in the research site, keeping an open mind about how ethical procedures should be adapted as needed.

Key methodological questions about researching educational dialogue

The overview in the previous section points to some key questions about how researching educational dialogue may move forward methodologically.

- What are the basic requirements for researching educational dialogue, taking dialogic principles into account?
- How can the outcomes of dialogic engagement be researched?

- What is the impact of changes in technology, and increasing access to different forms of hardware and software?
- What are the **affordances** of approaches to research emphasizing strong connections to practice and dialogue with stakeholders?

The first two questions are based on the belief that sufficient groundwork has now been done in the field of educational dialogue to justify building on what is known to go further in researching processes and outcomes in more detail. For instance, we have a secure understanding that dialogue develops over time (Mercer, 2008), so what are the best research methods to trace dialogue over shorter and longer periods of time? We now know a lot about the structures of classroom dialogue, so can we develop improved research methods and designs to investigate learning outcomes in 'real-life' situations with many confounding variables? The third question, about the impact of new technologies, seems self-evident for keeping generally up to date, but are there more specific possibilities for capitalizing on technological affordances? For instance, could this include the improved capacity to observe fast-paced interactions in detail? Could it involve designing and researching new uses of technology with dialogic aims in mind, such as online discussions? The fourth question highlights the affordances of connecting research strongly with practice, that is, what do such research approaches appear to offer in relation to formulating and answering the research questions and aims? Building close connections between research and practice is already of general concern in current educational research (BERA, 2018b), but are there also ways of developing familiar research designs and methods to enhance dialogic communication with stakeholders? Some answers to these questions are summarized in Table 4.1 which draws on the previous discussion with a few additional references.

Literature review as a dialogic research method

Literature review is an important dialogic research method in its own right. Some types of literature review bring authors' voices to the fore, such as 'narrative' or 'configurative' approaches

Table 4.1 Methodological questions and developments in researching educational dialogue

Methodological question	Dialogic aspects	Research developments
1) What are the basic requirements for researching educational dialogue, taking dialogic principles into account?	a) recognizing essential temporal and contextual aspects of dialogic conversations b) understanding theoretical variations in research interests and levels of analysis c) actively taking account of differing language structures, terminology and cultural practices in talk, including multimodal dialogue, non-verbal communication, silence	a) extending analysis of simple 'IRF' (initiation-response-feedback) sequences in teacher–student talk to examine chains and spiral structures of dialogue; concordance techniques for scanning texts (see Chapter 6) b) clarifying different approaches to observing talk with different purposes and RQs in mind c) conducting and synthesizing more international studies; attending actively to discourse and translations; attending to different forms of communication beyond speech, and to silence (e.g. Schultz, 2009)
2) How can the outcomes of dialogic engagement be researched?	a) contextualizing dialogue and learning outcomes b) understanding the nature of academically productive dialogue c) taking account of social aspects of thinking	a) developing designs that capture existing variation, different subject domains and activities b) conducting rigorous intervention studies in relationship with assessment of quality of learning c) developing assessment and evaluation instruments and practices based on dialogic theory (see Chapter 5)

3) What is the impact of changes in technology, and increasing access to different forms of hardware and software? (see review by Major, Warwick, Rasmussen, Ludvigsen & Cook, 2018)	a) recognizing technological affordances for dialogic engagement b) shifting attention between micro- and macroanalysis of dialogic interaction c) tuning into details of social interaction; activating memory and knowledge; joint focus of attention	a) capitalizing on increasing access to different forms of hardware, software, Big Data and techniques for technology-mediated dialogue (see Chapters 7 and 8) b) developing generic and bespoke software to support coding, video analysis and so on c) connecting with thriving areas of educational research, such as 'professional vision' and 'noticing' in classrooms, to focus and drive new technological uses (e.g. Gröschner, Seidel, Kiemer & Pehmer, 2015)
4) What are the affordances of approaches to research emphasizing strong connections to practice and dialogue with stakeholders?	a) communicating and co-researching with practitioners b) enhancing dialogic involvement of research participants	a) applying robust research designs that are based on research-practice collaboration, e.g. design-based research and lesson study b) reviewing familiar research methods for dialogic opportunities for groups and individuals who may have different ways of communicating

(Gough, Thomas & Oliver, 2012; Onwuegbuzie & Frels, 2016). These typically summarize and discuss theoretical, historical and/ or methodological aspects of the topic in question using a range of sources that are sufficiently diverse to explore a range of trends, assumptions and conceptualizations. In other approaches authors are less overly present, such as 'systematic' reviews that are designed to identify and evaluate all the relevant research evidence on a topic, potentially resulting in a clear statement of results. In keeping with dialogic principles, we see literature review in terms of its role in the use and production of knowledge, and authors' perspectives should be visible. Reading published work may give access to what others know, but thinking and writing about it then inevitably involves the construction of new ideas.

Thomson[1] has written extensively about academic writing, especially for doctoral students, pointing out that developing a literature review involves the extension and consolidation of different domains of knowledge:

- substantive knowledge from your discipline, or disciplines

- knowledge about your readers

- knowledge about the kind of text that you are writing

- knowledge about the kind of rhetoric that you have to use

- knowledge about the process of writing

- knowledge about scholarship and you as a scholar

Thomson argues that this writing needs to be more than a 'laundry list' of relevant sources, because a literature review inevitably involves the writer's interpretations. So a simple list of what others have written is incomplete without commentary. In another blog,[2] she refers to Kamler and Thomson's (2014) metaphor of the dinner table, suggesting that 'the literatures in the journal article can be thought of as a select dinner party with the guest list composed of people who can't be left out, and those who are going to be most interesting to talk to. As dinner party host you also control

---

[1]https://patthomson.net/2018/06/11/why-is-writing-a-literature-review-such-hard-work-part-one/.
[2]https://patthomson.net/2015/02/04/writing-course-the-literatures/.

the conversation and of course, you don't assassinate or poison the guests but conduct any disagreements in a civil manner.' This metaphor seems potentially dialogic, but it is still a one-way process in which the 'guests' cannot talk to each other or respond to you as writer. However, there are now some emerging models of publishing built explicitly on dialogic principles, including open dialogues in journals and open peer reviews for journal articles.

There are many practical guides to reviewing research literature, with detailed advice on searching, selection and making sense of different sources. Useful tactics include the following:

- formulating questions to ask of the literature, based on what you already know and your conceptual framework of how different theoretical ideas, practices, factors and processes relate to each other

- targeting searches on areas of main interest (e.g. Padilla, 1992)

- flexibly generating different combinations of 'keywords' to search journal databases

- browsing and 'hand searching' journals where relevant papers are often to be found (e.g. Erduran, Ozdem & Park, 2015)

- speed-reading papers for what is said about methodology (or whatever the perspective of interest may be)

- looking for information about the context and participants in empirical studies (including critical thinking about who is included and excluded)

- becoming aware of key authors in the field of interest, and following their work in their publications, websites and in person

- keeping dated records of searches conducted, recording results each time and noticing when lines of inquiry appear to be complete (i.e. no new material is appearing)

Successful engagement in reading other people's work depends on being aware of the understanding that one starts with. This is, however, not just to do with knowledge of research findings about the topic in question. It is a fundamental stance and disposition. Onwuegbuzie and Frels (2016) write comprehensively about being a 'culturally progressive literature reviewer'. This is based on their core understanding that 'every research study is (a) conducted on one or more cultural groups (e.g. ethnic groups, age groups, neighbourhoods, businesses, educational institutions); (b) conducted *by* one or more researchers representing one or more cultural groups; and (c) a product that is consumed (e.g. read, replicated, applied) by people representing one or more cultural groups' (pp. 74–5). In presenting literature review as a culturally progressive and ethical commitment, Onwuegbuzie and Frels's argument can be seen in dialogic terms. Making sense of a field of research is an intrinsically human activity, not a mechanical process, and there needs to be an active effort to understand and respond to other perspectives. There is also a communicative and potentially dialogic element in the choice of sources and the presentation of findings. Onwuegbuzie and Frels advocate a multimodal approach to literature review which combines different semiotic systems: linguistic, visual, audio, spatial, gestural. They give the example that a webpage, for instance, might have written language, pictures, music and sound effects, maps, moving images (p. 79). They summarize the key principles with their MODES acronym for different sources of information (p. 80):

M Media – visual representations
O Observation(s) – visiting locations
D Documents – printed and digital texts
E Experts in the field – interview prolific authors
S Secondary data – surveys, censuses, etc

This is an integrated process of consultation and response which extends beyond reading to include visits and discussion with knowledgeable experts as well as reference to different types of written material. In Onwuegbuzie and Frels' view, the researcher can ideally be an original, critical and ethical thinker, and a culturally progressive, reflexive and multimodal researcher. These core aspects of one's identity could be seen as the foundations of learning through research.

Reflexivity brings out another dialogic element, which is to value (and potentially challenge) the knowledge that each person adds from their own experience. Simon and Goes (2013) take this further, arguing,

> Truly innovative literature reviews go well beyond simple summaries of source material. A thorough and innovative literature review presumes that knowledge is cumulative, and that the researcher not only stands on the shoulders of others in exploring a topic of study, but generates critical and substantial value in the act of reviewing (p. 297). … [It] engages the researcher in a critique *of* the system, challenging assumptions within the system and conventional ways of thinking about a problem to generate new insights and new directions for logic and research. … The researcher engaged in

Box 4.4 Investigating a collaborative approach to literature review

Kahn, Wareham, Young, Willis and Pilkington (2008) report on their collaborative approach to literature review on reflective practice and PD in higher education (HE) which took place in several stages to embed practitioner perspectives from the start. The review team included HE programme directors with responsibility for leading PD programme and some previous experience of research. Each member of the review team focused on a defined area of literature on reflective practice, giving particular attention to studies that articulated how approaches to reflective practice were actually implemented. Review team members were asked to summarize each study using a proforma that explicitly sought their views about practice and they were interviewed in an interim evaluation. This sustained dialogic engagement allowed new perspectives to emerge including some unplanned observations. For instance, the interim interviews suggested that practitioner reviewers' initial signs of reluctance to judge research outcomes could be understood in terms of their adherence to highly contextualized and interpretive beliefs about practice-based knowledge in contrast to 'scientific' realist orientations to empirical knowledge. The authors conclude that in this sort of dialogic process it is important to take account of reviewers' different conceptions of the epistemological meaning of literature review, bearing in mind the range of disciplinary origins in the team.

this type of thinking views the literature review as a *debate* and *dialogue* between different ideas and different authors. (p. 299)

This can result in lasting transformation through appreciating and responding to other perspectives through dialogic engagement that potentially deepens or transforms understanding. Certain key stakeholders may be excluded for several reasons: they are not asked to be involved, they have no time to take part, they lack motivation or confidence to contribute their own views. So there is a need to include different voices in the review process and attempt to reduce privileging of some voices over others. Research has been conducted on this process, see Box 4.4.

Concluding remarks

In this chapter we have discussed the ways in which engagement with published research about educational dialogue, together with other research activities such as seminars and conference discussions, can become a dialogic process that supports the collective development of knowledge and understanding through the active and reflective 'translation' of ideas between different contexts of research and practice. Literature review is seen as a dialogic research method which brings certain core practices to the fore:

- respectful critical reading of other people's work
- actively searching for different sources of knowledge and ways of thinking, in readings, conferences, social media, and day-to-day conversations
- paying close attention to discourses and uses of terminology
- exploring new opportunities for engaging in purposeful discussions to clarify thinking, understand differences and, perhaps, help to solve problems
- willingly taking on the role of reviewing other people's writing for publication, as part of one's responsibility to academics, professionals, politicians and the wider public
- keeping abreast of the open agenda in education and research, especially in the digital age (see *Research Methods*

for Education in the Digital Age in this series, by Savin-Baden & Tombs, 2017) with new opportunities for sharing work, including new developments such as open peer review[3]

In terms of methodological decision-making, this chapter raises questions for planning a research project and then justifying the approach adopted:

- What may be offered by particular combinations of research methods?

- What are the trade-offs in deciding on research methods and focusing data collection at different levels for analysis?

- What theoretical position is informing the research planning? Is there a good match between theoretical beliefs and methods in use?

- Are there opportunities for interdisciplinary research, both in reviewing relevant literature and in working with other researchers?

We hope that this chapter's review of methodological developments and the importance of the literature review process not only helps to position the different chapters of this book but also encourages different forms of dialogic engagement in reading other people's work and contributing in turn to educational dialogue as a living field of study.

---

[3]https://www.nature.com/nature/peerreview/debate/nature04991.html.

CHAPTER FIVE

Dialogic Participation and Outcomes: Evaluation and Assessment

Ayesha Ahmed

Introduction

There are three important questions to address as a starting point for this chapter:

Why do we want to assess dialogue?
What do we mean by the construct of dialogue?
How should we assess dialogue?

Assessment is all about gathering evidence from which to make decisions. According to Harlen (2006), it is 'deciding, collecting and making judgements about evidence relating to the goals of the learning being assessed' (p. 87).

There are a number of possible reasons for wanting to assess dialogue. We might want to assess the quality of a dialogue in order to find out how dialogic the interactions are in particular classrooms, or to find out whether a group of students is having a productive dialogue, for example. The purpose of this sort of assessment of dialogue could be to provide teachers and learners with a way to judge dialogue among their students in order to help them to improve their dialogic skills. Alternatively, or additionally, it might be to enable us to look at the relationship between dialogue and an assessed learning outcome.

In any of these cases it's important to ask: What is the **construct** of dialogue? This needs breaking down further into: what do we mean by good quality dialogue and what might progress look like? We could consider quality to be a more *productive* dialogue, and this could be productive in terms of a specified outcome, such as deeper understanding of subject content, better take-up of ideas discussed or other resultant learning. Alternatively we could consider quality in terms of the dialogue skills themselves as evidenced by characteristics of the interactions such as level of engagement of participants, longer turns or use of a particular type of utterance such as questioning, reasoning or elaboration. Quality is most likely to be a combination of these things as outcomes will interact with features of the dialogue.

An important aspect of understanding what a construct consists of is building a picture of what progression looks like. For dialogue this could involve forming a concept of 'good' and 'poor' for various dimensions of dialogue, or it could be more nuanced and describe levels of quality in the form of learning progressions (e.g. see Wilson, 2009). Another way of thinking about progression is to consider the *frequency* of occurrence of certain features or dimensions of dialogue within a theoretical framework in which some of these features are considered more valuable or desirable than others. The question of what we mean by 'good' is fundamental to thinking about any assessment. It sits alongside the 'why' question in addressing the issue of purpose, and it sets conditions for the third question: *How* should we gather evidence of dialogic participation and of outcomes of dialogue?

In assessing dialogue we are making judgements about 'performances' which can consist of both the features and the results of the dialogue. Going back to the definition of assessment above, we are making judgements about observable evidence, and in the case of dialogue the evidence is complex and hard to capture. This of course affects the kinds of judgements we can make.

Let's take the two issues of complexity and difficulty of capture in turn. The complex nature of the evidence is that it is multilevel, multimodal and involves multiple participants. We are assessing interactions that are difficult to attribute to individuals as they occur in the dialogic space (see Wegerif & Mercer, 1997a), and assessors need to pay attention to multiple characteristics of the interaction that may occur simultaneously. For valid assessment, we need observables, and these need to be captured either by live observation, or by video recording, both of which present challenges in terms of available resources and the potential effects of the presence of an observer and/or recording device during dialogic interactions.

The challenges above, of defining the construct, of capturing observables and of deciding on a method for making judgements, all relate to issues of **validity**, the central concept when considering any assessment. The most widely used definition of validity is that given by Messick (1989) as 'an overall evaluative judgment of the degree to which empirical evidence and theoretical rationales support the adequacy and appropriateness of interpretations and actions on the basis of test scores and other modes of assessment' (p. 6). More recent theorists (e.g. Kane, 2001) have argued for a more pragmatic view of validity, linking it to the process of validation. Kane suggests an argument-based approach in which we must form a validity argument in order to give us warrants for the claims and *inferences* that we make from an assessment. Inferences are critical, because with dialogue assessment (as with much if not all of educational assessment), we are attempting to 'measure' something that is not easily quantifiable. We need to try to ensure that the inferences we make from the available evidence of the construct are as sound as possible.

A critical aspect of validity is the **reliability** of judgements, and again, in the case of dialogue, there are significant challenges to be recognized when considering the accuracy of our judgements of quality. These relate mainly to the issues described above, of capturing evidence and of making judgements when there are multiple participants. We will return to these issues after discussing some examples that illustrate research methods for the assessment of dialogue.

Example 1: Developing an Oracy Assessment Toolkit

This example involves assessing the quality of dialogue for the purpose of improving the teaching and learning of oracy skills. Dialogue and oracy are distinct but related constructs. Dialogic teaching, as a pedagogical approach, is distinct from the teaching of oracy as part of a curriculum (see Mercer's unpacking of this distinction at http://bit.ly/oracydialogue/). The construct of oracy consists of the skills involved in speaking and listening. Participating productively in dialogue can be seen as a subset of these skills, and one context in which this may occur is within a dialogic classroom setting.

The Oracy Assessment Toolkit was developed as part of a **design-based research** project[1] in which methods for assessing oracy in schools were researched and piloted. The project began with a conceptual (rather than empirical) approach to mapping the construct of oracy, based on the literature and on expert **focus group** discussions. The result was the Oracy Skills Framework (Mercer, Warwick & Ahmed, 2017) describing generic oracy skills divided into four categories: physical, linguistic, cognitive, and social and emotional. Tasks and assessment schemes were piloted to sample skills from across the framework, with one of these being a Talking Points task in which dialogue among three participants was assessed. Talking Points are statements (rather than questions which may imply there is a right answer) posed in order to prompt rich discussion in which participants aim to come to an agreed shared viewpoint (see Dawes, 2011).

Once we had a conceptual framework, we then applied an empirical approach to the sampling of the construct and the design of the methods for assessment. The three tasks (the Talking Points dialogue, individual presentations, and a paired instructional task) were trialled in schools with 11- to 12-year-old pupils in England. Teachers, researchers and oracy experts assessed performances using both live observation and post hoc video observation. Judgements were recorded on a basic observation sheet containing a sample of skills from the framework for each task. Teachers and researchers could rate the performances on a three-point scale for each relevant oracy skill. This was followed by focus group discussions with the judges, stimulated by the video data.

---

[1] See www.educ.cam.ac.uk/research/projects/oracytoolkit.

The trialling process allowed researchers to decide which skills were the most appropriate ones to sample in the assessment of each task, and to improve the design of the tasks to elicit the evidence needed. The design of the method for evaluating the dialogue, that is, the criteria and system for scoring, was also based on evidence from the trialling. Trialling took place in a school in which oracy was central to the curriculum, as well as in two schools with a more traditional curriculum.

Another important aspect of the methodology for developing this assessment was a comparative judgement (CJ) exercise in which judges made paired comparisons of performances, resulting in a rank order which was used to validate the scale. This method originated from the work of Thurstone (1927) and has recently become prominent again in educational assessment (see e.g. Pollitt, 2012). It can be used to validate assessments of a construct (in this case teacher and researcher ratings of the skills) by comparing rank orders produced by the original method and the CJ method. This exercise confirmed that teachers were able to judge pupils' contributions to dialogue (and performances in presentations and instructional tasks) in terms of the individual oracy skills in a way that was consistent with **holistic judgements** of the performances. With this method we can ensure that we preserve meaning even when making assessment decisions about discreet skills that comprise the construct.

The next stage was to communicate the scale so that other teachers could use these assessments with their pupils. This was done by providing exemplar video material for each task, illustrating the skills in evidence and describing the performances in terms of these skills. Below are two short extracts from one of the Talking Points tasks. The students (aged 11–12 years) are discussing whether or not they agree with the statement:

"Some people, like footballers, get paid too much."

Extract 1

C: *I think we should move on to 8, 'cos it...*
Y: *Yes.*
C: *... connects up. Right, erm, it depends, like, erm, football is, like, when you have so many good players, that they have good players and they get paid 'cos they're actually good.*

Like people get quite, footballers get conned [0:08:35.4] because, depending on how much salary they have. Er, Rooney has £300,000 a week and, erm, yeah, like, that could be different to people, like, people with lower wages might be, like, 'Oh, that's not fair,' but he's a person that's talented and I don't think that you need to argue with how much they get paid. It's just because they're, like, good at, they're good at that sport. They might not be as good as you.

Z: *I actually disagree with you on this one, erm, because Mr B, erm, showed us, er, erm, a website which showed how much Rooney gets paid, which is unbelievable. But I don't actually think that Rooney's got that talent, and I'm not going to go into football, but, like someone like a nurse is right now getting paid lower, getting paid less than how much Rooney makes and a nurse saves lives, give advice and, like, saves people from having diseases, whereas footballers just shoot a ball in the net.*

Y: *So, which, if that's the [0:09:42.9], then I agree with you, because some people, like footballers, get too much and so I can see C nodding his head, saying, 'No, no, no, no, no,'...*

C: *[Shakes head]*

Y: *... but, like, I think that rather than people throwing a ball on a pitch, erm, like kicking a ball to put it in the net, 'Ah, you've got a goal in,' and, yeah, and you get, like money is not always the solution to everything, because, like, sometimes being a nurse and a footballer, let's be honest, which one's more important? Being a nurse, isn't it, C?*

C: *Mmm [nods head].*

Y: *Yeah, 'cos, 'cos you have to deliver babies and stuff like that, whereas if you're being a footballer, is it that important? It's not the most important thing. Yes, it could, yes, it might be a dream that you might want, but, like,... [sighs], I can't explain it.*

C: *Right, erm, I, kind of, agree with you guys now. A, a footballer trains at least two times a week and plays either one or two matches which are up to 90 minutes a week, but if a nurse, a nurse has a shift for, like, 12 hours and that's, the difference between that is, is...*

Y: *[0:10:52.5].*

C: *... between a footballer, is just constant, and then, erm, a nurse gets, like, paid yearly, round, I don't know, I don't know how much a year, but a nurse gets paid yearly. But, like, erm, Messi gets £500,000 a year and he probably plays twice a week or, and trains twice a week, which, I think, comparing, is unfair.*

Y: *Yeah.*

C: *[Nodding]*

Y: *So, I think, overall, we all, kind of, agree with this.*

C: *Mmm [in agreement].*

Z: *Yeah.*

Y: *Yeah.*

C: *Z, do you want to pick one, because you haven't picked one yet?*

Extract 2

G: *Yeah. Some people, like footballers, get paid too much.*

J: *Well...*

D: *Well, I don't think, I don't, you know...*

G: *A lot of footballers get paid quite a lot of money for just...*

D: *I know, but...*

G: *... kicking the ball around.*

D: *... but, technically...*

J: *Yeah, that, yeah.*

D: *... but, technically, you can't really blame them, because...*

J & G:*Yeah.*

D: *... it's actually the managers of the club, they...*

G: *yeah.*

D: *... pay them. You know, but, also, if you're, if it means that much to them to have players playing for them and winning, maybe, you know, they're prepared to pay that much money.*

G: *Yeah.*

J: *Yeah. It depends if you have that much...*

G: *Yeah.*

J: *... money.*

D: *Yes.*

G: *Like, if you think about Wayne Rooney gets paid £500,000 a week now.*

D & J: *Yeah.*
G: *That's the, and, like, how much would he give to charity?*
J: *Yeah.*
D: *Yeah.*
G: *It would be about, like, a, not even about an eighth of the money he'd give to charity.*
D: *Yeah, erm…*
J: *Yeah… like, they'd have to get, they'd have to use that money just not on them, not just on themselves…*
G: *Yeah.*
J: *… and…*
G: *But for other people as well.*
J: *Yeah.*

A clear contrast can be seen between these two examples of dialogue: Extract 1 is from a school in which oracy is an integral part of the curriculum and students are explicitly taught skills of group discussion. Differences can be seen, for example, in the turn-taking and the length of turns. Within those lengthy turns in Extract 1 the students are responding to each other by elaborating on each other's points and asking questions, as well as justifying their own points by giving reasons for their ideas. These differences can be evaluated using the Oracy Assessment Toolkit to identify evidence of particular oracy skills in the dialogue. This can then be used to provide feedback to students on how to improve the dialogue.

The generic assessment toolkit developed in this study is available online at www.educ.cam.ac.uk/oracytoolkit for teachers to use during live observation in the classroom to score individuals' oracy skills on Talking Points and the two other tasks. The scheme provides an observation sheet on which teachers can rate performances by giving a Bronze, Silver or Gold rating on each oracy skill sampled for the task. The use of multiple tasks sampling different skills allows teachers to build up a profile of a learner's oracy skills. A profile of skills is more appropriate than an overall score for oracy as it makes little sense and is of little use to aggregate levels of performance on different aspects of this construct.

One of the aims of the project was to encourage more teaching of these skills in schools. Providing a way for teachers to assess these skills and for learners to self- and peer-assess should make it easier for teachers to integrate these kinds of activities into the curriculum. This work has been taken forward by Voice 21, a charity campaigning to raise the status of oracy in schools across the UK, in order to encourage schools to make oracy an important part of their curriculum.

Example 2: The relationship between classroom dialogue and learning

This large-scale study funded by the Economic and Social Research Council and reported in full in Howe, Hennessy, Mercer, Vrikki and Wheatley (2019) was designed to investigate the relationship between pupils' learning outcomes and the nature of dialogue in their classrooms. Rather than involving any intervention, dialogue was assessed in a naturalistic classroom setting. The researchers observed lessons in seventy-two Year 6 classrooms (pupils aged 10–11 years) in England. Two lessons were recorded in each classroom (two of English, mathematics and science). The dialogue from these lessons was transcribed and coded using a scheme based on Hennessy et al.'s (2016) SEDA scheme for coding educational dialogue on a turn-by-turn level (see Chapter 6 for more detail on this scheme).

The purpose of the coding in this case was to be able to form a notional scale of dialogicality so that researchers could look at the relationship between the quality of the dialogue and various learning outcomes of the pupils. The construct in this case was derived empirically: by observing the dialogue that was occurring naturally and then using a coding scheme to categorize what was observed at the utterance level and counting frequencies of these individual codes. This approach was grounded in a sociocultural theoretical framework informed by literature on the characteristics of theoretically productive dialogue (e.g. Alexander, 2008; Mercer & Littleton, 2007). The data from the coding, along with holistic lesson-level ratings, were then used to investigate the relationship between characteristics of dialogue and pupils' learning outcomes.

The outcome measures used were attainment on national assessments in mathematics, grammar and reading (end of primary school tests) along with a science test and a reasoning test designed by the researchers. Pupils also completed the PASS (pupil attitudes to self and school) questionnaire on attitudes to school and self as learner (GL assessment, 2013). An important aspect of this study was the consideration of the many potential **confounds** to measuring the effects of classroom dialogue on these learning outcomes.

Eliminating the effects of confounds is important for ensuring validity for any assessment; it means ruling out the role played by other, independent factors operating in the setting that may be related to both of the variables of interest (i.e. dialogue quality and student outcomes). This can be seen in terms of Messick's (1989) twin threats to validity: construct irrelevant variance (CIV) and **construct under-representation** (CUR). Confounds that can cause variation in scores that are due to something other than the construct of interest are potential causes of CIV; in this case, such variables were categorized and controlled for. For example, pupil characteristics such as prior attainment and motivation were controlled for with a **pre- and post-test design**. Confounds related to teacher characteristics such as homework set, feedback given and behaviour management were accounted for by using a teacher questionnaire. Confounds related to student characteristics or home background (such as parental support with homework) were accounted for by using a child questionnaire.

Addressing potential confounds in this way was critical to the design of the study as without this any variation in outcome measures could have been due to factors other than the construct of interest, dialogue. Because of the complexity of classroom dialogue, studies designed to evaluate it are vulnerable to threats of CIV, so it is important to be as rigorous as possible when considering possible confounding factors. The threat of CUR was less of an issue in this design as whole lessons were recorded, providing rich data on the dialogue occurring in each classroom.

In terms of Kane's argumentation approach to validity, it is important that the inferences made from the coding of the dialogue are supported by rigour in the way in which the codes are applied. Reliability checks carried out during the coding allow confidence in the consistency of coding decisions. These coding decisions are the critical judgements in this case, as frequency of codes is what makes up the 'scoring' system for assessing the dialogue. It was through the coding process and subsequent analyses that the variables making up the construct were identified. This empirical approach to de-constructing the construct of classroom dialogue by coding at the speaker turn level allows us a way to assess the quality of dialogue and therefore to look at the relationship between dialogue quality and learning outcomes.

Holistic lesson-level ratings were also used to score lessons on a three-point scale (0–2) on five dimensions, one of which was level of Student Participation. The inclusion of these holistic ratings is important in order to capture those features of the ethos within a dialogic classroom that cannot be captured at the more fine-grained level of turns. Ratings of different aspects of dialogue quality across exchanges, episodes or lessons rather than frequencies of codes could alternatively be used for all categories.

Once coding was complete, **multiple regression analysis** was carried out in order to investigate the relationship between dialogue (dependent variable) and confounds (independent variables). **Multilevel modelling** was then used to isolate the effects of different aspects of dialogue. This is a useful technique when variables are structured in a hierarchy, in this case with students clustered in classes, and with outcomes at the student level and dialogue at the class level. Each dialogue variable was analysed separately, followed by analysis of the interactions between key dialogue variables and their interactions with Student Participation.

As in the previous example, a process of validation was carried out in which experts were asked to rank episodes of dialogue using holistic judgement (although not using CJ in this case). The rank order of productivity of the dialogue was found to be consistent with results of the coding.

Results of Howe et al.'s (2019) study showed that when Student Participation (as rated in the lesson-level holistic ratings) was high then high levels of Elaboration and Inviting Elaboration, and high levels of Querying, were productive in terms of learning and attitudinal outcomes. However, they were not productive when Student Participation was low. This illustrates the importance of exploring the interaction between holistic-level judgements and finer-grained analysis. Parallels can be seen in the scoring of language assessments in which holistic and analytic approaches to marking are combined to preserve score meaning and therefore the validity of inferences made from the assessments (see e.g. Harsch & Martin, 2013, for a discussion of validity issues relating to scoring approaches).

Howe et al. (2019) also used an observation tool for group work whenever it occurred in the lessons. This involved recording instances of specific features of the discussions: proposals, elaborations,

All pupils were involved in the group work interactions	
Groups did not split into subgroups	
There was a significant amount of pupil–pupil on-task talk	
Pupils showed a positive attitude towards working together in a group	
Group interaction involved sharing and building on each other's ideas	
Group interaction involved justified reasoning	
Group interaction involved constructive evaluation of each other's ideas	
Pupils tried to reach consensus or compromise	
Group work involved productive discussion and/or conflict	
Group work roles were not detrimental to pupil group working	
Rating: 1 = Not true, 2 = Partly true, 3 = Very true	

FIGURE 5.1 *Group work rating scale.*

justifications, disagreements and consensus. This was done using a **time-sampling** technique throughout the group session. At the end of the group session a rating scale[2] was used for the overall quality of the group work as depicted in Figure 5.1.

This allowed the researchers to look at the relationship between the quality of reasoned discussions in the group work and scores on the pupil outcome measures; reasoning during small group work proved to be a strong predictor of learning.

In a separate project, Ahmed and Johnson (in preparation) developed an assessment tool for teachers to use to assess secondary school students' participation in group work involving problem-solving in secondary school lessons. See www.aqa.org.uk/groupwork for details of this resource designed for formative assessment purposes. Specific feedback can be shared with individuals on how to improve their collaborative skills by understanding more about the features of group discussions that result in better collaboration.

---

[2]This scale was adapted from that described by Kutnick and Blatchford (2013); it proved highly reliable (81 per cent agreement between researchers after rigorous training). Ratings were averaged across the ten scales to obtain an overall index of group work quality in each classroom.

The Instructional Quality Assessment (Junker et al., 2006) offers a further example for rating classroom dialogue, related to Accountable Talk (see Chapter 6 for more details). In this case four levels are described for a number of aspects of lesson dialogue. This includes a Participation dimension – along with Linking Contributions – as part of 'Accountability to the Learning Community'. It also employs similar 4-point scales to rate 'Accountability to Rigorous Thinking' and 'Accountability to Knowledge' (as reproduced in Box 5.1).

Box 5.1 Accountability to Knowledge rating scale

Junker et al.'s (2006) rating scale: How effectively did the lesson talk build Accountability to Knowledge?

Asking: Were contributors asked to support their contributions with evidence?

4 There are 3 or more efforts to ask students to provide evidence for their contributions, including questions that seemed academically relevant.

3 There are 1–2 efforts to ask students to provide evidence for their contributions that seemed academically relevant.

2 There are one or more superficial, trivial efforts, or formulaic efforts to ask students to provide evidence for their contributions.

1 There are no efforts to ask students to provide evidence for their contributions.

N/A Reason:

Example 3: Developing an English-speaking task for second-language learners

This example illustrates the use of research into dialogue to inform the design of an assessment, followed by research into the patterns of interactions produced during the assessment, in turn informing an understanding of dialogue in this context. The context is a test of second-language English speaking using paired dialogue: the Cambridge First Certificate in English, now known as B2 First.[3]

Two candidates and two examiners are involved in the paired test, with one of the examiners participating and the other observing. This allows both a two-way dialogue between the candidates and a three-way dialogue with one of the examiners participating. Both of the examiners score the test at the end: the participating examiner gives a global mark using a holistic scale and the observer uses an **analytical mark scheme** to score specific aspects of the dialogue. Scales are based on the Common European Framework of Reference for Languages (CEFR). Candidates are asked to imagine a specific scenario, for example, a town that wants to attract more tourists, and then to discuss ideas and questions relating to this in their pair for about two minutes. Examples of prompts for the paired discussion task can be found on the Cambridge English website referred to above.

Galaczi (2008) studied transcripts of thirty pairs of test-takers, using **conversation analysis** to investigate the co-constructed interactions that occurred. Looking at topical sequences in the dialogue, she found that the higher-scoring pairs of candidates were those in which interactions were collaborative, whereas lower-scoring pairs had interactions that were parallel rather than collaborative. Collaborative interactions were characterized by high mutuality and equality of exchanges. In further research Galaczi (2013) expanded this work to include listener-support strategies such as back-channelling, and the importance of turn management strategies.

This sort of work aims to bring empirical findings from analysing dialogue to use in the practical application of test design. It provides evidence for the validation of the scale descriptors used for scoring the individual test-takers on 'Interactive Communication', allowing us to understand which features of dialogue are important for different levels of performance. The inferences that can be made from the results of these tests are made sounder and fairer by gaining an understanding of the relationship between characteristics of the dialogue and scores on the test.

---

[3]http://www.cambridgeenglish.org/exams-and-tests/first/.

Example 4: Assessment for Learning

Baird, Andrich, Hopfenbeck and Stobart (2017) discuss theories of assessment and theories of learning as being 'fields apart', arguing that theories of assessment used as a basis for validity arguments should be informed by theories of learning. Considering dialogic approaches to teaching and learning and linking these to theories of formative assessment is one way to bring these fields together.

Whether or not an assessment can be called 'formative' depends on the way in which it is used. Black (2015) discusses how tests carried out near the end of a topic can serve a formative function 'through the specific use of interactive dialogue' (p. 165). 'Engineering effective classroom discussions' was one of Wiliam and Thomson's (2007) key methods for implementing assessment for learning (AfL) in the classroom. With reference to the Kings Medway Oxfordshire Formative Assessment Project (KMOFAP) Black identifies the importance of dialogue in the implementation of formative assessment strategies but calls for more detailed evidence of the type and quality of dialogue used for AfL in future studies.

The key point here is that if dialogue is effective in terms of actual learning then it is likely to be interactive and informative for the teacher and learner, which in turn means that it will be effective in terms of assessment. Hence good learning *equals* good assessment in a dialogic classroom. Dann (2014, 2017) provides a comprehensive discussion of the effects of learners' interactions with the feedback they are given in the classroom, and the importance of considering assessment as an aspect of learning. The Teacher-SEDA scheme (Vrikki, Kershner et al., 2018) is a version of Hennessy et al.'s (2016) SEDA coding scheme that has been developed specifically for teachers to use to identify features of classroom dialogue, and one of the aims of this is to increase teachers' understanding of and support for productive dialogue. This in turn can contribute to more productive assessment strategies being used by practitioners in the classroom.

Assessing dialogue means assessing a dynamic construct. It is changing as we assess it, it involves an interaction, it is multi-agent and multimodal. This is not the same as 'dynamic assessment' as defined by, for example, Sternberg and Grigorenko (2002), but it does mean that if we are assessing something dynamic, and it is changing as we assess it, then its assessment is inevitably also dynamic.

Poehner and Lantol (2005), in their discussion of the implementation of dynamic assessment in a language classroom, are clear that one of the goals of dynamic assessment is to modify the performance of the learner. While acknowledging the threat of such an aim to test reliability in the psychometric sense, they stress the importance of the integration of assessment and teaching, with mediation that is adjusted as the learner responds to it. Dynamic assessment approaches are based on the premise that we cannot assess how well a child can do something without also observing the social interaction or intervention in which they are progressing with this skill. The result of this approach is that dialogue between teacher and learner is an essential part of the assessment as well as of the learning. What the learner reveals about their knowledge, skills and understanding during the dialogue is what is observed and assessed.

Similarly, Ahmed and Pollitt's (2010) support model for assessment involves assessing performance based on the amount of support needed to complete a challenging task rather than following the more standard models of assessment based on judging the quality of final performance or measuring the difficulty of completed tasks. In the case of the Support Model, prompts are delivered within a digital platform, in response to students' previous responses to the task. Learning occurs during the assessment as students complete a challenging task with support. Espasa, Guasch, Mayordomo, Martinez-Melo and Carless's (2018) study of the dialogic potential of feedback also points to the provision of support *during* task completion rather than after.

There are obvious challenges with these approaches, particularly with respect to reliability, for any high-stakes assessment. But this does not mean that we should discount using such strategies for assessment decisions that have an impact on what is taught and learned in the classroom. Considering the nature of dialogue during assessment and feedback could be the key to understanding how to improve the integration of assessment and learning.

Concluding remarks

The examples discussed above illustrate a range of approaches to assessing dialogic participation and outcomes. When considering how to approach the assessment of dialogue, the first question, as with any assessment, must be: What is the purpose of this assessment? Following this, considerations of validity are paramount: are we preserving validity throughout the assessment process? Can we make valid inferences based on the results of this assessment? As part of the validity question we must also pay attention to issues of reliability (of coding and other judgements) and manageability (of observing and capturing dialogue).

Looking to the future, technological advances allow us to do much more with data from large-scale assessments than was previously possible. When students engage in online dialogue as part of an assessment, the problem of capturing the dialogue is removed. In fact we have the opposite issue of a wealth of data and the need to make decisions about what to focus on. For assessment purposes this is an opportunity to analyse students' response processes in a way that can be highly informative for assessment design. A number of the chapters in Von Davier, Zhu and Kyllonen (2017) address this issue, notably Graesser et al.'s chapter on assessing interactions with conversational agents. As more educational dialogue occurs in digital environments, new opportunities will emerge for the assessment of dialogue.

The commentary below by Gordon Stobart emphasizes the importance of focusing on the questions that we hope to answer when designing an assessment of dialogue, considering why they are important questions and whether our assessment instruments are fit for purpose.

Expert commentary

Dialogic participation and outcomes: Evaluation and assessment – a commentary

Gordon Stobart, Institute of Education, University College London, UK

We have known about the value of effective dialogue since Socrates but education has made limited use of it, preferring more didactic and teacher-controlled approaches. There has, however, been a steady flow of research which demonstrates the power of effective dialogue. I suspect a reason that more research hasn't been done in this area is that it looks intimidatingly complex to conduct. This chapter makes an important contribution by showing some of the ways in which we can validly research educational dialogue and increase its impact. A powerful message which emerges from it is that research does not need to be constrained by a narrow range of methods – the researcher's task is to ask specific questions and, in order to answer them, seek methods and instruments that are fit for purpose.

The chapter does not rush into describing possible methodologies, rather it takes a step back and asks fundamental validity questions about why we may want to assess dialogue and what we mean by dialogue. Only when we have clarity about these questions do we start looking for fit-for-purpose methodology. With a concept as broad as 'dialogue' this is essential – what is the purpose of our research, what are the specific questions we want to try and answer?

When it does examine some of the research methods that have been used, it offers us four examples of different approaches, each with a different purpose, which in turn is reflected in the research methods used. These powerfully illustrate the importance of the need for fitness for purpose of the instruments used in research – do our instruments measure what we claim we are looking for, can we validly answer our own question?

In the case of the Oracy project this meant developing and validating appropriate instruments. The first step involved developing a conceptual framework, thus developing a consensus on what oracy involves. This led to the construction of an assessment instrument for oracy skills that was developed in conjunction with teachers and validated using comparative judgement methods. The methodological point here is that for some research questions we may have to devise our own instruments. Simply choosing an off-the-shelf measure designed for a different purpose may run foul of Messick's CIV; it may measure something else.

The second example tackled the complex relationship between the quality of classroom dialogue and educational outcomes. Any research into the impact of a single variable, in this case classroom dialogue, on learning outcomes in classrooms is inevitably complex because other factors will be contributing. While the research was based on systematic (and relatively straightforward) classroom observations, a great deal of secondary analysis had to be conducted to handle confounds. Thus, factors such as prior achievement, teacher characteristics and student background may provide alternative explanations of the findings. One of the key issues in the validation of any research findings is to consider possible alternative interpretations of the data. In this case the researchers used a raft of measures that would allow them to factor in, and evaluate the contribution of, these other variables. This process also included statistical techniques such as multilevel modelling. To be credible, a relatively simple observational strategy has to be supported by complex techniques if a causal question is to be validly answered. It's worth noting that the researchers were willing to use established instruments (e.g. the PASS questionnaire) when they addressed confounding variables.

A different research purpose is found in the third example. The intention here is to assist in the development of tasks to be used in a second-language test focusing on paired dialogue. Here the research sought to use conversation analysis to assist the development of scale descriptors by identifying the important features of performance at different levels. This approach offers an interpretation of already collected data, offering a better understanding of the concepts being addressed.

Encouraging classroom dialogue may be part of broader pedagogical approaches such as AfL. The research approach here might best be seen as a form of action research – how can teachers' appreciation and use of dialogue be encouraged? Are there coding schemes that would be appropriate in working with teachers on this?

Hattie (2012) has come up with some salutary findings about the quality and nature of classroom dialogue. The classes studied in a variety of national contexts were dominated by recall questions from the teacher (about 70 per cent) with very few open-ended questions for discussion. Student responses typically took less than five seconds to give and on average had three words. Following this up, I have looked at research findings from the last 100 years and found that little has changed in the patterns of classroom questioning (Stobart, 2014). Is this still the case in classrooms in England?

What Chapter 5 illustrates is the range of methodological possibilities when investigating aspects of classroom dialogue. The first two examples in particular provide cutting-edge methodologies for investigating specific research questions. Both were funded research projects staffed by a team of experienced researchers. For the individual researcher (who may, for example, be completing a higher degree) this may seem very intimidating, prompting questions of 'how can I match these levels of resources and complexity?' My response would be 'you can't – so let's look at more manageable research questions that can be answered by small-scale research'. So observational classroom research may be descriptive rather than trying to draw causal inferences, and improving oracy might seek to replicate the reported research by applying the toolkit in a different setting.

This takes us back to powerful opening questions about why, what and how we research classroom dialogue. Based on these, my own three questions are the following:

1. What question(s) do we want answering?
2. Why are they worth investigating?
3. Will our methods and instruments be fit-for-purpose and manageable given our resources?

What this chapter does is to show us how varied and creative we can be in researching dialogue. There can be no methodological straightjacket in this area, we are invited to use our imagination, as well as the creativity of others, to explore the questions we have.

CHAPTER SIX

Analytical Coding Schemes for Classroom Dialogue

Sara Hennessy

Introduction

How do we know high-quality classroom dialogue when we see it? There is arguably a broad consensus – albeit with some divergence around the edges – concerning the central features of dialogue that are productive for learning (Howe & Mercer, 2016). These features can serve to open up a 'dialogic space' in which different perspectives can be explored and critiqued, and meaning can be jointly constructed by the participants; contributions are chained; students feel comfortable and encouraged to contribute. Whether these characteristics are present in classroom interaction can be investigated using various methodologies and methods, including the two main traditions of **linguistic ethnography** and **sociocultural discourse analysis** (Mercer, 2010). These are very different – but complementary – to the more systematic approaches to analysis, primarily at the **micro-level**, namely turns or utterances in dialogue, on which this chapter focuses.

A common way to determine whether our impressions as researchers or teachers are grounded in actual instances of productive forms of interaction is to categorize interaction systematically. This is what we mean by 'coding' it, chunk by chunk, often categorizing each speaker's turn separately. This means looking at the discourse 'moves' – invitations or statements – that teachers and students commonly make to achieve particular goals when communicating with each other. Systematic observation of this kind helps us look at whether and how the dialogue promotes learning, whether everyone is participating and so on.

Researchers may develop their own list of categories, that is, coding scheme, or they may reuse or adapt one. To create or modify one, they draw on a starting conceptual framework and research questions (based on the literature and sometimes their own experience of classrooms), often combined with preliminary classroom observations, to create a set of relevant categories that seem to be frequently occurring. There is typically a lengthy period of trial and refinement, which is often an inductive as well as a deductive process; this means that initial constructs from the literature might be expanded, qualified, reformulated and exemplified using authentic examples from recordings of (oral or written) dialogue. Thus, what is already known interacts with what is observed in the particular setting; ultimately an exhaustive set of categories emerges. Then the scheme is finalized and systematically applied across a dataset (usually across lessons) to characterize specific features of the interaction that keep recurring. This usually takes place at a turn-by-turn or utterance level.

In recent years, researchers have typically used video recordings rather than only live observation to identify speakers more easily and capture dialogue more accurately. With this method the researcher benefits from seeing who is speaking (see also Chapter 9), from visual cues including gaze, gesture and facial expression, from capturing interactions with artefacts, and above all, from the ability to replay the recordings. Video analysis is ideally undertaken in conjunction with transcripts, but transcription is time-consuming, so researchers increasingly code directly from video using specialized software such as (open source) Elan[1] or the (highly sophisticated, allowing synchronous playback of multiple modalities, but pricey) Observer® XT.[2] In a recent study carried out at Cambridge by Howe, Hennessy,

---

[1]https://tla.mpi.nl/tools/tla-tools/elan/
[2]https://www.noldus.com

Mercer, Vrikki and Wheatley (2019), we found that direct video coding in Elan took around a third longer (with a twelve-category scheme) than using a transcript because of needing to replay the recording more often, although we saved a lot of time and money on transcription. However, we can only use the transcribed lessons for further analyses involving searching for keywords and patterns (as elaborated below); the videos alone are unsuitable.

While many researchers create and adapt coding schemes, publications rarely report on the trials and tribulations of developing and applying them in practice, leading readers to assume that the process must have been straightforward. This chapter outlines and problematizes some of the methodological issues arising. It is illustrated partly by the work of a team at Cambridge University in collaboration with Mexican colleagues (Hennessy et al., 2016) in developing and trialling the Cam-UNAM Scheme for Educational Dialogue Analysis (SEDA). Two other fine-grained schemes are also introduced: Accountable Talk® developed by a team at Pittsburgh (Michaels & O'Connor, 2015) and Transactive Discussion (Berkowitz & Gibbs, 1983). The dialogic 'quality' of one transcript is also examined from the perspective of each scheme and how the schemes differ or overlap with each other is discussed. Note that key examples in this chapter focus on whole-class dialogue, but the issues and techniques could equally relate to peer group dialogue.

Systematic coding schemes: Some strengths and weaknesses

The advantages of coding approaches are summarized in Table 6.1. For some research purposes, systematic coding is the *only* feasible method. For example, relating dialogicality and participation levels to learner outcome measures, as in our own recent work, requires **regression**-based statistical analyses, a large-enough sample to make them meaningful, and reducing the data down to a manageable number of dialogue variables that can be applied across the dataset (Howe et al., 2019: see summary in Chapter 5). Variation in the quality of dialogue across different lessons and classes means that analyses benefit from being repeated over time.

Table 6.1 Strengths and weaknesses of coding dialogue

Pros	Cons
Lots of lesson data can be handled, searched efficiently and reduced to highlight the key characteristics of dialogue	Meanings and intentions can be ambiguous; coding may be misleading or categories may not be straightforward to apply
Coding shows up turn-taking and other patterns, commonalities and variation that the casual observer might not easily perceive	Classroom norms and the underlying social dynamic and emotional aspects of learning may be hard to characterize
Changes (in teacher practice, student participation or learning) can be charted over time	The temporal nature of dialogue is lost when coding of separate turns or utterances is then compiled out of context since original talk is no longer visible; this may conceal how speech acts are chained and influence each other
Student groups/teachers/lessons/ classrooms/subject disciplines/ schools can be compared using a single measure; generalizability is increased	Starting with certain categories can introduce researcher bias and limit observation of other forms of interaction

Mercer (2010) and others point out that coding has its limitations. 'The most serious are the problems of dealing with ambiguity of meanings, the temporal development of meanings, and the fact that utterances with the same surface form can have quite different functions' (p. 4). It follows that treating all similar-looking utterances as repeated instances of the same speech event has its limitations. Identifying decontextualized moves in isolation and counting frequencies over a large dataset rather than analysing how moves co-occur and are chained within exchanges (e.g. Lefstein, Snell & Israeli, 2015; Wells, 2009; Wells & Arauz, 2006) cannot tell us much about how participants in dialogue *respond* to each other's contributions. In teacher–student dialogue it is also hard to know whether particular student moves are self-initiated or (indirectly) prompted by teachers or peers. Likewise, coding tells us little about the quality of teacher–student relationships (Boyd & Markarian,

2015), the underlying dynamic of learning in that classroom and the associated instructional stance of a teacher – how dialogic or monologic it is. Yet, while the limitations of coding lead many researchers to avoid it, we must be careful not to go to the other extreme of 'anything goes'.

In our own work we tried to capitalize on the complementary strengths of several approaches, drawing on the key concepts embedded in coding schemes, keyword analyses and narrative accounts, and ultimately producing a tool for systematic turn-by-turn analysis. The open-source Cam-UNAM Scheme for Educational Dialogue Analysis (SEDA, pronounced 'sedda' as in Spanish) is described below and compared with other established schemes.

What researchers do alongside or after coding

Seeking rigour and using complementary methods can strengthen the coding approach, especially when exploring the temporal nature of dialogue and interpreting the findings to understand any patterns emerging. Our team's systematic analysis of a very large dataset (over nine thousand minutes of lesson time) required a minimum team of four full-time coders to complete the work within the timescale. However, a set of lesson-level **rating scales** was also devised to determine whether there was a conducive classroom climate for dialogue (see Chapter 5).

Coding of moves may be used to identify more dialogic **episodes** to subject to further microanalysis (Lefstein et al., 2015). Detailed qualitative or narrative analysis of episodes can be extremely informative. Here, the researcher can 'go beyond the data' to interpret the patterns and functions of dialogue, bringing in prior knowledge of other classrooms and synthesizing the findings with literature; theory thereby interacts with methodology. The analysis still requires rigour; for example, the interpretation is backed up by close reference to the excerpt itself and counter-examples may be sought.

Coding may also be followed by frequency counting and/or **descriptive statistics** in order to compare different groups, lessons, subjects or classrooms. Durations of moves and turns are easily compiled if transcripts or video analysis are time stamped, and these can be revealing, especially where student turns are longer. Researchers might look at ratios of dialogic (or 'transactive' (see definition below)) compared to non-dialogic (or non-transactive) forms of interaction, as undertaken by Howe et al. (2019) and Berkowitz and Gibbs (1983). In larger-scale work, correlational statistical analyses can be used to determine the association of certain types of dialogue or frequency of contribution with learner characteristics (e.g. socioeconomic status or linguistic capability) or achievement measures.

A coding alternative or complementary systematic approach is to count the relative frequencies of occurrence of particular **keywords** or phrases (Mercer, 2004). Specialized **concordance** software such as AntConc assists this process (some qualitative data analysis packages such as NVivo[3] offer some similar facilities). Thus researchers can compare the relative incidence, repetition and form of use across contexts and see which words tend to occur together ('collocations').

Related to this but further foregrounding the temporal aspect of dialogue is **sequential analysis** of chains of interaction moves (using a computer programme). 'Lag sequential analysis' calculates the probabilities of certain moves following other moves; this requires a very large data set so will not be feasible for many researchers but offers insight into the kinds of responses that open and closed questions provoke (Lefstein et al., 2015).

Epistemic network analysis (ENA) is another method with powerful potential for exploring the sequential patterns of classroom dialogue. It is a form of '**quantitative ethnography**' (Shaffer, 2017), integrating in-depth, qualitative analysis with statistical tools to handle large datasets and multiple data sources. Specifically, it models the connections made by each participant between ideas. Differences in individuals' or groups' ENA scores can be statistically tested, for example, to show that students who better understood the relationships between particular ideas or issues spent more time talking about them, or to show that teacher practices or perspectives changed after a dialogic intervention. See

---

[3]https://www.qsrinternational.com/nvivo/.

Box 6.1 for details. Very large samples are unnecessary although the more data there are per participant, the better.

Box 6.1 Epistemic network analysis – the nitty-gritty of how it works

Moving 'stanza' windows – defined as overlapping sequences of four to seven lines (capturing majority of references back) – highlight connections between codes in any one referring transcript line and those in its recent temporal context. The researcher visually represents the similarities and differences emerging using network graphs for each participant (Shaffer, 2017, p. 349). A series of (quite complex) mathematical calculations using the bespoke open-source tool nCoder[4] allows the researcher to examine both the content and density of connections in each network. A significant difference indicates that the pattern observed would likely characterize the rest of the data from that participant group, for example, class, warranting generalization within the data.

In a similar vein, Wagner and González-Howard (2018) proposed that **social network analysis** (SNA) can be applied to classroom discourse data. Rich information about discourse can be derived from network measures such as density, reciprocity of dialogic moves and centrality of individuals. Further analytic techniques include looking at positions/roles and clusters/subgroups, correlations between individual attributes and network measures, and longitudinal analysis to measure changes over time. Network analyses benefit from complementary contextual information gathering and may be followed up with interaction analysis too; that combination allows researchers to examine how individuals are included or excluded from dialogue. SNA underpins analysis of discussions within the online Knowledge Forum environment, discussed in Chapter 7. However, SNA only measures the structure of interactions between individuals in a group, not their content.

---

[4]The nCoder web tool is available at www.epistemicanalytics.org .

Methodological issues

This section outlines some of the common dilemmas faced by researchers addressing the challenges derived from 'the complexity of doing credible, compelling, rigorous classroom discourse analysis' (Park, Michaels, Affolter & O'Connor, 2017, p. 19).

Scope

All discourse versus dialogic forms. Some schemes extend to all forms of discourse (Boyd & Markarian, 2015; Wells & Arauz, 2006), according to research purpose. In our own work we usually categorize dialogic interaction only. Adding a 'non-dialogic' category of interaction (excluding monologue) in our latest scheme enabled us to measure the ratio of dialogic to non-dialogic interaction in each lesson too (Howe et al., 2019). When only dialogic forms are coded researchers must decide what to do about the gaps and whether to code for pauses or the lack of a contribution following an invitation. Pauses (minimum two to three seconds typically) are usually indicated on transcripts and we find this helpful as it signifies 'wait time' or 'thinking time' allowed for participants to respond. Other nuances can be taken account of during follow-up qualitative analyses if the coding misses them. Note that no scheme can be fully comprehensive; in Chapter 7 we discuss incorporating multimodal interaction.

Teacher and/or student dialogue. Some schemes relate to teacher discourse moves only (e.g. Accountable Talk (Michaels, O'Connor & Resnick, 2008) and the Analyzing Teaching Moves (ATM) Guide (Correnti et al., 2015)) or to student moves only (Functional Analysis of Children's Classroom Talk (FACCT): Kumpulainen and Wray (2002). Some code student and teacher moves differently (Boyd & Markarian, 2015; Fishman et al., 2017). Sedova, Sedlacek and Svaricek (2016) coded only four, mixed indicators to assess change after their professional development intervention in the Czech Republic: student talk with reasoning, teachers' open questions of high cognitive demand, teacher uptake, and open discussion. Other schemes like SEDA analyse moves solely according to their function within the dialogue rather than to role of the speaker, recognizing that teacher and student roles are potentially malleable (cf. Freire, 1971).

Some schemes focus on the highly significant 'third turn' or 'follow-up' move in triadic dialogue, usually executed by teachers. Dialogue is chained, of course, so the third move can trigger another exchange, as in the 'spiral IRF cycles' identified by Rojas-Drummond, Torreblanca, Pedraza, Vélez and Guzmán (2013) or the teachers' Rejoinder and Initiating moves categorized by Correnti et al. (2015: see Figure 6.1).

Wells' (2001) framework focuses on the *relationship* between teacher and student moves versus the quality of participants' contributions to the discussion. The framework is immensely detailed and lengthy and thus it is not fully described or applied in this chapter, but of most interest for coding dialogic interaction are the *Student Link* section and the follow-up moves *Clarification* and *Invitations for clarification* (Box 6.2). This identifies occasions on which a student explicitly makes reference to a previous contribution and describes the nature of the connection.

Box 6.2 Selected follow-up moves in Wells's (2001) coding framework

Student Link

A Adds to a previous contribution with an example, anecdote and so on.
C Challenges or counters it with an objection or alternative.
E Extends it by developing, justifying or generalizing it.
O Makes reference but does not make connection explicit.

(Invitations for) clarification

R Repetition using the same or similar words.
I Identification of what s/he intended to refer to.
C Confirmat ion/denial of the validity of a previous utterance.

In practice either teachers or students can execute any of these moves. So, there are several options for the researcher, and as with all of these methodological decisions, the choice must depend on research purpose.

Appropriate grain size: Unit and level of analysis

Strategic decisions about **granularity** are needed, again according to purpose. For instance, if we wanted to know what kinds of questions students ask during whole class discussion (on the rare occasions that they ask any), coding each question would be sensible. To see how those questions are responded to, we need to scrutinize sequences of dialogue in some way. Interaction can be categorized at three levels (see Box 6.3).

Box 6.3 Levels of analysis of dialogue

Micro-level: *clause/sentence/utterance/turn*
Meso-level: *exchange/sequence/topic/stanza/episode*
Macro-level: *lesson/lesson sequence*

Even within the meso-level, definitions of terms can vary. An **episode** is variously described as a change of activity, theme or communication approach (Sedova et al., 2016) or a change of (some permutation of) purpose, topic, orientation or participant structure (Hymes, 1972: 'communicative event'; Nystrand, Wu, Gamoran, Zeiser & Long, 2003; Wells, 2001). However, several topics may be simultaneously open and intertwined within an episode (Linell, 2001). Wells defines a *sequence* as a nuclear exchange (two or three moves) and all the *exchanges* that are bound to it through their meaning and function. Lefstein et al. (2015) assert that interactional structures of three or more turns constitute the optimal unit of analysis. Nystrand et al.'s (2003) term 'dialogic spell' moves beyond the mechanical chunking of lessons to focus on episodes of active discussion in which students play an active and sustained role in discussing ideas and posing questions. Thus, interaction sequences may be coded only when they are *predetermined* to be dialogic. A key point to stress is that the **micro-, meso- and macro-levels** of coding are not mutually exclusive and can be fruitfully combined in order to overcome their respective limitations.

Micro-level coding

Working at the micro-level is demanding but also illuminating since it allows the researcher to carry out detailed, systematic analyses of what participants actually do and say. In our own recent work, we have used the turn level since a change of speaker can be reliably distinguished whereas the boundaries of an utterance may well be more ambiguous. However, a long turn includes multiple utterances with unique functions and linguistic forms, and for more detailed coding the utterance may be a more appropriate unit (Park et al., 2017). Applying multiple codes to one turn obscures the part of the talk they each refer to, while prioritizing to avoid multiple coding of a single turn disadvantages long turns if codes are later counted. Counting multiple instances of the same code within a turn reduces inter-coder reliability, however, compared to binary coding of presence/absence.

The features of dialogue at this micro-level include 'communicative acts' (Hymes, 1972), 'speech acts' (Searle & Vanderveken, 1985) and 'talk moves' (e.g. Michaels et al. 2008). These are all identified by their function within an interaction, namely the speaker's expressed intention (e.g. elaborating or predicting); researchers usually code initiating moves regardless of the actual response. A communicative act obtains its status from the social context and is defined by the minimum number of utterances or actions needed to reflect its function. When developing SEDA, we broke down a turn comprising several sentences, or even a single sentence, into smaller units or phrases, if necessary, allocating each a line in the coding spreadsheet, applying two or more codes in sequence within a turn (Hennessy et al., 2016). Segmentation is not always straightforward, however. Our own most recent scheme and several others focus on dialogue 'moves' that signify and support both social and cognitive processes; for example, a move can involve both reasoning and listening and responding to others (Greeno, 2016; Resnick, Michaels & O'Connor, 2010).

Some researchers prefer to offer slightly looser indicators for dialogue. For example, seminal work by Nystrand et al. (2003) in secondary classrooms in the United States used the Classroom

Language Assessment System, CLASS 2.0, to identify three key teacher discourse moves: (1) authentic (open) questions; (2) uptake of previous responses and (3) high-level evaluation involving follow-up questions. Questions from students proved especially effective for learning. Even broader codes can be applied at the meso-level; procedures are similar.

Macro-level analysis: Clustering, charting and rating categories

In larger schemes, related micro-level categories are often grouped under headings or clusters (thematically or functionally related codes). Accountable Talk categories are linked to teachers' goals in orchestrating whole-class talk (see Figure 6.2). SEDA has thirty-three codes clustered into eight groups such as *Make reasoning explicit*, *Positioning and Coordination, Connect*, and the optional cluster *Express or invite ideas* (see Table 6.3). These help to maximize reliability (see next section) and practicability, allowing the researcher to count frequencies more easily too since codes within a cluster are hierarchical and thus mutually exclusive (although two or three clusters may apply). Moreover, offering fewer, broader grained clusters is more useful for time-poor practitioners. Note that the current SEDA clustering is fairly pragmatic and to some extent arbitrary. It is the third iteration we went through. Researchers really need to make their own decisions about clustering, and these may be formed deductively, that is, derived from the literature. Decisions about clustering are paralleled by decision-making about the granularity of codes themselves, which varies considerably. Combining and splitting codes and expanding or reducing their scope and hence definitions – to best fit the data – are inevitable parts of the iterative process of developing a scheme.

Correnti et al. (2015) offer an unusual, alternative strategy to simple counting, involving calculating the cumulative sum of positive, neutral and negative teacher moves. These are categorized according to their close proximity with other moves (e.g. uptake can be diluted if it co-occurs with other kinds of moves such as Repeat and Provide Information within a single turn) and plotting it on a graph to show progression. It is unclear how subjective or reliable these evaluations are though. Another variant (Figure 6.1) displays the actual single or multiple codes emerging in each turn

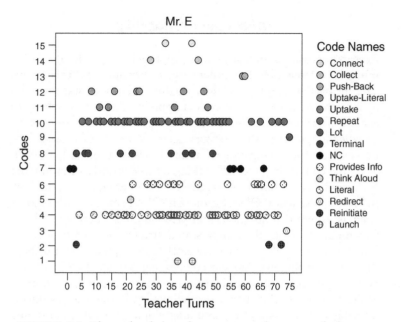

FIGURE 6.1 *Chart of coded teacher turns over the course of a lesson.*
(Reproduced from Correnti et al., 2015, p. 328, with kind permission of the author and American Educational Research Association ©2015)

using coded symbols, again charting progression across teacher turns in a lesson. This offers an evocative graphical representation of not just density of specific moves (fifteen categories) but co-occurrence within turns and spacing throughout the episode. It gives an instant and holistic overview of the interaction in the lesson. Again this is potentially helpful for teachers as well as researchers to scrutinize.

More fine-grained approaches are not necessarily more fruitful. The limitations of micro- and meso-level coding outlined above highlight the benefits of considering broader lesson-length categories or rating scales. Recording presence/absence of forms of dialogue may be complemented or even replaced by a *continuum-based model* to capture those features of the ethos within a dialogic classroom that cannot be captured at the move level, for example, levels of student participation and teacher direction (Howe et al., 2019).

Inter-coder reliability

Researchers using systematic coding approaches typically attempt to minimize **inference** levels in order to maximize inter-coder reliability. This means that they try to tighten up their definitions and examples to maximize the chances of coders applying the same category to each turn or utterance. This is especially applicable for large datasets or when employing other coding assistants. Levels of success vary, however, and achieving high reliability levels is notoriously difficult and time-consuming, typically taking up to 6 months or even more for a complex scheme. One 'relatively low-inference' tool, the Low Inference Discussion Observation (LIDO) scheme[5], includes moves such as using open questions and providing reasoning or evidence to support a claim; these may sound straightforward to identify, but experience tells us they are not! 'Open questions' are more difficult to distinguish than closed ones (e.g. Myhill, 2006) and how complete or coherent does a reason need to be before it 'counts'? Some researchers classify reasons by quality. In one study, students offering correct, complete, and unambiguous explanations and challenging or building on other students' ideas performed better in mathematics (Webb et al., 2017). However, the finer grained and more complex a coding scheme, typically the less reliable it will be simply because there is more room for discrepancy and error. Levels of inference and potential over-interpretation need to be monitored carefully. Identifying clusters before individual codes is more reliable than coding directly.

Reliability is usually measured using a statistical technique such as Cohen's kappa (for pairs of coders) or Krippendorf's alpha (for multiple coders) on a subset of the data and reported – although it is often omitted – even when categories are very few (e.g. Sedova et al, 2016). Questions arise about who takes part in reliability trials, is the scheme intended for use 'cold' by researchers new to it (more generalizable), or is it confined to a small team who have worked closely together on establishing common understanding and ironing out their discrepancies over a long period (more common and easier)? Such researchers sometimes use consensus coding or social moderation: two or more coders resolve any discrepancies

---

[5]http://ccdd.serpmedia.org/lido.html.

between them through discussion. However, the degree of agreement between them or the potential for use by other teams is unknown. Note that Shaffer (2017) argues that strictly speaking, segmentation itself should also be tested for reliability (unless speaker turns are the **unit of analysis**).

Reliability test results cannot be assumed to generalize to the rest of a dataset, except when there are very frequent codes and large test samples (Eagan et al., 2017). Interpretations of the same lesson by different researchers from different perspectives or backgrounds may vary considerably, possibly despite a common research question. We have had experience of asking a number of established experts in the field to comment on the dialogue in the same set of five diverse transcripts in terms of its potential productivity for learning in each case; we received some directly conflicting comments in return – albeit along with considerable consensus. Note that this exercise assisted us with *validating* our coding scheme; while reliability is commonly measured, **validity** checks are rarely reported in this field. Unwarranted assumptions based on initial interpretations of the literature abound. Likewise, **relevance** is important. A systematic literature trawl and mapping against other commonly used analytic schemes distilled out all of the key concepts emerging and underpinned development of SEDA (Hennessy et al., 2016).

Examples: Applying three analytic schemes to classroom interaction

I now apply three schemes – varying in scope and granularity – to the same excerpt from a primary school science lesson, in order to illustrate the process for coding dialogue and explore the relative merits of different schemes. This episode ('Is tap water different to rain?') was chosen from our recently collected dataset of naturalistic lessons in classrooms in England because it contains an open task and student contributions in which participants take account of each other's ideas.

Context. The school is located in a very deprived area of London; students work above the expected national levels in English and mathematics. The Year 6 class has thirty children aged 10–11, all of whom are eligible for free school meals and twenty-nine of whom have English as a second language, although twenty of those are reportedly fluent or near fluent in English. The excerpt lasts 5 minutes 34 seconds and comes from a lesson on the water cycle. The lesson activities are listed in Box 6.4. The excerpt (see Table 6.2) begins with a small group discussion eight minutes into the seventy-two-minute lesson (713 turns in total), and the video clip can be viewed at https://sms.cam.ac.uk/media/2827690 (excerpt begins after 9 seconds). Groups comprise two to six pupils seated around tables.

Box 6.4 Water cycle lesson activities

- Small groups discuss agreement with statements concerning the water cycle on the board, then feed back to the class.
- **Excerpt: Students' feedback on the statement that 'Water in a tap is different than water that falls as rain.'**
- Teacher presents her water cycle model and asks students to build their own models in groups.
- Students record predictions of what will happen according to their models, then share those with the class.
- In groups – and then in the whole class – students label parts of the water cycle diagram using keywords.
- Teacher presents facts about the water cycle and students take notes.

The only intentional departure from the published schemes in this coding exercise is that 'invitations' are identified rather than 'questions' wherever utterances clearly invite a response.

Example 1: Scheme for Educational Dialogue Analysis (SEDA)

The – rather ambitious – aim of developing the Cam-UNAM SEDA scheme was to offer a framework for analysing dialogue can be adapted for many different research purposes and applied to diverse educational settings: any age phases, subject areas, activities with and without digital technology use, and contexts including whole-class,

Table 6.2 Coded excerpt from a primary science lesson on the water cycle

Line	Time stamp	Agent	Utterances	APT	Transact	SEDA
97	0:08:19	T	'Water in a tap is different than water that falls as rain.' Mmm, what do you think? Have a little chat on your table.	Partner talk		E1 Invite opinions / G1 Encourage student-student dialogue
98	0:08:26	Class	((Start talking))			
99	0:08:31	T	((Moves to table))			
			[37 secs of group work cut]			
118	0:09:08	T	So what do you think? Do you agree with this person or do you disagree?	Agree/Disagree	O TQ	I2 Invite elaboration/ agreement with another's view
119	0:09:11	Abdakirim	Disagree.		S RQ	
120	0:09:12	T	You disagree?	(Agree/Disagree)	(O TQ)	
121	0:09:15	Ishra	No, agree.			
122	0:09:16	T	So you think water in the tap is different to water that falls as rain? And what specifically are the ways that you think it's different? Because you can't affect the temperature ((counting on fingers))? Is that all?	Say more	O TQ	I6 Invite elaboration

123	0:09:28	B3	And the tap, it can go quickly.		S RQ	E2 Make other relevant contribution
124	0:09:31	T	So you can affect the rate of the flow of the water?	So, are you saying?	OTQ	B1 Elaborate another's contribution
125	0:09:33	B3	Yeah.			
126	0:09:34	T	We can't affect rain?	So, are you saying?	OTQ	I6 Invite elaboration
127	0:09:34	Ishra	Rain comes from clouds.		S RQ	E2 Make other relevant contribution
128	0:09:35	T	Rain comes from clouds? Where does tap water come from?	Say more??	OTQ	I6 Invite elaboration
129	0:09:39	B3	You can't control the rain.		S RQ	B1 Elaborate another's contribution
130	0:09:38	Ishra	The tap.			E2 Make other relevant contribution
131	0:09:39	T	What, it's just magically in the tap?	Challenge or counterexample	OTQ	P5 Challenge viewpoint
132	0:09:41	Abdakirim	The pipes.			E2 Make other relevant contribution
133	0:09:41	Ishra	The toilet.			E2 Make other relevant contribution

				Challenge or counterexample		
134	0:09:44	T	It comes from the toilet? ((Chuckles)) I don't know what tap water you're drinking, Ishra.		OTQ	P5 Challenge viewpoint
135	0:09:51	B3	(Inaudible) but we can drink tap.		S RQ	E2 Make other relevant contribution
136	0:09:51	T	OK. Well let's talk about it.			
137	0:09:53	T	((Moves to front of class)) ((to class)) 3, 2 ((puts lights on)), 1, ((picks up pot of name sticks)). OK, again, there were some very interesting discussions ((indicating to back table)) on this table. Let's see who's going to share their thoughts. ((Picks out name stick)) Isma, what were you saying on your table?			E1 Invite opinions
138	0:10:11	Isma	We think that (inaudible).			
139	0:10:16	T	So you think that they're different? So you agree with this person ((pointing to interactive whiteboard)), that water is different? In what way did you think it was different? What was your example? … Just tell us again because I don't think everyone can hear you, darling?	Agree / disagree, Say O TQ more		I2 Invite elaboration/ agreement with another's view (also I4 Ask for explanation but I2 trumps I4)

140	0:10:29	Isma	That (inaudible).		
141	0:10:33	T	Tap water is clean? Is rain water clean, inSay more your opinion?	OTQ	I6 Invite elaboration
142	0:10:38	Isma	(Inaudible).		
143	0:10:39	T	Mmm ((holds ear))?		
144	0:10:40	Isma	Not that much.	S RQ	B2 Elaborate own contribution
145	0:10:41	T	It's not as clean as tap water? So you thought that they were different, so you agreed with this person? OK, that's good thinking. ((Pulls out another name stick from pot)) Nabil, what did you think on your table?	So, are you saying? OTQ	E1 Invite opinions
146	0:10:51	Nabil	Erm... I think tap water is clean because...		
147	0:11:05	T	You think tap water is clean? So are you So, are you saying? / OTQ agreeing with Isma?	Agree/Disagree	I2 Invite elaboration/ agreement with another's view
148	0:11:08	Nabil	Yeah.		

#	Time	Speaker	Utterance	Code	Description
149	0:11:09	T	So you think they're different ((indicating to interactive whiteboard)) 'cos tap water is clean and you don't think rain water's clean? OK, did you have any other thoughts about it on this table? ... Anyone want to help Nabil out?	OTQ / Add on (last utterance)	R1 Explain another's contribution / E1 Invite opinions
150	0:11:21	TA1	Come on, what (inaudible)?		
151	0:11:24	T	Who would like to share their idea ((to whole class))? We're going to call this table ((indicating to front table)). Come on, what (inaudible)) 'dozy, we've not woken up yet' table. Ayisha?		E1 Invite opinions
152	0:11:29	Ayisha	I wasn't really sure, but I think that rain water is clean, but then the air is- Like, in the city, there is loads of petrol and the air is polluted. So then the rain gets dirty.	S RQ	R2 Explain own contribution
153	0:11:45	T	Oh, you think-		
154	0:11:45	Ayisha	Then-		
155	0:11:47	T	OK, so do you agree or disagree with this, then ((indicating to interactive whiteboard))?	OTQ Agree/Disagree	I2 Invite elaboration/ agreement with another's view

#	Time	Speaker	Utterance		Code	Category
156	0:11:50	Ayisha	I'm not sure.			
157	0:11:52	TA2	Well, you were wondering about what does that person mean in terms of 'different'.		OTS	B1 Elaborate another's contribution
158	0:11:56	T	Ah, that's interesting, isn't it?			
159	0:12:00	TA2	But we didn't think it was too specific, so we were wondering.		OTS	B1 Elaborate another's contribution
160	0:12:03	T	Yeah. So what did that person actually mean? They didn't explain their idea very well. I think that's a fair point. They just said, 'Well, water from the tap is different from water that falls as rain.' On this table ((indicating to back middle table)) you were talking specifically about what you think they might have meant. Does one of you want to explain your ideas? Go on, Ishy.	Explaining what someone else means	OTQ	I2 Invite elaboration/ agreement with another's view / C1 Refer back
161	0:12:18	Ishra	Er, when you have water in a tap, you can control the power and if it's hot or cold, but you can't control rain.		S RQ	R2 Explain own contribution

162	0:12:27	T	Ah, OK, that's interesting. So you're saying it is different because, when water comes out of a tap, you can affect the rate of the flow? You can affect the temperature? Amin, do you want to build on that idea?	So, are you saying? / O TQ Add on	R1 Explain another's contribution / I2 Invite elaboration/agreement
163	0:12:35	Amin	I think it's similar as well, because rain is drops and you can make drops come out of the tap.	O RQ	P6 State (dis)agreement / R2 Explain own contribution
164	0:12:42	T	Oh, so, if rain's falling as drops, depending on how much you open the tap, you could make it around about the same amount of flow? Yes, I suppose you could. Towha, last idea from you, then we're going to move on.	So, are you saying? O TQ	R1 Explain another's contribution / P6 State (dis)agreement
165	0:12:53	Towha	I think water from a tap is actually the same as rain water, because I had a thought that, in most of this water that we have now, comes from the River Thames, but where did the River Thames come from? The only real way you can think about is that it came from rain, and the water from our taps is just a filtered version of that water.	S RQ	R2 Explain own contribution

166	0:13:12	T	Ah, so you think all water, ultimately, comes from one place? Does all water come from the River Thames?	So, are you saying? / OTQ Say more	I6 Invite elaboration
167	0:13:19	Class	No.		
168	0:13:20	Ishra	It comes from the toilet.	S RQ	E2 Make other relevant contribution
169	0:13:23	Class	((Giggling chatter))		
170	0:13:24	T	Ishra thinks all water comes from the toilet.		
171	0:13:29	Class	((Giggling chatter))		
172	0:13:31	T	((Finger to lips)) Well, I don't know about you, but I think it's really important that we have this lesson because I'm not going to give away any of the answers, but I am going to say all water does not come from Ishra's toilet, and I think we're all going to be very glad about that.	STS	G3 Introduce authoritative prospective
173	0:13:45	Class	((Laughs))		

group and paired work. It is framed at the 'communicative act' level, with its thirty-three categories clustered as outlined earlier (see Table 6.3 for a summary). Development of the scheme in the UK and Mexico over a three-year period is detailed by Hennessy et al. (2016) and the full scheme is freely accessible to other researchers; versions for technology-mediated learning contexts (Tech-SEDA) and teacher professional development (Teacher-SEDA) are being tested. Teacher-SEDA (http://bit.ly/T-SEDA) offers time sampling and related coding and other tools for teachers to use.

For the purposes of another project recently undertaken at Cambridge, SEDA categories were radically condensed and reformulated to create a new scheme (CDAS: Cambridge Dialogue Analysis Scheme) that had fewer (twelve), broader categories (Vrikki, Wheatley, Howe, Hennessy & Mercer, 2018). There the aim was large-scale analysis based on frequency counting, in order to conduct regression statistical analyses of the relationship between dialogic pedagogy and student outcomes. For the exercise in this chapter, the full thirty-three-code SEDA was used.

Example 2: Accountable Talk or academically productive talk

Accountable Talk® holds students responsible for integrating their own reasoning and knowledge with that of peers; participants prioritize development of ideas, including robust reasoning and use of evidence, over presentation and defence of their own position. It is promoted as 'academically productive talk' (APT: Michaels & O'Connor, 2011; Michaels et al. 2008) by its originators in Pittsburgh. This scheme focuses on the third turn or uptake moves, offering alternatives to Evaluation in the classic IRE sequence. The nine moves (see Figure 6.2) include challenging ideas and offer the original speaker the opportunity to modify the original idea, if necessary (Park et al., 2017). It is important to note that the scheme is not actually designed as an analytic scheme for researchers but as a professional development tool. It is intended to help teachers recognize and use more moves to sustain discussion while being inclusive and responsive to student contributions. It categorizes teacher moves only, although APT moves intentionally open up further turns for students, positioning them as thinkers and holders

Table 6.3 Cam-UNAM Scheme for Educational Dialogue Analysis (SEDA)

Cam-UNAM SEDA Condensed version © 2016: Cluster and Code Summary

	I – Invite elaboration or reasoning		R – Make reasoning summary
I1	Ask for explanation or justification of another's contribution	R1	Explain or justify another's contribution
I2	Invite building on/elaboration/ (dis)agreement/evaluation of another's contribution or view	R2	Explain or justify own contribution
I3	Invite possibility thinking based on another's contribution	R3	Speculate or predict on the basis of another's contribution
I4	Ask for explanation or justification	R4	Speculate or predict
I5	Invite possibility thinking or prediction		
I6	Ask for elaboration or clarification		B – Build on ideas
		B1	Build on/clarify other's contributions
	P – Positioning and coordination	B2	Clarify own contribution
P1	Synthesis ideas		
P2	Evaluate alternative views		C – Connect
P3	Propose resolution	C1	Refer back
P4	Acknowledge shift of position	C2	Make learning trajectory explicit
P5	Challenge viewpoint	C3	Link learning to wider contexts
P6	State (dis)agreement/position	C4	Invite inquiry beyond the lesson

	RD – Reflect on dialogue or activity		G – Guide direction of dialogue or activity
RD1	Talk about talk	G1	Encourage student–student dialogue
RD2	Reflect on learning process/ purpose/value/outcome	G2	Propose action or inquiry activity
RD3	Invite reflection about process/purpose/value/ outcome of learning	G3	Introduce authoritative perspective
		G4	Provide informative feedback
	E – Express or invite ideas	G5	Focusing
E1	Invite opinions/beliefs/ideas	G6	Allow thinking time [optional when not verbally explicit]
E2	Make other relevant contribution		

of positions. I am including it in this exercise despite its different objectives because it is a well-known and respected typology of moves that adds a complementary perspective to the other schemes on interpreting the extract.

Example 3: Transactive discussion

Transactive discussion, again developed by American researchers, has been defined as reasoning that operates on or transforms another's reasoning, that is, there is *active cognitive engagement with others' ideas* (Berkowitz & Gibbs, 1983). Use of transactive reasoning in groups of peers – characterized by clarification, elaboration, justification and critique – is associated with more sophisticated moral reasoning (ibid.; Kruger 1993), improved problem-solving performance (e.g. Goos, Galbraith & Renshaw, 2002), and creative music composition (Hewitt, 2008). A balance between the self- and other-oriented transacts categorized by Kruger is deemed optimal (Gweon, Jain, Mc Donough, Raj & Rosé, 2013) and this is more prevalent in contexts with trust and respect between students (Azmitia

Goals for Productive Discussions and Nine Talk Moves

Goal One Help Individual Students Share, Expand and Clarify Their Own Thinking

1. Time to Think
- Partner Talk
- Writing as Think Time
- Wait Time

2. Say More:
"Can you say more about that?" "What do you mean by that?"
"Can you give an example?"

3. So, Are You Saying...?:
"So, let me see if I've got what you're saying. Are you saying...?"
(always leaving space for the original student to agree or disagree
and say more)

Goal Two Help Students Listen Carefully to One Another

4. Who Can Rephrase or Repeat?
"Who can repeat what Javon just said or put it into their own words?"
(After a partner talk) "What did your partner say?"

Goal Three Help Students Deepen Their Reasoning

5. Asking for Evidence or Reasoning
"Why do you think that?" "What's your evidence?"
"How did you arrive at that conclusion?"

6. Challenge or Counterexample
"Does it always work that way?" "How does that idea square with
Sonia's example?" "What if it had been a copper cube instead?

Goal Four Help Students Think With Others

7. Agree/Disagree and Why?
"Do you agree/disagree? (And why?)" "What do people think about
what Ian said?" "Does anyone want to respond to that idea?"

8. Add On:
"Who can add onto the idea that Jamal is building?"
"Can anyone take that suggestion and push it a little further?"

9. Explaining What Someone Else Means
"Who can explain what Aisha means when she says that?"
"Who thinks they could explain why Simon came up with that
answer?" "Why do you think he said that?"

Adapted from: Chapin, S. O'Connor, C., & Anderson, N., (2009). *Classroom Discussions: Using Math Talk to Help
Students Learn, Grades 1-6.* Sausalito, CA: Math Solutions Publication

TERC

**The Inquiry Project: Bridging Research &
Practice** Supported by the National Science
Foundation Copyright 2012, TERC. All Rights
Reserved.

FIGURE 6.2 *Academically productive talk moves.*

*(Reproduced from Park et al. (2017) by kind permission of the authors.
Scheme was adapted from Chapin, O'Connor & Anderson (2009))*

& Montgomery, 1993). Transactive discussion highlights differences between participants' mental models (Azmitia & Montgomery, 1993), a crucial aspect of productive dialogue, which can cause cognitive conflict. A common theme that emerged from the analyses of six problem-solving transcripts in the study by Goos et al. was related to *challenge* – a key feature of the other two schemes trialled as well, that is known to promote learning. Almost all of the research using this scheme features pairs, however, while I apply it to teacher–student dialogue. The coding here is tentative; this is a new scheme for me, it is not straightforward to apply in this context, and others may have assigned different codes to the same excerpt!

Berkowitz and Gibbs (1983) identified eighteen codes; subsequent researchers have tended to simplify this scheme. I test out the version used by Goos et al. (2002: following Kruger, 1993). Three types of transacts were coded and the orientation of each transact was also noted (see Box 6.5). Note that 'passive' is a slightly odd term; basically it does not imply that participants behave passively, but simply that they *respond* to others' direct questions to them.

Box 6.5 Transacts and orientations

TS: spontaneously produced *transactive statements*
TQ: spontaneously produced *transactive questions*
RQ: passive *responses to transactive questions*
O: operations on one's partner's ideas *(other-oriented)*
S: reasoning directed at one's own ideas *(self-oriented)*

Interpreting the coding

What does the coding tell us about dialogic quality?

This episode was chosen because it seemed to contain the hallmarks of what theorists would consider productive dialogue. Indeed, although APT only applies to teacher turns, we can see that most teacher turns in this excerpt attract codes from all three schemes, indicating high dialogicality, so it offers a fair comparison of the schemes. Only one teacher turn was not coded with any scheme. Likewise most of the student turns are coded under SEDA and as transactive. Interaction in this excerpt is teacher-led as is typical in primary schooling. However, the teacher poses a series of reasonably authentic and uptake questions (Nystrand et al., 2003) that signal to students her interest in what they think and know and that invite their contributions.

Excluding the four inaudible contributions and lines of class laughter, there are fifty-one speaker turns in this excerpt: twenty-eight from the teacher, twenty-one from students and two from a teaching assistant. None of the schemes is intended to cover all of the contributions made or all of the moves in a teacher's pedagogical repertoire; each focuses only on the dialogic elements; this makes it easier to observe dialogicality. The very high proportion of transactive invitations (TQ) coded confirms that the teaching has a dialogic intention; this is corroborated by the high proportion of teacher turns coded with APT moves, the spread of APT moves used and the number of SEDA clusters (albeit a smaller proportion of codes) applied, indicating that a wide range of moves was observed (see Table 6.4). The APT coding is particularly striking given that all APT moves are basically invitations intended to open up a space for dialogue after student contributions, so, for instance, and in contrast with standard analytic schemes, coding does not cover teacher elaboration or revoicing of a student's idea in itself but only *invitations to students to respond to peers' contributions* in these ways or to *verify the teacher's perception of their viewpoint*. To 'count' as a genuine example of revoicing there should ideally be a pause for student response after the invitation. The teacher in this science class speaks quite rapidly and the video indicates that wait time is low. Indeed in the whole lesson she only once pauses for at least three seconds (the APT threshold for 'wait time'). Thus codes 'So are you saying?' and 'Explain what someone else means' do not actually apply in several potential instances where a less strict scheme such as SEDA would suggest a code (e.g. the teaching assistant comments in Lines 157 and 159). Nevertheless the former code has been applied to many turns in the excerpt where rising intonation indicates that the teacher is checking her understanding, although she quickly follows her verification question with another kind of question (e.g. Lines 147, 149).

In some turns (e.g. Lines 124, 126) the teacher seems to add new substance to her revoicing as she draws inferences about what the student means; in APT this is coded 'So, are you saying?' since the scheme does not have an exactly matching category, although these turns have elements of 'Say more' too. Likewise some contributions coded 'Say more' (e.g. the second utterance in Line 166) go a bit beyond the simple repetition or attempt to get students to say more that define this category; they are too far removed from the student contribution to be a revoicing, and yet not far enough to (obviously) be a totally new and unrelated question (O'Connor, personal communication) – illustrating a typical coding dilemma.

How do the schemes compare in coverage?

The coded excerpt in Table 6.2 indicates that there is considerable overlap between schemes, for instance, invitations for elaboration or reasoning in SEDA and 'So, are you saying?' in APT are also always 'O TQ' transacts. Table 6.4 shows that the three schemes had approximately even coverage of teacher turns. Only five out of twenty-eight teacher turns (plus two of the teaching assistant turns, which are coded but not counted) were coded just with one or two schemes rather than all three. Encouraging student–student dialogue is not coded as transactive, for example. However, there are some further gaps that do not immediately show up when other codes are applied to different parts of the same turn; for instance, revoicing without adding additional information (145, 166), even when verifying a viewpoint, is not coded as such in SEDA. The only five turns to be coded under one scheme alone were all coded in SEDA using Express opinions or Invite opinions. It was recognized by the SEDA developers that these codes are not intrinsically dialogic – although they can play an important role in conveying understanding and progressing the dialogue through stimulating a response – hence the E cluster is optional. If it had been omitted, match between schemes would have increased further and the slight edge of SEDA regarding coverage of both teacher and student turns (see Table 6.4) would have basically disappeared. Nevertheless, SEDA coding is more fine-grained (and hence more time-consuming!) and it

Table 6.4 Coverage of the excerpt by the three schemes

	APT	SEDA	Transactive dialogue
No. teacher turns coded	20/28	21/28	18/28
No. student turns coded	NA	12/21	9/21
Total no. turns coded	20/49	33/49	27/49
No. scheme categories applied	6/9	13/33 codes; 7/8 clusters	4/6
Overlapping codes applied	Invite elaboration of/agreement with own/another's views; elaborate/build on prior contribution; challenge viewpoint; explain/verify another's contribution; encourage student–student dialogue		NA
Unique codes applied	Revoicing/ repeating without adding additional information ('So, are you saying?')	Refer back; express opinion; invite opinions; introduce authoritative perspective	NA

NA, not applicable.

illuminates the nature of all of the dialogic moves in a little more detail. Transactive categories are broader, so cannot so easily be compared with other schemes.

The self-/other orientation proved interesting. The coding using SEDA and APT shows that most often (in six turns) the teacher asks for elaboration of/agreement with another's views, and she sometimes elaborates contributions or invites opinions. In turn, students spontaneously volunteer multiple opinions. Yet, as we often observe in classrooms, reference to others' prior contributions is generally only implicit. Thus, under our fairly strict coding rules which strive to maximize reliability, the contributions were coded as self-oriented in Transactive Discussion and SEDA rather than as elaborating others' contributions.

Indeed, while nine student turns were coded as transactive, eight of them were self-oriented passive responses; these are typically statements that clarify, elaborate, evaluate or justify their own thinking. Other-oriented statements, questions and responses that represent an attempt to understand a partner's thinking are highlighted in yellow in the Transactive Discussion column; a quick glance down the column shows immediately that while they are impressively frequent, all except one of these derive from the teacher (or a teaching assistant). Student turns were coded using four of the eight SEDA clusters but overall their moves were less dialogic and diverse than the teacher's and they issued no invitations. Having examined dialogue across seventy-two classrooms in our recent project, we know that this is typical of teacher–student interaction with this age group at least, while most of the (surprisingly limited) work on transactive reasoning has previously been applied in studies of peer groups. Even in the study of pairs of 10- to 11-year-olds composing melodies (Hewitt, 2008), students rarely asked each other transactive questions. Moreover, where the teacher sought agreement in the excerpt, it was usually related to the statement on the whiteboard (a virtual 'other') rather than to peers' opinions. Discussion between peers was encouraged explicitly only a couple of times in this episode, in Lines 147 ('So are you agreeing with Isma?') and 162 ('Amin, do you want to build on that idea?'). Again, we know this is typical.

Finally, the dialogue is relatively inclusive of multiple voices: eight learners participate during this five-minute lesson segment. The few extended student explanations are not coded under APT of course, so gaps inevitably do arise in that coding. Confining scope to teacher moves – specifically to *teacher invitations that are follow-up moves* – in APT is wholly purposeful in a scheme designed primarily for professional development rather than for research on teacher-student dialogue. Nevertheless it means that a very sizeable proportion of the interaction cannot be systematically considered, if teachers wanted to use coding to understand how students are responding to their moves.

Joining up the dots

We need to look more qualitatively and holistically at chains of interaction to judge the quality of dialogue properly. Space does not permit a full qualitative analysis here, but the process can be briefly illustrated using one nicely dialogic sequence spanning Lines 160–6 and sharing some immediate thoughts. Note that other researchers will likely generate some different comments, and further layers of analysis could be undertaken, but this hopefully offers a flavour (for longer examples, see Hennessy et al., 2016).

The teacher begins by referring to the talking point on the board and comments that the explanation there is impoverished (Line 160); use of this virtual participant probably depersonalizes any disagreement. In the same turn she refers back to a pertinent contribution that she heard when circulating around the groups and then brings this into the arena of whole class discussion. This gives it status and illustrates – and progresses – the cumulative nature of dialogue over time. Students respond (Lines 161, 163, 165), reasoning explicitly. The teacher listens to each and further explains their contributions to the class (Lines 162, 164), using a questioning tone which signals a request for verification and room for disagreement. However, wait time is very limited. In the final line (166) the teacher verifies what Towha is saying in her lengthy contribution in Line 165, and implicitly challenges her by inviting the class to comment on the validity of her idea. Overall, the teacher makes a range of dialogic moves, especially invitations, while retaining tight control over the course of the dialogue. Students seem happy and supported to contribute their ideas.

To conclude, there is strong overlap between the coding outcomes from the perspectives of the three schemes, plus some nuanced differences. In the sequence in Lines 160–6 and indeed across the excerpt, SEDA drills down the furthest and occasionally brings in unique codes such as *refer back* (Line 160). The transactive coding offers an immediate overview of the kinds of interactions and orientations observed, while mapping directly onto SEDA coding. Both highlight the explicit positioning in Line 163 where Amin's other orientation 'O RQ' breaks the pattern that otherwise goes O TQ (teacher) – S RQ (students) – OTQ – S RQ and so on. APT illuminates the teacher moves only but illustrates the variety of moves aimed primarily at getting students to share, expand and clarify their thinking. We could of course have coded using only SEDA clusters instead of the detailed codes, and the outcome would have approached the broader level of granularity that coding with APT afforded: the three clusters of Invite Elaboration, Reasoning and Positioning featured across Lines 160–6.

Finally, readers may be interested to know that we tested out the same three schemes on the excerpt in a coding workshop in our department, with colleagues and doctoral students. Others may likewise benefit from seeing and discussing the pros and cons of the various schemes through such an exercise too (using these or other examples and schemes).

Concluding remarks

This chapter has introduced some of the systematic coding schemes for analysing classroom dialogue at the micro-level and outlined some of the methodological issues arising in design and application to authentic interaction. The key message is that 'there's more than one way to skin a cat' – here this somewhat unpleasant (!) English idiom means that researchers need to make their own decisions after reflecting upon the potential consequences of different pathways and tools for their own specific research purposes, and a certain amount of trial and error. An increasing range of options is available, including complementary and alternative methods to systematic fine-grained coding. We have to acknowledge that coding – and all the data processing and trials that go with it – is inevitably time-consuming and sometimes taxing, but it is also very rewarding and often highly illuminating of patterns in the dialogue that may not otherwise come to light. It is invaluable for largish datasets in particular.

Most of this chapter has focused on analysing talk. There is a pressing need to expand coding tools to capture interactions where material resources and knowledge artefacts, especially digital artefacts, are pivotal participants in the dialogue. Indeed, our deliberate use of the broader term 'dialogue' rather than 'talk' in this book is partly intended to convey its multimodal nature. The next chapter shares some thoughts on the methodological implications.

This chapter has become very long – apologies readers – yet it inevitably remains partial. I am grateful to Adam Lefstein and Matan Barak for their insightful commentary below, and for bringing the all-important non-cognitive dimensions of dialogue to the fore. Their creative suggestions around researching issues like power and voice add a welcome, complementary perspective.

Links

A condensed version of SEDA is available at http://tinyurl.com/SEDAcondensed, the cluster descriptors are at http://tinyurl.com/SEDAclusters and the detailed coding scheme is at http://tinyurl.com/SEDAfull. The scheme is openly available under a CC-By-4.0 licence (international): http://creativecommons.org/licenses/by/4.0/.

Acknowledgements

Many thanks to Cathy O'Connor for checking the application of APT to the excerpt and for her helpful comments on the ambiguities arising. SEDA was developed and trialled by a large team through a British Academy-funded collaboration between colleagues at University of Cambridge and the National Autonomous University of Mexico (http://tinyurl.com/BAdialogue).

Expert commentary

Tradeoffs and dilemmas in coding classroom dialogue

Adam Lefstein and Matan Barak, Ben-Gurion University of the Negev

The chapter provides a wonderful introduction to the nitty-gritty details of selecting, testing, refining and using an analytic scheme for coding classroom dialogue, and the sort of judgements – and trade-offs – this process entails. In our commentary we discuss some of the issues the chapter raises for us, and challenges facing this field as it moves forward.

First, perhaps a word about where we're coming from. We conduct research on classroom dialogue from broadly linguistic ethnographic and pedagogic perspectives. We are likely located near the 'divergent' edges of the consensus about central features of productive dialogue that Hennessy mentions in the chapter introduction. Not that we're opposed to critical exploration of multiple perspectives, joint construction of meaning and elicitation and examination of reasoning – it's just that we think that dialogic pedagogy encompasses further dimensions, such as interpersonal relations, **epistemological** stance, the realization of voice, shared power and even aesthetics (Lefstein & Snell, 2014). We don't want to lose sight of these dimensions, even though they are awfully hard to pin down in a reliable coding scheme – more on this below.

We very much appreciate how Hennessy highlights throughout the chapter the trade-offs involved in choosing and adapting a coding scheme. Our natural, ethnographic instinct is to employ a scheme with a comprehensive scope, which includes multiple categories and values, in order to account for the many facets and nuances of classroom discourse and interaction. However, each added variable adds complexity, thereby increasing coding time and reducing reliability. Achieving reliability is easier with codes that focus on surface-level behaviors – for example, overlapping speech or a two-second pause. But was the overlapping speech an interruption or cooperative backchannelling? Does the pause reflect wait-time or interactional trouble? Once we move from surface-level behaviors to attributions of meaning our reliability plummets. Unfortunately, many researchers (and reviewers) tend to think about coding issues in rather technical terms (e.g., What is an acceptable Kappa score? Which program should I use for transcribing?). The chapter helpfully orients readers to coding as a set of trade-offs and dilemmas that require careful consideration in relation to research aims, resources and theoretical assumptions.

Consider, for example, an intriguing moment in the episode that was analysed in the chapter. During the small group segment the teacher asks where tap water comes from, and one of the pupils, Ishra, answers, 'the toilet' (Line 133). The teacher responds incredulously, 'It comes from the toilet?' and then chuckles as she says, 'I don't know what tap water you're drinking, Ishra,' before transitioning from the small group to whole class discussion.

When Ishra says, 'the toilet' in Line 133 she gestures with her hand in what appears to us as an illustration of the flow of water. While the teacher moves away, Ishra, inaudible in the recording and with her back to the camera, repeats the gesture, suggesting that she continues to explain her point to the other group members. Three and half minutes later, the teacher asks, now in the plenary, about the origins of water and Ishra reiterates that it comes from the toilet: see Lines 166–73. The teacher – in a tone of good humour – clarifies that this is not the case (Line 172). In this sequence the class appear particularly engaged and enthusiastic; they enjoy the joke. Something important is happening here, but it is not captured by the various schemes examined in the chapter, which focus exclusively on the cognitive aspects of classroom dialogue. First, having a good laugh performs important social functions: capturing the students' attention, having fun, bringing the class together and placing students at ease. Sidorkin (1999), in his 'three drinks theory', suggests that this sort of joyful looseness is essential to the development of dialogue. Second, the teacher relates the rather theoretical comparison of tap and rain water to the students' home lives, suggesting with scatological humour that they'd best know the origins of their drinking water. Third, we wonder how this sequence positions Ishra: might she see herself as the object of derision rather than the author of the joke? Fourth, we infer from her persistent raising of the point that she was attempting to field a legitimate idea, which was marginalized perhaps inadvertently for the sake of a laugh. The resulting 'dialogic space' does not include her voice (Segal & Lefstein, 2016).

But how if at all might we reliably code these sorts of issues? It is impossible to develop codes to describe the intricate and nuanced social relations that we've just begun to explore in our brief discussion here. But we could certainly code for laughter, and perhaps also for heightened involvement. More difficult, but not impossible, would be to code for which voices and ideas are expressed, and how they are taken up by the teacher and/or students in the unfolding interaction.

Returning to coding as trade-offs and dilemmas, it is entirely reasonable to decide not to attend to these non-cognitive dimensions of dialogue. Indeed, for most research programs that would be the wisest choice. However, the challenge remains: how do we avoid reducing our approach to dialogue to the coding scheme we have elected to use? Hennessy discusses the importance of post-coding analyses, but in our experience it is difficult to shake free of the analytic infrastructure that we so meticulously develop and train ourselves to use. Moreover, in the life cycle of a research project, the coding scheme typically dictates the main research findings and themes, which are then 'illustrated' with qualitative analyses (chapter 3 in Nystrand, Gamoran, Kachur & Prendergast, 1997, is a nice exception to this rule). We suggest that perhaps a *pre-coding* stage, in which researchers respond openly and holistically to the episode, might be a useful antidote to the totalizing tendencies of a priori schemes. Or, alternatively, you could add to the coding process additional columns for researcher annotation with regard to more 'qualitative' issues, such as social dynamics, pupil identities, power relations, the development of ideas and so on.

We thank Hennessy for presenting here the state of the art of coding classroom dialogue. Thinking ahead, here are some of the key challenges we hope will occupy Hennessy, her readers and the rest of the field in the coming years:

- *The movement of coding schemes between research and pedagogical tools.* We were intrigued that Hennessy took the 'talk moves' developed by Michaels, O'Connor and Resnick as part of the *Accountable Talk* program and used them to code talk for research purposes. This shift should not be taken for granted, since the purposes, resources and standards of pedagogical and research tools differ considerably. For example, the nine talk moves are designed as tools for teachers to elicit, probe and extend student ideas in classroom discourse. They are designed for working with teachers, and hence they focus exclusively on teacher talk. However, the teacher moves are intended to lead to changes in student participation, so if as researchers we wish to study their effectiveness we would want to focus on student responses. What is sensible and appropriate as a professional development tool becomes inadequate as a research tool. Likewise, the opposite move, from research to pedagogy, requires careful adaptation of tools according to the needs, conditions and standards of teacher professional development.

- *Meaningful coding of student talk*. Most existing coding schemes focus primarily on teacher talk, in part because teacher talk is so much more predictable and orderly than student talk. Nevertheless, student talk is the heart of classroom dialogue, and we need to devise meaningful and reliable means of investigating it on its own terms.

- *Coding quality of ideas*. Likewise, most schemes focus on functions – for example, argument, evidence, explanation, refutation, question – rather than on the content of ideas. But ultimately we value these functions to a large extent because they can improve the quality of thinking and ideas. How might we be able to directly code and track the quality of thinking and ideas?

- *Tracking individual student voices*. Overwhelmingly, existing coding schemes treat students as a group, or at best differentiate between boys and girls. But students experience classroom lessons as individuals, and it is significant who is addressing whom, and how individual students' participation, ideas and voices develop over time.

CHAPTER SEVEN

Methods for Researching Technology-Mediated Dialogue

Sara Hennessy

Introduction

Using technology with a dialogic intention opens up new kinds of opportunities for learners and teachers to share, explain, justify, compare, critique and reformulate ideas. Technology-mediated learning changes the nature of dialogue itself. A recent landmark-scoping review of seventy-two international research studies, many informed by a sociocultural perspective (see Chapter 2) outlines the key ways in which classroom dialogue and digital technology can interact to influence learning (Major, Warwick, Rasmussen, Ludvigsen & Cook, 2018). This review indicated that using digital technologies can enhance productive classroom dialogue in a number of specific ways: see Box 7.1.

Box 7.1 How technology can enhance classroom dialogue (Major et al., 2018)

- exposing learners to different perspectives, for example, using microblogging to help students with limited prior knowledge tap into others' perspectives or prompting learners to consider the 'audience' (where known!) when contributing to an online forum;
- supporting learners to build knowledge together, including through creating shared digital artefacts (elaborated below);
- learners using dialogue to express metacognitive learning and to think about others' thinking when responding to their contributions;
- learners using dialogue to scaffold understanding of their peers;
- supporting collaboration and creating an increased sense of community.

The myriad uses of digital technology to support learning through dialogue raise methodological challenges, particularly for analysing large-scale research. Technology introduces additional modes of communication ('multimodality': Jewitt, 2006) that all need to be taken into account and that may operate simultaneously; for example, learners explaining their thinking orally and gesturing as they make a contribution in a digital environment. Modes are loosely bounded, not discrete units. In any interaction, one mode can take on high intensity (weight) and change the action, and along with the number of modes and their interrelationships, this contributes to modal density – which itself can ebb and flow (see the seminal work in this field by Norris, 2004). Approaches to analysing dialogue arising within and across modes must be flexible in order to allow for potential rich new forms of dialogue that emerge when it is supported, transformed or constrained through technology use. Researchers may need new methods to capture such 'multimodal dialogue'. There is also often dialogic interaction away from the technology that acts as a 'priming' mechanism to allow students – without teacher involvement – to rehearse their ideas (and justify their reasoning) before bringing them to the whole-class arena (Ravenscroft, 2007). Examples include pair discussion or using mini-whiteboards to storyboard ideas (see Figure 7.1)

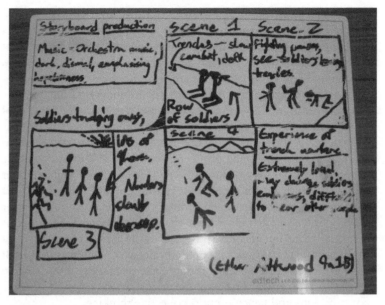

FIGURE 7.1 *Storyboard to dramatize a war poem in a secondary history class.*

before publicly sharing them via an interactive whiteboard or IWB (Hennessy, Warwick & Mercer, 2011). Or, 'offline' peer group discussion or individual writing may follow up activity using the technology. Offline activity needs to be captured by researchers too if their interest is in the whole learning process and its outcomes.

An essential part of any analysis of dialogue – indeed of learning – in technology-mediated contexts is identifying the specific features of common educational technologies that are considered to support or constrain learning: these are the 'affordances' of the technology for particular learners achieving a particular learning objective in a particular setting at a particular point in time using a particular pedagogy. Affordances are fluid and context-dependent. A useful way of understanding affordance is as a set of broad categories pertaining to a range of 'action possibilities' presented by an object or scenario that may apply *across different technologies*, but that can in turn inform analyses of the 'enacted affordances' of a *specific technology*, that is, whether and how the affordances are actually manifest in situ (Major & Warwick, in press).

To illustrate this, a powerful affordance of educational technology for learning through dialogue is (potentially) its support for continuity and deepening of a dialogue over time – in contrast with both oral and traditional print media. As elaborated below, provisional knowledge artefacts created using digital media have a material permanence of form that helps to underpin 'the recursive reflection and revision that is so important a characteristic of knowledge building' (Wells, 1999, p. 116). The IWB technology has proprietary software allowing archiving of the 'flipchart' – series of screen images – including any annotations or modifications made during a lesson. These can then be revisited and manipulated later in the lesson or lesson sequence, offering a major advantage over the transient records made on ordinary wipe-clean whiteboards or blackboards. A similar affordance characterizes online, synchronous discussion fora, but of course the traces of the dialogue look different in that context, and how they are later drawn on will manifest itself differently too. In each case, though, the technology use can help learners and teachers to create meaning within chains of dialogic contributions and hence support collective thinking.

The scoping review by Major et al. (2018) showed that the majority of studies of classroom dialogue and digital technologies collect qualitative data (especially those conducted in primary schools) or use mixed methods (predominantly in secondary schools). Quantitative data collection alone cannot capture the complexity of dialogic interaction in a technology-mediated environment. It should be acknowledged though, that this is a field still in its infancy; few tried-and-trusted techniques exist and there is no consensus approach. Our team at Cambridge, working with colleagues in Hong Kong, Norway and Wales as well as others in England, is presently grappling with the challenges. The remainder of this chapter shares some of our progress and thinking to date. The chapter is illustrated by exemplars derived mainly from a series of studies focusing on researching dialogic use of interactive display screens.

How can we analyse multimodal dialogue?

The main objective is to build up a sophisticated picture of the complexity of interaction in any given technology context, to examine its dialogic quality and relate this to learning where possible. Ways to tackle this that have proved productive include examining the artefacts that teachers and, especially, students create during dialogue; identifying the affordances for the particular technology and context; analysing and integrating the interaction taking place via different modes (including audio/video recording and transcribing speech and action, capturing and analysing digital texts and images of digital artefacts and offline activity); categorizing multimodal interaction sequences using an adapted scheme for **coding** dialogue or qualitative **thematic analysis;** interviewing participants using **stimulated recall** – or **think-aloud protocols** – in order to learn more about the thinking underlying the interaction; automatic **data mining** techniques, for example, using **screen capture** software; and integrating the outcomes across the different analyses through **interpretative narrative. Critical event analysis** is often employed as part of these methods. Complex is indeed the word! These approaches are outlined below. Not all of them may apply in a particular setting; of course, they are simply options, and there will be other possible approaches too.

Capturing interaction with artefacts

We think with and through artefacts. (Säljö, 1995, p. 91)

It can be very helpful to think about how digital representations might embody knowledge as it gets developed, transformed and manipulated by teachers and learners through a dynamic process of shared, dialogic inquiry. While language is seen as the highly flexible 'master tool' that mediates learning (Cole, 1994), the dialogic space in which thinking is linked to exploring and reflecting upon difference is more fundamental than words (Wegerif et al., 2010). Other forms of interaction besides talk contribute to learning that is mediated by technology use. Such learning is often supported by teachers and learners actively creating what I have called 'digital knowledge artefacts' (Hennessy, 2011). Artefacts vary enormously in format and include objects created on an IWB (e.g. a mind map) and wikis or online forum discussions where the need to externalize ideas prompts students to offer deeper explanations (Lipponen, 2000). Artefacts are provisional, interim records of the evolving collective (social and cognitive) activity and hence the ongoing dialogue. Thus these 'improvable' objects (Wells, 1999) are supportive devices for learners' emerging thinking, rather than finished products of dialogue – in keeping with conceptions of dialogue as unfinalizable (Bakhtin, 1986). These shared objects of activity 'materialize' the interaction between individual expertize and communal knowledge (Hakkarainen & Paavola, 2007). They embody the knowledge that is developed and externalized through multimodal interaction, often including talk – which may be supportive but rather ancillary, and insufficient alone.

Artefacts are important to researchers of dialogue because they are an intrinsic part of dialogic turn-taking. Hence 'turns with artefacts' enter into the interaction (Jordan & Henderson, 1995, pp. 64–6). For example, children grabbing and relinquishing the mouse constitute significant moves in collaborative problem-solving using a computer (Sacks, Schegloff & Jefferson, 1974). In contexts of interaction with material or digital resources, topics tend to stay alive much longer, and lengthy pauses are common (Jordan & Henderson, 1995). Indeed the nature of dialogue changes. Researchers may wish to investigate how artefacts and technologies support or constrain particular participation structures (Jordan & Henderson, 1995). Orientation to a digital device may radically change how participants are physically oriented or relate to each other in comparison to group interaction around a table. The impact varies with both the physical setup and the technology: desktop computers, interactive display boards or tables, and handheld devices like tablets (and the number of participants sharing them, of course) all afford different participation structures and combinations of talk, gesture and digital object manipulation that the researcher needs to prepare for. Control of the manipulation (notoriously gendered) and ownership of artefact creation and modification are further variables that influence the course of dialogue and may be of interest to researchers.

Artefacts generally provide physical, permanent records of collaborative activity and ideas that can remain visually accessible and be usefully *revisited or referenced* during subsequent activity. These objects of joint reference make learning histories and trajectories more visible and support the *continuing ('cumulative') dialogue over time* – across lessons as well as within. Artefacts can also be built upon or modified (e.g. through annotation) to become new artefacts; this is a form of *elaboration or building upon others' ideas.* Of crucial importance too for analysing dialogue is the argument that revisiting or comparing digital knowledge artefacts *makes the difference or agreement between perspectives more salient.* This helps participants to *make understandings and reasoning explicit* to peers or the teacher and to *coordinate, challenge or evaluate ideas* (Hennessy, 2011).

Readers may recognize the themes in italics here as cornerstones of dialogue, as elaborated in earlier chapters, especially Chapter 6 where they formed components of systematic coding schemes. I argue that technology use actually extends the way that dialogue is conceptualized through bringing in new modes of interaction with others' ideas. This moves us beyond traditional spoken dialogue and even beyond verbal language as a wide range of graphical and other representations (images, diagrams, graphs, drawings, multimedia presentations, simulations, animations, concept maps) all become potential modes of communication.

Examples can be drawn from our research group's past work on how the IWB, a tool ubiquitous in classrooms in England (typically used for whole-class teaching) offers a dialogic space in which mediating artefacts play a major role (Kershner, Mercer, Warwick & Kleine Staarman, 2010; Mercer, Hennessy & Warwick, 2010). Figure 7.2 offers an example from a secondary English classroom activity involving transforming a poetry text, which began with a brainstorm exploring learners' interpretations of a character's feelings. Figure 7.3 depicts a drawing built up cumulatively by six students aged 12–13 in turn each adding elements perceived to be typically present in a trench during wartime. Talk was minimal during the drawing process; this succinct, collective symbolic representation was instead 'drawn into being' (cf. Floriani, 1993). Finally, Figure 7.4 shows how students aged 9–10 engaged in dialogue about where to place a glow-worm in a categorization of objects as light sources or reflectors.

Capturing artefacts supports the research process as more data become accessible compared to offline settings. Data overload is a possible risk, though, and with all of the methods outlined in this chapter, researchers need to be guided by the research question(s) at all times. This includes deciding at the very start what is key to record and transcribe, before the analysis can begin. Further data selection may of course be required later using criteria relating to the question. For instance, Ingulfsen, Furberg and Strømme (2018)

FIGURE 7.2 *Brainstorm exploring feelings of character in poem: Secondary English lesson.*

analysed in depth only three sequences after initially examining general patterns in forty-nine student–teacher interactions around real-time graphing of pH levels of water under two conditions.

Part of the planning task for the researcher is to consider how to *capture the artefacts and interactions/modifications of them as they evolve* since they are not static – for instance, using screenshots, photographs, video recordings or direct screen capture (e.g. of IWB lesson flipcharts before and after annotation). It is challenging to capture the posts and links progressively added in an online environment without automatic data capture of some kind. Moreover, in themselves, jointly created artefacts – however richly they represent the developing understanding – tell us only part of the story. We need to consider the activity and talk that surround their evolution, and, where possible, delve more deeply into their meanings. I go on to suggest some ways of doing this.

Analysis of video and screen recordings

Still images of artefacts are static, of course, and capturing the dynamic processes of multimodal interaction in a permanent format

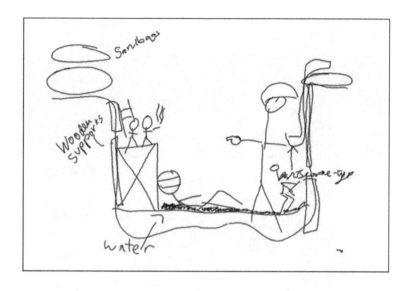

FIGURE 7.3 *Collective drawing of trench in secondary history lesson.*

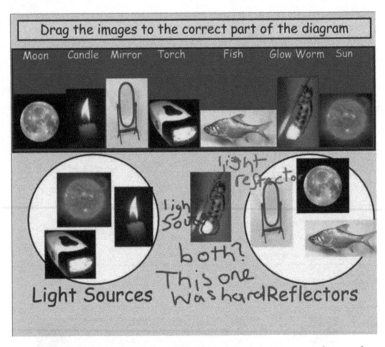

FIGURE 7.4 *Using an IWB in thinking about primary and secondary light sources.*

may well be desirable. Highly effective methods for this include (a) audio/video recording of the whole activity, depicting the learners themselves, and/or (b) automatic screen capture of the activity in the digital environment, often including audio recording. The IWB and many computer operating systems have a very simple screen recording facility built in, for instance; like video recordings, this allows action replay in real time and still image capture from the recording.

Video recording in technology contexts raises some issues of its own, especially where desktop or portable computers are involved. Researchers must decide whether to focus the camera on the screen or the learners. Many use two cameras simultaneously. Then, if screen capture is used, can it be linked with other recordings? The picture-in-picture procedure allows two or more recorded images to be merged into the same file, with the secondary image appearing as a small inset of the primary image. Moreover, groups of students conducting inquiry, simulated or real-time experiments using computers need teacher support, especially for interpreting the outcomes and in making connections (Ingulfsen et al., 2018); thus, recording such support is important too. Capturing audio of sufficient quality is particularly challenging.

The T-MEDIA project carried out by Hennessy and Deaney (2009) offers an in-depth approach to analysing the footage and any other data and it illustrates the dialogic research stance outlined in Chapters 2 and 4. Video footage was collaboratively analysed with eight secondary school practitioners (co-researchers) in order to understand how subject learning might be mediated by interactive display board technology like the IWB. Independent video review of the same lessons was conducted by ourselves as university researchers, by the collaborating teacher-researcher who was filmed, by a colleague within the same subject department who also acted as co-researcher and by an academic subject expert in each area (English, mathematics, science, history). We undertook the video review using a pre-prepared summary of the lesson activity against a timeline (the content log) in each case, segmented after key changes of topic or activity (every few minutes). There were four phases of video review, as in Box 7.2. Note that our project was externally funded and covered teacher release time; for a sole researcher, an adapted version would be more feasible.

Analysis options for video recordings and related data include phenomenology (interpretation), thematic analysis and/or systematic coding that may be inductive, deductive or abductive (see Chapter 4). In T-MEDIA, for instance, the university researchers generated a set of preliminary deductive codes derived from the literature and our previous analysis of teacher mediation in another project with practitioners, using these in the first subject case study. Examples included *scaffolding* and *focusing*. They were illustrated with strategies from the teacher's own (first two) lessons. The tentative analytic scheme was iteratively refined during analysis of each subject case in turn, as new, inductive codes were integrated, meanings were negotiated and degree of fit with the data assessed. Analysis therefore involved a complex, recursive process of constant comparison (Glaser and Strauss, 1967).

The discussion above has focused mainly on capturing collective thinking; however, researchers may also be interested in the impact of dialogic technology-mediated activity on individual thinking and products. Or they may wish to probe more deeply into individual

Box 7.2 Phases of video review in T-MEDIA project

- *Phase 1: Independent review.* The various analysts reviewed the lesson video independently, adding commentary in note form to each segment of the lesson summary (see example in Table 7.1). The researchers and the teacher-colleague noted questions for further discussion with the teacher during subsequent review meetings. Questions were intended to clarify the teacher's rationale for a particular action or interaction, the underlying curriculum objectives, or views about the unique contribution of the technology, or to elicit further contextual information. Likewise the subject specialist(s) viewed the videos and formulated independent commentary.
- *Phase 2: Preparing a multimedia database.* The four individual reviews were collated and combined using parallel columns in a single table for each of the lessons. These were then integrated with relevant excerpts from teacher diaries and the other observational data collected, including interviews, videos, images of IWB flipchart slides and nondigital whiteboard representations, lesson plans and handouts, and observation notes. This **ethnographic**-style data formed an extended version of the 'video portfolios' employed by Maher and Martino, 1996). Specialists' written commentary was circulated too.
- *Phase 3: Team meetings.* We verified, compared and integrated our perspectives in a series of meeting dialogues. Lesson videos were available throughout on a laptop computer for reference to additional corroborating and contrasting examples. A key activity was identifying 'critical episodes' and discussing what made them more or less significant, and salient to different reviewers. Reference to video recordings, lesson materials and participants' own experiences increases 'ecological validity', that is, applicability of the outcomes to authentic classroom conditions.
- *Phase 4: Producing narrative accounts.* All data sources were integrated and coded with the final coding scheme by the university research team using qualitative analysis software. A final teacher interview further clarified issues emerging from the analysis or raised by specialists. The process culminated in an accessibly written narrative account for each subject area. These negotiated accounts produced 'intermediate theory', bridging

> between knowledge of specific settings and educational theory. They encapsulated the dialogic relationship between unique critical incidents and more general patterns that was referred to in Chapter 2.
>
> - *Encapsulating joint outcomes in multimedia resources.* Each account was ultimately represented in a digital professional development resource by a map illustrating the main themes identified, hyperlinked to selected video sequences and slides (reproducing whiteboard displays). Material for each clip included excerpts from the other data sources ('nuggets') and lesson commentary from all three groups. A further account compared pedagogical approaches across cases. These accounts were each expanded to prepare academic publications (including the book by Hennessy, 2014) with input from our co-researchers who – to a degree – became co-authors.

thinking processes while they contribute to group/class activity and dialogue. The following two techniques serve these purposes.

Stimulated recall interviews and 'meta-discourse'

Stimulated recall interview using digital artefacts or video clips is a very useful technique to tap into learners' thinking about an earlier activity, particularly in settings where they may not be verbalizing much (Lyle, 2003; Nind, Hall & Curtin, 2016). Images like those in Figures 7.2–7.4 provide a very powerful aide-memoire; a single annotated image can capture half an hour of activity and immediately conjure it back up for analysis. Participant-created artefacts carry more meaning and may offer the researcher more insight than videoed interactions created entirely by researchers; they offer a strong case for using stimulated recall interviews. The interview technique can also be used with selected video clips, though, or with video plus artefacts and other data pertaining to the same activity.

A key example comes from the study by Wegerif et al. (2010) of creative and critical thinking using dynamic online concept mapping in the Argunaut project. Creative student posts that initiated new threads were used along with the 'replay' function of the *Digalo* software tool in 'key event recall' interviews to revisit the steps leading up to a new contribution to the map. Students were asked what they were thinking and feeling at the time and why. Their reports indicated that the spatial layout made it easier to follow the whole discussion and see its strands, compared to previous experience with linear text-based conferencing environments. Having multiple themes and ideas and the links between them visible together in the mapping space had triggered new ideas. By focusing on branching events ('key dialogic moments') that had helped to widen the discussion, the interviews helped students to reflect on how they had learned through dialogue; all identified disagreement with others' posted ideas as a powerful motive for generating new perspectives and insights. The students' accounts **validated** the relationship observed by the researchers – through coding – between oppositions and subsequent emergence of new ideas. The interviews also revealed many oppositions that had not been explicit in the online dialogue.

Stimulated recall interviews are a form of dialogue in themselves, with the intention of probing into how learners solved a problem or constructed knowledge together. They not only capture the history of the dialogue but could be said to bring the artefact and its evolution into a new dialogue between researcher and learner. Of course, the interviewer, like a teacher normally would, is setting the agenda and leading so it is not a democratic form of dialogue. Moreover, the level of **inference** can rise when an interview becomes a dialogue in itself, and a degree of rigour in conducting and analysing the interview is important. There are also potential limitations of participants retrospectively reordering their accounts or being biased in their reports; however, stimulated recall remains a valuable tool for capturing accounts of decision-making in naturalistic contexts (Lyle, 2003). Innovative forms of video-stimulated discussion have been conducted (a) with teachers in order to support reflective dialogue about technology use and to interrogate scholarly theory together (Hennessy & Deaney, 2009), as alluded to above, and (b) in focus groups with teachers and learners reviewing lesson clips together during a three-way dialogue (Nind, Kilburn & Wiles, 2015). In both studies, critical events were selected by participants as well as researchers. The discussions of clips yielded pedagogical insights, more nuanced interpretations of classroom activity and provisional themes for subsequent coding across contexts.

A further example of dialogic stimulated recall is the 'meta-discourse' activity in the Knowledge Forum software environment (known as 'rise-above') whereby learners periodically review the collaborative knowledge-building discourse of the group or class. They evaluate its quality and make explicit reference to relevant previous contributions (discussion 'notes' posted on the forum 'wall') and links between them, using a built-in hyperlink function (Yang, van Aalst, Chan & Wen Tian, 2016). This process involves tracking, synthesizing and reflecting on development of students' own ideas; prompts are built into the system, for example, 'What I initially thought', 'How my ideas developed' and 'What I understand now and what questions need to inquiry further'. This meta-discourse can be captured in a reflection journal, in records of oral classroom discussion and in further portfolio notes subsequently added to explain individuals' knowledge advancement. The prompts provided for perusal of the Knowledge Forum discussion trace serve to stimulate reflections that are then recorded in the system for easy access by the researcher, although the other forms of data still need to be integrated manually.

Think-aloud protocols

Think-aloud method is similar in some ways to stimulated recall but it is carried out in real time. It has long been used in mathematics education research and other areas where individual problem-solving processes are of interest to researchers, but it holds significant potential for those looking at learner collaboration and dialogue in digital environments. Essentially, participants are asked to verbalize their thinking, reasoning and decision-making strategies as they engage in complex tasks, and this is recorded (Ericsson & Simon, 1993). The method can provide valuable, rich and detailed insights that are sometimes difficult to attain retrospectively when memory limitations and interpretations may interfere. There are some pitfalls: reports may prove to be somewhat incoherent since they are generated live, without filtering or reshaping, and verbalizing strategies may change them. Nevertheless they are likely to have higher validity than the more reflective, post hoc accounts that stimulated recall may provoke. Think-aloud is a labour-intensive and time-consuming method, though, like stimulated recall, so it is best employed with very small samples.

A Norwegian study by Siddiq and Scherer (2017) employed think-aloud in assessing upper secondary school students' social and cognitive skills while they were communicating and collaborating with peers in a digital problem-solving environment. Data comprised video recordings of students' screens capturing their actions and audio recordings of their thinking aloud. These were categorized using a large set of time-coded event and sequence codes, capturing the time spent on each task, the actions taken (e.g. creating a mind map) and the skills demonstrated (e.g. help-seeking). Charting individuals' actions against a timeline revealed how long each group spent collaborating, the relationship with the roles that individuals took and so on. The technique seems to offer considerable potential for researching dialogic interactions mediated by technology.

Characterizing affordances

The notion of affordance was introduced above as a means of highlighting the *potential* for use of an educational technology to support (or constrain) learning through dialogue. Features of software and technology may or may not be exploited by teachers or students in the ways that their designers intended since user agency plays a central role. Whether intentions and potential are realized or not is closely related to pedagogical outlook (e.g. Kennewell & Beauchamp, 2007). In one study of dynamic geometry software use in secondary schools, teachers were observed to handle the apparent mathematical anomalies of operating the software differently, depending on whether they saw these as anomalies to be capitalized upon or to be concealed in order to avoid confusion (Ruthven, Hennessy & Deaney, 2008). In the former case teachers saw anomalies as opportunities to challenge students' expectations about how the software would behave and to develop their mathematical understanding. A dialogic pedagogy may likewise drive teachers to exploit technologies in certain ways. Affordances vary with technology type (e.g. touch screens on tablets, interactive display boards or touch tables offer a very different learning environment to a desktop computer) as well as educational purpose and context. IWB-specific affordances include highlighting and annotation of images and texts by hand in real time during discussion (see Figures 7.2–7.4). Yet, there are some generalities emerging in the literature; Box 7.3 lists some examples of commonly identified affordances. Collectively, these can facilitate creating a shared dialogic space for collective knowledge building.

Box 7.3 Common affordances of technology for dialogue

- multimodality itself
- direct manipulation – the facility for engaging with concepts and processes through interacting with physical representations of them (e.g. manipulating magnitude of force in a simulation), affording easy experimentation
- dynamism – moving images and models of dynamic processes (e.g. animations, simulations)
- provisionality – knowledge objects are tentatively positioned, debatable, movable, improvable, reversible, unlike writing/drawing in an exercise book
- accessibility to a wide range of digital resources
- immediate contingent feedback offered by the technology: responsive to learners' input

---

A multimodal analysis table with parallel columns

We are beginning to collect a number of forms of data relating to a dialogic **episode** or lesson; these need to be integrated and any omissions identified. An extremely useful device is to create a multimodal analysis table where different kinds of data are recorded against a timeline of the lesson/session: each row depicts one time window. Density or absence of data in each cell is significant. All rows should contain the same kind of information (labelled consistently) and be self-sufficient so that reference to other parts of the table is not needed (e.g. school name might be repeated in every row pertaining to data from classes in that school), especially where frequency counting might be desired. Which types of data are included, and the criterion for **segmentation** (see Chapter 6), both depend on the research question and methods, of course. Likewise, depending on whether a **micro- or macroanalytic** approach is desired, rows could be differentiated by participant turn or discrete action, for instance, or they might be coarser-grained short sequences of related actions/interaction, perhaps lasting a few minutes. If the former, then a column can also be added for the unique sequence/communicative event identifier (to be applied to a number of adjacent rows) so that analysis can be conducted at both the micro- and meso-level. In any case, distinguishing who the participants are within each segment is essential; names or unique identifier numbers might be recorded, and a separate column might simply distinguish teacher from students. (This could help to see how equitable participation is, for instance.) Other metadata such as 'group name/number', 'class number' or 'organizational context (group vs class vs teacher and individual student)' might usefully be included in another column(s), if appropriate (Shaffer, 2017). Typically, time codes are included – transcription software (such as open-source 'Inqscribe') will stamp these automatically onto transcripts – and each row is numbered too for ease of reference. All of the decisions made about what to include in the table ideally need to be considered at the research design stage.

See the first five columns of Table 7.1 for illustration. The table depicts analysis during the T-MEDIA project of an episode of whole-class teaching taken from a secondary English lesson sequence (already referred to in relation to Figure 7.2). The first two (consecutive) segments are not differentiated by discrete turn/action (thus Columns 3–4 are blank), whereas the third segment (which followed an interlude of group work) is, simply by way of illustrating these two levels of detail for readers. Normally, of course, a single **unit of analysis** would be used throughout a study.

In this lesson focusing on metaphor, a set of words relating to the lifestyles of the personae in the poems by Duffy and Armitage that the class had studied was displayed on the IWB (Segment 1). The teacher, Jackie, asked four pupils to come up and assign the words to the briefcase or rucksack pictured on the IWB (symbolizing hitchhiker and businessman characters), using the drag-and-drop facility. Some terms whose meanings pupils were uncertain about were placed centrally after class discussion. Pupils generated their own examples during the course of a further lengthy class dialogue concerning the two contrasting perspectives, and the image was annotated accordingly.

The next columns of data include some form of records of the physical activity and speech/textual contributions, that is, the content of the interaction. Researchers will often want to transcribe the speech and prepare a written rough summary of the action: such a 'content log' provides a useful quick overview of the dataset and helps in locating particular sequences, issues or interesting segments to transcribe (Jordan & Henderson, 1995). In some of our studies we transcribe only selected features of the interaction that emerge as related to the analytic focus. Where close attention to the dialogue is needed though, verbatim transcription – including vocalization other than speech – is essential (unless using direct video coding software such as Elan). The data in the table will typically also include 2D images of artefacts where viable; again these offer a powerful aide-memoire for the analyst. In our own studies we have analysed multimodal dialogue by setting up parallel columns where images are aligned with summaries of the physical action and the oral dialogue against a timeline (see Columns 6–8 of Table 7.1). We might include pertinent observation notes, interview or diary extracts (Column 10).

Further columns contain the analytic elements – in our case a dialogue code (Column 9: see next section) and a commentary highlighting the affordances being exploited at the particular time, along with the teacher's strategies for supporting learning and creating a conducive climate for dialogue (Column 11). Text was coded to highlight the different perspectives. See further detailed examples in Hennessy (2014). In the actual analysis, extra columns were added for each commentator and additional data source, but these have each had to be condensed into one column (10 and 11) in Table 7.1. Again such complexity is unlikely to be appropriate for more modest studies; nevertheless the principle of tailoring an analysis table to the specific project participants, purposes and data types still holds. Lefstein and Barak (Commentary on Chapter 6) suggest that additional columns might include comments on issues such as social dynamics, pupil identities or development of ideas. A single table cannot of course include all of the data collected. (Indeed, extracts in Table 7.1 are

Table 7.1 Example of a multimodal analysis table

1 Segment no. (or line/turn no.)	2 Time	3 Agent T/Sa	4 Agent ID	5 Whole class / group / T-S	6 Action	7 Oral dialogue	8 Artefacts: Image / online dialogue	9 Codeb	10 Interview / meeting / diary extracts	11 Commentary / Affordances of technology for dialoguec
1	0:58:14–1:02:48			class	T reviews yesterday's work, showing images of briefcase & rucksack. T calls 4 Ss up to IWB to sort words into the right places; each S in turn moves one word over an image. Other Ss sometimes disagree with placement. Four words are ones people were unsure about: 'confined', 'philosophical', 'liberated', 'hedonistic'. T moves them back up to the list area for discussion.	T: 'Liberated': People were saying they didn't think it should go in the briefcase. What does liberated mean? Matt: Feeling free. T: Absolutely. It comes from the word… similar to it? P: Liberty. T: […] so if you're 'confined', what does that sound like? What might be confined? Luke: 'trapped'. T: Yes […] what is the person in Hitcher confined by? Natasha: His work […]T: So his work is trapping him […] T: 'Philosophical', what does that mean?' […] Boy: "Reflecting on subjects."		RB EL	**Team meeting notes:** T chose these 4 Ss because they wouldn't ordinarily volunteer. T reported that at this school there is a culture of Ss being quite happy to share ideas. Ss are often told how creative it can be and that things aren't usually right or wrong. It gives Ss confidence to analyse and evaluate different ideas – vitally important. **Diary:** T felt that with her support, and through building on each other's ideas:	R1: **Revisiting** using slide from last lesson to continue activity started then; selected Ss given the chance to demonstrate their knowledge of vocabulary relating to poem's themes **(public sharing)**. T solicits meanings of (and **elaborates**) remaining unknown words from rest of class **(filling in)**, using **annotation** to **record** for all Ss, again mixing her own terms in with Ss' phrases to create collaborative definitions (e.g. 'reflective, thoughtful'): **dialogic; public sharing.** R2: T's running commentary fosters **active involvement** of audience. Technology affords **provisionality:** T drags a couple of items back from briefcase to the main part of the board in order to ensure students understand the vocabulary. Pupils could make immediate changes to their choices.

T discusses meaning of each unfamiliar word, using question-and-answer. T annotates slide with key words, relates them to Hitcher in poem. T writes 'free' and 'liberty' on IWB T writes 'trapped' T writes 'reflective', 'thoughtful'	T: "Brilliant. So you're very reflective, it's about thinking. Reflective, thoughtful. So you think a lot about what you want out of your life…"	"The definitions that some of the pupils gave at this point certainly showed an increased understanding – which, as the group shared their ideas, built up to a fuller definition."	T: Class keen to correct mistakes but in a supportive way – opens up discussion about new vocabulary and about persona's lifestyles, developing understanding of poem. Other students able to share their knowledge – T draws on word roots and similarities to **scaffold** task. Ss keen to show their knowledge of how [new] words relate to poem… T **funnelling** through directed questions. **Reshaping Ss' thinking.**

						C: Ss are confident to contribute and move words around on the IWB even though not completely confident about answers. This allows the opportunity to **revisit** language already learnt and for further language extension. T continually offers alternatives and redefines language in relation to the poems. **Dialogic synthesis.**
2	1:29:44	T	class	T gestures (points, waves hand over phrases) to indicate categories printed on IWB slide: personae, mood/tone, society, language	T to class: What similarities can we say these poems have in terms of these four areas – the personae, speakers in the poems? What connections have you spotted? [...]	IC T: Shared analysis and comparison of themes across poems after discussion. R1: T solicits Ss' ideas and records, creating a joint representation of themes **(public sharing)**

Time		Speaker	Action	Dialogue	Code	Comment
1:30:10	S	Josh	Josh raises the poetry book and opens it briefly (presumably to remind himself what Education for Leisure was about)	Josh: The person in Stealing is bored, the Hitchhiker has got nothing to do so he sits around waiting for a lift, and in 'Education for Leisure'... is that the one where he squashes a fly?	SC	C: S confident to answer T's questions and expertly speaks about each poem when giving answer.
1:30:32	T	T	T writes on slide: 'bored', 'aimless'	T: Yes, so they are bored, they are aimless, any other adjectives that you'd like to say for all of them?	EL	R1: T records words reflecting students' responses, but not always using their own words
1:30:38	S	Amy	T writes 'careless'	Amy: 'Careless'		
1:30:44	S	Josh		Josh: 'They are all about making people angry, or hurting them'.	SC	

Time					Code	Notes
1:30:47	T	T	T writes 'cruel'	T: Cruel perhaps. What is the word we use for people who want to inflict pain on other people?	EL	T: T offers new vocabulary that Ss might find useful but only as it arose from discussion rather than giving them a word out of context. Relates word to content of poems. R2: **Dialogic interaction / synthesis.** T records
1:31:02	S	Boy		S: Is that terrorism?		S ideas and expands on them, including introduction of unfamiliar vocabulary. **Coaching / reshaping thinking.**
1:31:05-1:31:28	T	T	T writes 'sadistic - want to make others suffer'	T *(with slight laugh)*: Not terrorism! 'Sadistic' [. . .] Being sadistic means wanting to make other people suffer…		

---

a T = teacher; S = student

b RB = Reference back to prior contributions; IC = Invite coordination/synthesis of ideas; SC = Simple coordination / summary of ideas; EL = Elaborate/build on ideas

c R1 = Researcher 1; R2 = Researcher 2; T = teacher; C = teacher's colleague. Phrases in bold font denote affordances or other themes from the coding scheme for this lesson sequence.

abridged for reasons of space.) If appropriate, researchers could also add hyperlinks to data stored online.

Affordances can go in a separate column if desired: some researchers do this. Major and Warwick (in press) derived an initial framework of emerging affordances related to the 'Talkwall' microblogging environment and then, through inductive and deductive processes, coded the classroom activity for the actually 'enacted affordances' of Talkwall for promoting dialogic interaction, assigning each segment an affordance. Further refinement of the themes produced a final framework of enacted affordances that was applied across the data set.

In some contexts it may be useful to separate action *around* a technology – including control of it, such as taking/releasing a mouse (e.g. Cowan, 2014) – from action *within* the learning environment, in different columns (clearly this would not apply to immersive technologies). Yang, Wegerif and Pifarre (2013) did this in studies of Metafora, a visual language software tool supporting 'Learning to learn together'. Figure 7.5 shows a dynamic discussion map collaboratively constructed by primary school students conducting internet inquiries together on laptops. The map is another exemplar of a co-constructed digital artefact that enabled learners to read and interpret peers' perspectives. An example of 'action around' the activity recorded in the researchers' table was 'Mia stopped typing and Josh took the control of the laptop' while (in the same row) 'action in' Metafora included 'Josh made a link between Nodes (2) and (3)'. (Another column contained the verbatim talk accompanying these actions.)

The order of the columns is of course the researcher's choice and may reflect theoretical priorities or practical concerns. Use of a matrix in any case invites alternative non-temporal reading pathways, and allows connections to be noticed, for instance, between mouse control and gaze (Cowan, 2014). In Table 7.1 the columns are roughly increasing in level of inference as they move from left to right. Any two researchers given a particular lesson might independently record the same data and images in Columns 1–8. Consensus may decrease when choosing extracts for Column 10, and without a predetermined typology of affordances, those may vary too. The free-text commentary will almost certainly vary the most; here the decision-making becomes much more subjective. The research question will yet again guide researchers to identify

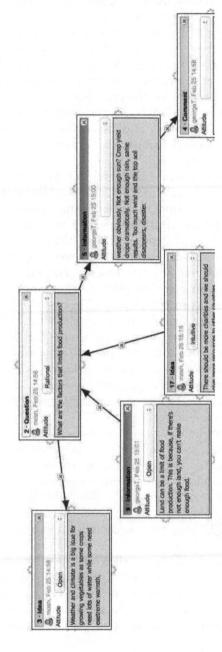

FIGURE 7.5 *Example of discussion map co-constructed using Metafora.*

affordances and decide what to note in their commentaries. We might be interested in how, say, a concept-mapping software tool helps students to make their reasoning and connections between ideas explicit in peer group dialogue. Direct manipulation of objects representing concepts and processes (as in Segment 1 in Table 7.1) would be an obvious affordance emerging in this case as students move and link the components. Provisionality would be very important too, as learners tried out different configurations until they felt satisfied with the map (see example in Figure 7.6). Commentary might focus on the sequence of actions and reasoning involved, any technical constraints arising or quality of the peer interaction.

Having a good initial appreciation of the functionality of the technology in question is desirable in order for the researcher to perceive the potential for exploiting it to support dialogue, and hence to identify missed opportunities as well as effective exploitation.

In sum, a dense tabular transcript of this kind can be demanding to read and interpret (Cowan, 2014) but offers an immensely rich and succinct way of representing and reducing multimodal data.

Coding multimodal dialogue

One way of analysing the interaction encapsulated in a table is to categorize or code it for dialogicality; a mixed-methods approach that then combines coding with the qualitative commentary can be very useful. Chapter 6 outlines the original systematic coding scheme developed by Hennessy, Rojas-Drummond and colleagues: SEDA. Many of the same categories can be applied in digital technology contexts, although here they are no longer primarily relevant to verbal contributions. For example, students might be 'building on others' ideas' in a very simple way when adding a link to a half-completed food chain (Figure 7.7). A further illustration is the set of features of the IWB that support 'focusing', another technology-specific affordance for dialogue; for example, the spotlight, blind and zoom facilities can be employed to direct learners' attention to a target part of the screen. Figure 7.8 depicts the well-known 'Armada' portrait of Queen Elizabeth I[1] discussed

---

[1]https://en.wikipedia.org/wiki/Armada_Portrait.

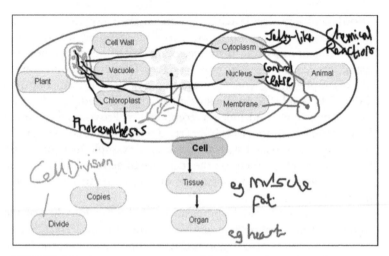

FIGURE 7.6 *Concept map annotated by learners in a science lesson.*

by a history class, and Figure 7.9 indicates that the teacher then spotlit a key portion of it, provoking dialogic discussion around whether it meant she 'rules the world'. See the code identifiers in Column 9 of Table 7.1. These codes are adapted from SEDA and their definitions and examples (the 'Tech-SEDA' scheme we are currently developing) are all described in terms of technology-mediated dialogue.

Once the data are coded, analysis may proceed through counting frequencies of codes and employing statistical methods to assess learning or through more qualitative methods of analysis (see Chapters 5 and 6 for debates around these and other options).

Readers may wish to try out applying other coding schemes to interaction mediated by technology and see how well they hold up. Our first trial applications of Tech-SEDA revealed the need to capture *gesture* (e.g. pointing at a screen). For example, Beauchamp, Joyce-Gibbons, McNaughton, Young and Crick (2019) found the immediacy of the (silent) flick gesture used by remote groups communicating using multitouch tables (to share clues for a history mystery task) built a memorable and motivating link that inspired meaningful collaborative interactions. Currently we incorporate gesture in the action column (see the first two lines of Segment 2 in Table 7.1) as it is intimately linked with

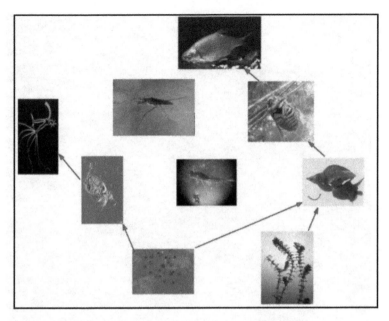

FIGURE 7.7 *Food chain created in a primary science class.*

physical interaction with technology. Goodwin (2007) argues that participants orientate themselves to a task through talk and gesture to a shared focal activity, and Mexican work identifies gesture as 'the main orchestration strategy to organise talk, electronic resources displayed on the IWB, and participation of students in a coherent whole' (Fernández-Cárdenas & Silveyra-De La Garza, 2010, p. 184). Our initial transcriptions of activity and talk in any context always incorporate recording relevant gestures in double brackets (following Jefferson notation: see Chapter 6) where these are deemed helpful for making sense of what happened, although gestures have not been coded explicitly or separately. This bracketing technique is commonly used, as seen in analysis of the three excerpts presented by Ingulfsen et al. (2018). This demonstrated the significance of teachers using pointing movements to highlight important features of graphs produced with data logging technology. Potentially, whole separate layers of analysis might be introduced for different communicative modes and signals (including facial expressions, gaze, pointing, other hand signals, head nodding/shaking, body

FIGURE 7.8 *Portrait of Queen Elizabeth I discussed in a secondary history class.*

FIGURE 7.9 *Spotlight feature of IWB used to zoom in on portrait of Elizabeth.*

position); these may provide important cues as to the affective, emotional state of the participants. Some multimodal transcription records gaze of each participant (and computer sound) in separate columns (Cowan, 2014). Prosody (e.g. intonation, pitch, volume, emphasis) is also very important to take into account, for example in distinguishing an invitation or query from a statement, and for inferring humour, impatience, hesitation and so on. Again, we record such cues in brackets.

A multimodal analysis table with parallel horizontal lines

An alternative method to the table with columns for representing the layers of multimodal interaction is using parallel horizontal lines that each represent talk or an activity positioned along a timeline from left to right, as in a musical score (Jordan & Henderson, 1995, offer examples). Spatial layout in this method allows the relationship of the various participants, modes or lines of activity to each other to be grasped at a glance, and moments of concentrated action within and between modes become more prominent (Cowan, 2014). Transcription of talk can be aligned with symbols representing detailed data capturing other modes, including duration and intensity of movements, and/or, again, with visual images such as miniature representations of artefacts being constructed or manipulated. Selected video stills in particular help to illustrate key features of the context and make salient information about the interaction which would take many words to describe, such as proxemics – distance between participants and from relevant objects (see Figure 7.10).

Integration and interpretative narrative

A reasonable number of table columns can help us begin to get a grip on the otherwise elusive and highly complex components of dialogic interaction between learners, teachers and digital technology. However, populating the columns alone, however numerous and detailed they are, cannot adequately embody meaning. Even the chain of argument built up in chunks in cases where communicative

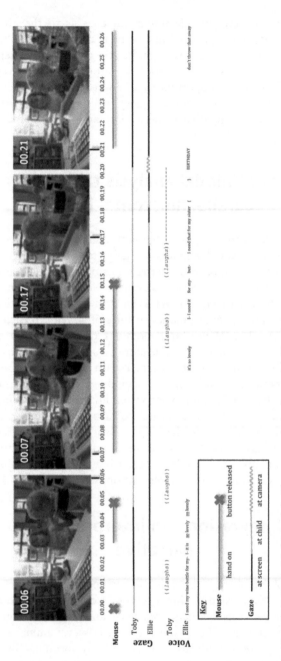

FIGURE 7.10 *Multimodal video transcript using a timeline layout.*
(Reproduced from Cowan (2014) by kind permission of the author and Taylor & Francis ©2014)

events each have their own analytic commentary spanning several rows are fragmented in one sense. As argued (and illustrated) in Chapter 6, we need to complement systematic analyses with interpretative narrative that spans the whole lesson or session in order to investigate how actions and interactions were stimulated by what preceded them in the sequence, and to show holistically and convincingly the role of technology use in mediating the dialogue.

We can also exploit technology ourselves in working with an analysis table: using a spreadsheet programme like Microsoft Excel enables us to hide certain columns, to filter data by participant, to sort the rows in order to group lines assigned the same affordance, to count frequencies of particular categories and so on. We find spreadsheets immensely useful even when we work with transcripts alone without other data. Simply being able to display so many columns is valuable while even a Word document in landscape format may prove too physically constraining. More sophisticated uses of technology include the statistical modelling underlying ENA, introduced in Chapter 6.

Concluding remarks

Dynamic, multimodal interaction within a technology environment – and capturing the artefacts that learners create and modify as they build knowledge together – affords some unique opportunities for learners to make their thinking more visible and to deepen dialogue. This can offer researchers greater insights than when investigating offline interaction where verbal language is usually foregrounded. However, it introduces methodological complexity, especially where talk decreases. It could lead to data overload without careful concentration throughout on the research question and the phenomena of key importance, helping to guide selection of data for transcription/processing and analysis.

Many researchers combine different methods, including manual and (semi-)automated methods of analysis, as mentioned in Chapter 6 in relation to corpus linguistics. **Machine learning** techniques correlate adequately but not yet impressively with human coding, meaning they complement rather than replace them (Kelly, Olney, Donnelly, Nystrand & D'Mello, 2018). Automation is impeded by technical issues such as background noise, dialect variation, multiparty talk and lack of visual cues, along with the difficulty of determining intent when coding speech acts in isolation. Nevertheless, future development in this field will be most exciting as it will lessen the burden on researchers faced with complex data sets.

The examples in this chapter are mainly classroom-focused but the methods are considered largely generalizable to other contexts of technology use; online dialogue specifically is addressed by Wegerif in Chapter 8. The methods detailed above illustrate some of the work to date and are certainly not in any way prescriptive. It would be very interesting to hear readers' ideas and strategies too as this area of dialogue-oriented research is relatively underdeveloped. The commentary by Manoli Pifarré Turmo below brings in her own experiences of using some of the methods outlined above in the context of analysing small-group work in a shared digital environment. This provides some helpful illustration, stressing the importance of analysing multimodal interaction including physical proximity, and raising the notion of a multi-voiced analysis.

Links

Video clips related to some of the above examples and artefacts depicted appear in the collection of clips at https://sms.cam. ac.uk/collection/1085164 and the T-MEDIA online professional development resources at http://t-media.educ.cam.ac.uk/. Further sample tables and other information about the T-MEDIA project are also visible there: choose T-MEDIA Project - Video Review - Grid Example within each subject resource. Further data pertaining to the lesson featured in Table 7.1 and related lessons are available in the online English resource.

Acknowledgements

The T-MEDIA project was funded by ESRC (ref. RES000230825) during 2005–7.

Metafora was developed by a consortium of seven international partners led by Baruch Schwarz in Israel. See https://cordis.europa. eu/project/rcn/95596_en.html.

Expert Commentary

Reflections on researching technology-mediated dialogue

Manoli Pifarré Turmo, University of Lleida, Spain

Interactive technologies have specific features that enable the creation of a tangible dialogic space (Wegerif, 2007) to foster collective knowledge creation. The dialogic space can embody physical action (through direct and visible manipulations), cognitive representations (through the construction of shared digital knowledge artefacts) and emotional relationships (through multimodal shared experiences). Furthermore, this multifaceted dialogic space is co-built using, simultaneously, different modes of communication (e.g. oral, gesture, written) and multiple symbolic languages (e.g. images, graphs). Research has shown that this multifaceted and multimodal co-created dialogic space opens up and supports learners' opportunities to be engaged in a high-quality interaction that can have a positive impact on students' learning.

Educational research needs to develop appropriate methods to capture the complexity of the learning processes that arise when students interact dynamically and multimodally in a technology-mediated learning context. Sara Hennessy in this chapter presents some key research issues that are crucial when you are attempting to study this complexity. Based on my research experience in this field, I would like to highlight the following five remarkable issues that researchers have to bear in mind when investigating technology-mediated dialogic interactions: (1) clear research focus; (2) use of mixed methods; (3) collection of different types of data; (4) generating a holistic picture of technology-mediated interaction and (5) developing a **multi-voice analysis**.

First, a clear research focus is the key in any study. However, this is a challenge that sometimes needs some work on exploring your experimental data. In this endeavour, the creation of a multimodal analysis table, as proposed in the chapter, can be a valuable tool to re-focus and refine a research question. This type of analysis table allows the researcher to experiment and simulate different ways to organize the data, to include different types of data and different ways to interrelate the data that can generate new insights on the phenomena under study.

Second, using **mixed methods** (e.g. Mercer, 2004) may involve qualitative analysis of the basic data that remain throughout the whole learning process. This allows the analysis of the nature and functions of dialogue in promoting learning and thinking over time. Qualitative analysis can then be integrated with quantitative analysis, usually in the form of codes or categories that help to give a macro perspective of the educational processes. This research strategy can support the design of larger-scale empirical studies to implement and evaluate dialogic technology-enhanced pedagogy.

Third, multimodal, multi-symbolic and multiple forms of interaction and communication that technology can afford are crucial to collecting different types of data. The chapter gives some clues on different sources of data collection that can spark new insights on technology-mediated dialogue. The main ones are online and offline interaction, screenshots and screen video recordings, verbal and gestural interaction, peer interaction and teacher–students' interaction, and students' voice and perceptions (stimulated recall interviews and think-aloud protocols).

In my experience of analysing small-group work in a shared digital technology environment in which students combine face-to-face interaction with technology-mediated interaction (such as iPads, laptops) in a classroom, I detected that it is essential to find ways to capture and synchronize computer screen recordings with verbal and nonverbal interaction videos. I found that sometimes students did not communicate much orally when they were working synchronously in a shared digital space, however through nonverbal interaction, students showed high levels of engagement in the task: clearly, it could be observed that students read others' contributions, looked at each other, and facial expressions (such as smile and nod) indicated acceptance of others' contributions. At other times, participants indicated collegiality in overcoming challenges by moving closer to a student who showed difficulties and together solving the problem. These observations are similar to the findings in other studies (e.g. Sakr, 2018) which have claimed that body movement and the gaze of participants directed towards the common work undertaken in the technology environment, acted as an external reference point of the common work.

Fourth, the analysis and understanding of the complex dynamic and multimodal interaction within interactive technologies require developing a holistic picture of that interaction. In order to reach this objective, I agree with Sara Hennessy on the value of creating a multimodal analysis table. This type of table enables researchers to organize and manage the different types of data collected. In my research, multimodal analysis tables have been crucial for (1) refining the research question, as mentioned above, (2) building a coherent picture about what is happening in the technology context, (3) identifying the key educative variables that can play a role in technology-mediated dialogic interaction, (4) dismissing irrelevant data, (5) building a coding scheme or categories that can help to understand the context under the study and (6) developing claims of the research that will help to present the data and main results of the study meaningfully.

Finally, dialogic education claims that holding different perspectives together is a resource to promote the emergence of new ideas (Wegerif et al., 2019). Therefore, the research of technology-mediated dialogue should introduce different voices into analysis of the data and construction of an interpretative narrative about the learning processes developed. This analysis has to be carried out in collaboration with other researchers, but also, among other educative agents such as teachers or students.

As a final remark, previous dialogue-oriented research has shown that the period of time in which students work together is an important variable because dialogue is constructed and progressed over time (Alexander, 2008). Technologies afford that all actions and ideas can be saved and revisited and, therefore, can support the progressive and cumulative aspects of dialogue. Accordingly, dialogue-oriented research has to consider how technology mediates not only the emergence but also the progression of dialogue over time. Again, the construction of a multimodal analysis table can be extremely useful to capture how dialogue features unfold and change across time and how technology affords it. In our recent study (Pifarré & Li, 2018) about how students developed learning-to-learn together skills (L2L2) in a wiki project, constructing an analysis table facilitated the investigation of the inter-relations between the four L2L2 skills identified during two different modes of collaboration (face-to face and online collaboration). It demonstrated how these skills were collaboratively developed as the wiki project progressed. Further research about how dialogue can progress over time in technology-mediated environments is crucial information for designing effective technology-enhanced dialogic pedagogy capable of improving students' learning processes.

CHAPTER EIGHT

Researching Online Dialogues: Introducing the 'Chiasm' Methodology

Rupert Wegerif

Introduction

Whenever I have a question about almost anything now, I do not just ask the people around me but I find myself typing, or speaking, into Google in order to see what comes back to me. This works really well for many practical problems like how to change the LED lights in my new home or finding simple new HTML code to improve my personal website. Where there is a single correct answer this kind of learning is not obviously dialogic, but often my questions lead me into vicarious participation in online dialogues, with questions like 'What is the best pub in Cambridge?' and 'What is the significance of the speed of light being a constant?' Asking about this last one, for example, led me to an interesting debate on a website called Quora where each utterance in the dialogue was about one year apart. A participant, PG, posed a similar question to mine in 2015, HK put forward a considered response in 2016 and JL challenged this with an alternative view in 2017. This is clearly a dialogue, but it is different in many ways from more familiar face-to-face dialogues. When PG posed the question he was not speaking to anyone in particular or even to a particular community of people but to anyone and everyone who was interested enough to read his question. Indeed he was not just speaking out to people. Many bots or non-human agents will have read his message and decided, through their programming, whether to respond or not. I do not think that either HK or JL were bots pretending to be humans, but it is always possible. From PG's point of view the 'interlocutor' or other voice in the dialogue that is being addressed is not so much a person, or a defined group of people, but more of an indefinite horizon of otherness with no clear boundaries either in space or in time. An analysis of this educational dialogue in terms only of the recorded utterances of PG, JL and HK would miss this experiential aspect, the experience of being in dialogue not with a person but with an unknown horizon. It would also miss the role of the many listeners to the dialogue. Quora shows that several hundred people have read PG's question and the answering posts. Each reader of this dialogue will have had to interpret it in relation to their own context and motives and so, implicitly at least, they will have formed a response which continues the dialogue. These 'lurkers' or 'read-only participants' such as myself, might therefore, be thought of as vicarious learners.

It is clear that the internet supports new kinds of dialogue very different from the more familiar face-to-face type of dialogue. There is the now very common new kind of dialogue described above in which someone throws a question out, an answer comes back, and the dialogue grows without it ever being possible to completely define the participants and so to draw a boundary around the space and the time of the dialogue. Bots or automatic agents can participate in online dialogues in ways that cannot always be easily distinguished from the contribution of human-embodied voices. Further, images, music and videos can be part of internet-mediated dialogues. It is easy to find on YouTube apparent dialogues in which the spoken or written word, if it is present at all, is subservient to the multimedia nature of the utterances; threads of videos linked by titles such as 'Yoga Challenge' or 'Silly Salmon Challenge', for example. Bakhtin defines dialogues as interactions where the answers give rise to further questions (Bakhtin, 1986, p. 168). In that sense these YouTube threads can be viewed as dialogues. Many such threads have an educational intent and educational consequences. Another more embodied form of dialogue with educational intent that is worth mentioning is online concept mapping (e.g. https://hcii.cmu.edu/research/lasad). Here the dialogue is not only verbal but also spatial since the positioning of utterances in relation to other utterances is a key part of the dialogue (Wegerif et al., 2010).

By contrast to these new online forms of dialogue, face-to-face dialogues might appear much easier to grasp. If, for example, you want to research three children talking in a classroom, you can record the event and treat it as something with a boundary, a location and a clear content which is limited to the audible talk, all of which can be transcribed. But perhaps this apparent obviousness of face-to-face dialogues is misleading. Howe and colleagues reported research in which it seemed that children learnt something about science issues from engaging in challenging small-group dialogues but only after quite a long time had elapsed (Howe, 2009; Howe, Tolmie & Rogers, 1992). It seems from this that even the educational implications of face-to-face dialogues cannot be so easily bounded within space and time. Perhaps the fact that dialogues are taking on new forms on the internet might help us to go beyond the apparent obviousness of the image of dialogue as consisting of face-to-face 'talk' in order to explore that which is most essential to the educational nature of educational dialogues.

As we discussed in Chapter 2 of this book, understanding in a dialogue involves the inextricable combination of two perspectives: being outside and being inside, being objective and being subjective, both at the same time. Being inside and being outside are both required for understanding within a dialogue but they cannot be reduced into one single composite perspective. There is an unbridgeable and irreducible gap between them. This is what I have elsewhere referred to as 'the dialogic gap'; the gap between perspectives in a dialogue around which it is possible to switch in perspectives from being on the inside speaking outwards to being on the outside listening inwards (Wegerif, 2013). The experience of understanding is a product of the creative tension between these two perspectives. It is always a risky achievement. The experience of not understanding is also common. Understanding is a creative response. Voloshinov suggested that insight is like a spark that occurs out of the tension of the charge between two different terminals (Voloshinov, 1973, p. 102). But I think we need to go a little further with this metaphor and say that insight is a fire ignited in kindling by a spark. Given the tension between two terminals sparks will always occur but if the kindling is damp or too chunky, or for many other reasons, a fire will not always spark into life. Sometimes, for many reasons, a creative response does not arise out of the tension of a dialogue and all we are left with is the, often uncomfortable, feeling of the tension.

In the remainder of this chapter I develop this insight about the dialogic nature of understanding into a methodology for researching online dialogues and dialogues in general. In the next section I show what is gained and what is lost by taking a more outside-in stance towards online dialogues. Then I look at what is gained and lost by taking the less common inside-out or 'online ethnography' approach which attempts to get inside the experience of participants in online dialogue. Finally, I argue for the value of a new 'chiasm' approach that combines an outside-in approach with an inside-out approach in a principled way, holding them both together in tension in the hope that this tension will spark insight and understanding in the reader. This chiasm approach is then illustrated using content from a recent research project that involved online blogging between schools around the world.

Outside-in and inside-out studies of online learning

The large majority of research papers published about educational dialogues online take an outside-in approach confining the data they use to what I think of as the electronic traces left behind by a dialogue. This is true not only of learning analytics approaches to studying interactions on MOOCs (Massive Open Online Courses) and other online courses (Ferguson, 2012) but also to so-called 'qualitative' analyses of the 'social construction on knowledge' in online **communities of inquiry** which code and count online utterances and do statistics on the results (Gunawardena, Flor, Gómez & Sánchez, 2016).

It is common to ask of a research method 'what is it good for?' But sometimes a more perspicuous question is 'who is it good for?' Whose interests does it serve? Outside-in perspectives are about comparing different things. 'Does Course A or Course B lead to higher scores?' is a classic outside-in sort of question, for instance. This sort of finding is very valuable to policymakers who have to make decisions on whether to invest the limited time and resources available to them in Course A or Course B. Learning analytics can be used to look at the impact of specific features of an online course design: 'Do learners show better understanding in the feedback exercise after they have looked at the video or after they read the text?' is the sort of question an outside-in approach could answer. This is very useful to educational designers.

The curious thing is that the one group of people this sort of 'outside-in' approach, if applied on its own, does not serve very well is educational researchers. Evaluating if a course works well or if a design feature functions properly is a normal part of the development in every area of enterprise and does not, on its own, count as research (http://www.oecd.org/sti/inno/Frascati-Manual.htm). I know this because, when I was in charge of research in a university faculty I had to make the case for whether or not funding we received should be coded as 'D' for development or 'R' for research. While policymakers often seem content to know that Course A worked better than Course B in getting the result they wanted, educational researchers also want to know why Course A worked better. Similarly, while education designers might find it useful to know that their video feature worked better than their text feature in promoting a specific learning objective, an educational researcher would want to unpack this to find out exactly why this was happening. Evaluations of the impact of design features can be part of research but only in the context of applying a rigorous and thought-through design-based research (DBR) strategy (see Chapter 2).

The danger in applying a pre-established code to data is that you must already assume that you know what is important and what is not. If you code every utterance in terms of a theory you are unlikely to learn something new about learning because the data that would enable you do that are filtered out by your coding procedure. In the field of education there are many questions of such uncertainty and debate about causation or the question of what is important to learning, and, indeed, what is learning, that it is probably more useful to focus on good theory generation than on theory testing.

On the whole most outside-in research approaches such as applying a pre-prepared coding scheme are not able to be sensitive to the temporal developmental processes that are at the heart of learning (Mercer, 2010). To give an obvious example, the meaning participants give to the term 'spin' at the beginning of a course on quantum mechanics might be very different from the meaning given to the same term at the end. That developmental or emerging change in meaning of one word might be key to analysing the learning on the course. It is hard to capture that sort of change over time through coding and counting or other outside-in research approaches.

The solution to the problems with outside-in research approaches might appear to be inside-out approaches such as online ethnography. An example of this is a study of 'the social dimension of asynchronous learning networks' (Wegerif, 1998). This claimed, on the basis of a few telephone interviews with participants on an online course, to have discovered educationally significant features of their shared experience such as a shift from feeling like an outsider to feeling like an insider, occurring around a threshold experience which involved taking responsibility for some group learning online. There are many more recent examples of online ethnography which take an inside-out perspective focusing on students' experience of learning (see Varis, 2016, for a useful survey of this growing field).

Just as outside-in research can be criticized, so can inside-out research. One possible criticism, applied commonly to much ethnography, is that of bias and cherry picking. In any presentation of an online ethnography (Hine, 2000) particular bits of discourse will be selected and focused upon, but how were these selected? How can the reader of the research trust that they offer a true reflection of what happened online and not something concocted by the researcher? Back in 1994, before most online dialogic education research, the linguist Michael Stubbs made some criticisms of Douglas Barnes's work which are still relevant to online ethnographies. Barnes's seminal research reported and commented upon episodes of talk in classrooms. He used this research to introduce the idea of 'Exploratory Talk' (Barnes, 1976) which influenced later dialogic education reported upon in this book. While studies based on the presentation of fragments of recorded dialogue can be insightful and plausible, they raise 'problems of evidence and generalisation' (Stubbs, 1994). It is often not clear, Stubbs continues, how such studies could be replicated and compared, or how they could lead to cumulative progress in the field. Qualitative discourse analysis, in the tradition of Barnes, must rely on presenting short selected texts. Yet educational research often seeks generalizations, and evaluative comparisons, which cannot rest only on these samples. This is why, as Hammersley has argued, qualitative analysis can be effective for generating theories but not so effective for testing them (Hammersley, 1992). In contrast, the quasi-experimental research designs which are often associated with the use of coding schemes and other quantitative measures can offer explicit tests of hypotheses and systematic comparisons. This is particularly evident in studies that show the link between dialogic talk in classrooms and educational attainment (Nystrand et al., 2003).

Dynamic-Inverted-Pyramid analysis in the context of classroom talk

As a very early career researcher visiting Mexico in 1997 I was given a problem to solve. Professor Sylvia Rojas-Drummond and her team had collected data in two different classrooms, recording and transcribing the talk in the classroom at regular intervals over a term. The classrooms were comparable in every way except that one had been using the 'High-Scope' approach which emphasizes active learning through problem-solving. This target class had performed better in examinations. Sylvia asked me to help her analyse the data in order to understand why the High-Scope class did better. Given two largish sets of transcripts ('corpora' in the jargon of linguistics) in a language that I was only just beginning to be able to read, the first thing I did was turn to concordance text analysis software in order to compare them with each other. I looked at the total amount of talk over time, the amount of student turns at talk versus teacher turns at talk and the patterns of key words and phrases. This comparative analysis produced evidence of differences in patterns of language use but, of course, did not indicate how these differences related to the difference in exam results. To understand the learning in the different classrooms we switched the process of text analysis from a top-down to a bottom-up approach. Just using the evidence of the transcript, as that is all we had, and reading them as if we were vicarious participants, we searched for apparent learning episodes and tried to understand them. We found student utterances indicative of breakthroughs in understanding shown, for example, in utterances where they explained things to the teacher or to each other and then we explored the linguistic context meaning simply the words used around this incident. We found features of language that seemed relevant, for example, people asking open questions such as 'porque?' (why?) or the teacher saying 'vamos a ver' ('let us see'). We then saw if each feature seemed correlated to learning episodes or not. The point here was not to simply count the occurrences of types of language but to explore the contextualized use of language. For example, the same phrase, 'vamos a ver' that apparently led to learning in the High-Scope data was only used in the official classroom data to turn students' eyes to the blackboard where the answer was written for them. This dynamic combination of top-down and bottom-up analysis of the data, facilitated by electronic text analysis with the use of concordance software, was presented as the 'Dynamic-Inverted-Pyramid' or 'DIP' method (Wegerif & Mercer 1997b; Wegerif, Mercer & Rojas-Drummond, 1999).

I mentioned briefly above how Hammersley noted a research cycle in which exploratory bottom-up research sometimes led to theories which could be tested in a second stage of top-down research. This is what we realized we were doing with the DIP method, only the cycles of theory generation and theory testing were very rapid. Exploring the data from the point of view of the learners we came up with conjectures such as that the teacher saying 'vamos a ver' was relevant to later learning experiences and we tested this conjecture by looking at all the contexts of 'vamos a ver' across all the data. This did not only show us that it was relevant, yes or no, but also why it was relevant, for example, how it worked differently in the High-Scope class from in the normal class. In this way, using electronic text analysis, we brought the context of theory generation much closer to theory testing. We called this method 'dynamic' precisely because it involved a rapid iteration between bottom-up theory generation and top-down theory testing.

Each micro-study incorporated the following five steps:

1. An episode of talk that is 'of interest' as it indicates learning
2. Language features selected as being potentially significant in this episode, features such as 'vamos a ver' or students initiating talk in a way that is picked up by others or even the length of utterances

3. All instances of the use of this feature, usually a word or phrase, in all the data are examined in their immediate linguistic context

4. The educational context of the use of these features is explored in more detail in all data

5. Quantitative differences in use between the two sets of data are abstracted from the full transcript data ending up, for example, with a simple comparison of how many times different terms were used in the data

The result of this was not just a simple figure of the statistical difference in language use between Group A and Group B but that headline figure closely correlated to a narrative story explaining why this was educationally significant. In the High-Scope data statistically significantly more 'vamos a ver' occurred from the teacher than in the normal class and we could show how and why that correlated to moments when students appeared to understand things and expressed their understanding.

We presented the DIP method using a triangle (Figure 8.1) as a way to integrate several levels of abstraction in the data. The most concrete data available to us in these examples was the full video and audio recording. Abstraction is the process of pulling selected features out of this most concrete level. Making an annotated transcription, for example, is the first level of abstraction from the full recording. Pulling lists of Key Words in Context (KWIC) out of this transcript is a further level of abstraction, and pulling just a count of words out of that KWIC list goes further still. The DIP method moves from a focus on the qualitative event, the point of the pyramid, out to more general and abstract measures such a count of words or other features of language in use, via a series of stages of the analysis of words in context (see Figure 8.1). Looking at the use of key words in context and exploring their collocations (the other words they occur with or the company that they keep) can be done quickly with computer-based concordancers using electronic transcripts.

This development and practice of the DIP method was influenced by procedures used to explore large amounts of language data in corpus linguistics (Durrant and Schmitt, 2010; Pérez-Paredes, 2017). This method works very well and we use it all the time. It was used and is still used, for example, to link talk in groups around specific

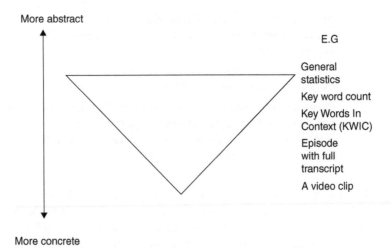

FIGURE 8.1 *Dynamic-Inverted-Pyramid (DIP) methodology.*

questions in a non-verbal reasoning test with the overall test scores of groups such that we could say not only which groups were better at reasoning together but also why, through an analysis of the talk moves and other factors that led them to be able to solve problems together (Wegerif et al., 2019; Wegerif, Mercer & Dawes, 1999). Recently we used it to explore the difference in language used in chat groups in a FutureLearn MOOC between Week 2 and Week 8. This as-yet-unpublished pilot work was done with the educational linguist Pascual Pérez-Paredes. Pascual was excited to find many changes in the language used over the six-week period that indicated increased complexity of thought. These included increased modality such as using 'would', 'could' or 'might' more and increased use of adverbs, adjectives and prepositions. If we had enough time, funding and access we would be able to link these apparently abstract and general changes in language use to specific learning incidents.

Chiasm: A dialogic research methodology

People sometimes say, 'it is all very good in theory but does it work in practice?' I have also heard the opposite asked as a joke: 'OK so it works in practice but does it work in theory?' I think this joke has truth in it and is relevant here. The problem with the DIP methodology is not that it does not work in practice, it works very well in practice; the problem is that it does not work well in theory, at least not for me. That is the real reason why I refer here to the DIP method in the past tense above and feel the need to move on to a new theoretical formulation which I call the chiasm method.

The idea of the DIP method is that we have a concrete learning event and then we abstract away key features from it, each level becoming more general as it becomes more abstract. For instance, we observe a learning event happening, then we abstract away just the video and sound with a recording, then we get this transcribed thereby abstracting away only the audible language, then we use the transcripts to look at keywords in a context of, say, ten words to either side to see if there are phrases and patterns, then we just count the keywords and perhaps correlate these with exam results to say that the language in this class over a term correlates with greater success on an examination. The trouble with this is that each level is not only an abstraction from the previous level, it is also a different view. Videos can show things you did not notice as an observer. Looking at language features in transcripts can show patterns of meaning that you would never notice in the different timescale of watching a video (Louw & Milojkovic, 2016). Exam results might be abstract and general in the same sort of way as word counts abstracted from classroom talk, but each are very different ways of looking at work in a classroom over a term. If a student or teacher were to write a short poem about their learning experience over that term would that not also be an abstract and general account? The more I thought about it the more it did not work.

The idea that everything can be mapped on a scale from the situated and concrete to the abstract and general is quite widespread. It is clearly articulated, for example, by Vygotsky in 'Thought and Speech' where he writes,

Imagine that all concepts are distributed at certain longitudes like the points of the earth's surface between the North and South Poles. ... The longitude of a concept designates the place it occupies between the poles of extremely graphic and extremely abstract thought about an object. Imagine further that the globe symbolizes for us all reality which is represented in concepts.

We can then use the concept's latitude to designate the place it occupies among other concepts of the same longitude – concepts that correspond to other points of reality. (Vygotsky, [1934] 1987, p. 228)

Vygotsky argued that education moved the student from the concrete and situated to the abstract and the general (Wertsch, 2013). I had read Vygotsky in the early 1990s as a PhD student and so this is perhaps where the idea for the DIP method came from. But although it appeared to work well in practice it was impossible to make sense of the many contradictions that it generated when I tried to think it through. Reading Buber, Bakhtin and Merleau-Ponty offered an alternative way of looking at what was going on that enabled me to understand why the DIP methodology worked so well in practice but within a very different theoretical framing (Wegerif, 2008). This alternative way of thinking about the methodology was not as a data pyramid but as a living dialogue between two incommensurate or irreducibly different perspectives; the perspective of the experience of students going outwards and the view from the outside trying to define and locate that experience moving inwards. This combination of an inside view looking out and an outside view looking in corresponds to Merleau-Ponty's concept of the 'chiasm' (as discussed in Chapter 2).

Chiasm describes the essence of a dialogic relation as one in which two or more perspectives mutually envelope each other and reverse about each other without merging. In a living dialogue the 'other' voice is not only a located individual within my field of consciousness but also an outside point of view – the other's gaze – that encompasses me and locates me. What we get in dialogue then is not just two separated and located voices interacting but an outside perspective looking in – as you look at me and locate me within your gaze – and an inside perspective looking out – as I look out at you and try to express my truth. These two dynamic perspectives reverse around each other as now I speak, perhaps defining you as a small part of my world, and then you speak, locating me as a small part of your world (Wegerif, 2013, p. 31).

Applied to the issue of research methodology this is related to the theme, which we referred to in Chapter 2, of the tension between an 'etic' or outside point of view defining the people who are subject to study and an 'emic' or inside point of view of the subjects of the study and how they experience the world. In dialogic terms the 'outside' or 'etic' perspective represents what Buber referred to as the objectifying stance of 'Ich–Es' or 'I to It relationship' that tries to locate and understand as if from the outside seeking, but never fully attaining, the ideal of an unsituated or universal overview. The 'inside' or 'emic' stance, by contrast, stems from Buber's 'Ich–Du' or 'I to Thou relationship' (Buber, [1923] 1958) that reveals contingent local meanings that can only be understood from within a dialogue (see Chapter 2). This insight is where the chiasm methodology begins. It is an attempt to rigorously and coherently map the links between stages of the inside-out perspective in relation to the outside-in perspective. If exam results and word counts say something about the course as a whole over a term, it would be interesting to juxtapose this with interviews with students or perhaps creative writing or multimedia expressions from students which attempted to express their experience of the course as a whole. If the claim is that particular phrases like 'vamos a ver' prompted learning activities, then it might be worth juxtaposing that with how the students felt about it using a technique like key event stimulated recall, as described in Chapter 7.

In the example above of the Mexican classroom there were no interview data. Nonetheless the chiasm methodology can be applied. The inside voice here should be understood as the unique meaning of learning events discovered in the transcripts or the 'ideographic' and the outside voice as the patterned and universal aspect of events or the 'nomothetic' (Larsen, 2012). The claim is that understanding comes from the dialogic juxtaposition of these two aspects held together in the creative tension of a dialogue where there can be no reduction to one side or to the other. Research in social science has frequently tried to reduce findings either to an outside view as in statistical correlation research, for example, or to an inside view as in some 'deep description' or phenomenological studies. In reality we can only make meaning of these studies through an, often implicit, dialogue between outside and inside perspectives. If the meaning we seek in research is only to be found as something that emerges in the dialogic creative tension between an inside and an outside perspective, then it follows that we should try to design empirical research in such a way as to bring these two perspectives into a fruitful or, mutually illuminative, relationship without allowing the generative tension to collapse into one sole perspective. In practice in this proposed methodology, as with the DIP methodology that it builds on, the findings of statistical measures are used to help focus in on those key events which need to be interpreted in order to understand where the measures come from and what they really mean, while, insofar as this is possible, the statistical measures are based upon and drawn out from those features of communicative events that interpretative analysis suggests carry causal significance.

Corpus linguistics on online blogging combined with interviews

We applied this chiasm research methodology to designing an evaluation of the Generation Global (GG) programme.[1] The GG programme is intended to build resilience against the narratives of violent extremism. Operating for more than seven years in more than twenty countries, it has reached over two-hundred thousand students aged 12 to 17. After a compulsory module teaching 'the essentials of dialogue,' classes engage either in team blogging or in facilitated videoconferencing with classes in other regions of the world, discussing issues that are central to religious and cultural differences. The team blogging involves placing students into teams in the GG online-learning community. In these teams, they talk with peers from other countries by creating short blog posts in response to predetermined prompts (or questions), and by commenting on each other's posts.

On the one hand, we sought to provide an evaluation of the impact of the programme that was rigorous and convincing as possible; on the other hand, we also sought to understand the processes whereby individual young people develop and change their attitudes towards others who are different from them. These twin aims require that we combined together in one methodology, two very different perspectives; one perspective looks at the experiences of young people in the programme as if from the outside, seeking to measure change objectively, the other perspective explores the same

[1]This research was funded by the Tony Blair Institute for Global Change. I have to thank my collaborators, Jonathan Doney, Phillip Durrant, Ian Jamison, Andrew Richards, Nasser Mansour and Shirley Larkin.

experiences as if from the inside, trying to understand how each encounter feels for the young people involved and what it means for them in the context of their lives.

In the overall study[2] the external objectively rigorous view was provided by a measure of dialogic open-mindedness, an instrument with thirty-six questions that we developed specifically for the project. The results of this evaluation enabled us to focus in on schools where the GG programme seemed to be having a strong positive effect and on schools where it seemed to be having little if any effect. Six schools in three countries were followed up with case studies including interviews with teachers and some students on their experience of the programme. Our ideal was to link the abstract scores on the measure with actual incidents that led to increased or decreased dialogic open-mindedness. However, because the focus of this chapter is on online research, we will focus on the evaluation of the impact of the online blogging which was just one aspect of the GG programme.

In the GG programme there are two main options for dialogue between schools. One is videoconferencing and the other is 'team blogging'. In team blogging, groups of four schools from different countries discuss world issues together. Before taking part in team blogging, students were asked to reflect on how they 'feel about people from those countries, communities, cultures and faiths you expect to meet when team blogging?' They were also asked to reflect on why they feel this way; 'write about things in your experience that have shaped your views'. Similar questions were posed after the team-blogging event. Quantitative data on how many blogs were written, read and responded to were also gathered.

A total of 1,140 reflections were filled in by individual students from more than 100 different schools. These were labelled as either 'pre-' or 'post-blogging' experience. Matching pairs of pre and post reflections had been made by forty-five individuals, enabling us to explore changes in attitudes through changes in language use. Analysis of this data using a combination of discourse analysis and corpus linguistic statistical techniques showed clear patterns of change in the way that language was being used.

---

[2]https://bit.ly/2VJnQ98.

The keyword technique enables the comparison of two sets of texts (corpora) to see how similar or different they are. Log-likelihood is a statistical measure of how surprising it is to see patterns of language in one set of data in the context of the language use in another set of data. In this case we looked at the difference in word use in the 'post' data as compared to the 'pre' data. The log-likelihood measure tells us how likely it is that the difference could have occurred by chance. A log-likelihood of 10.83, for example, translates as an event that is only likely to occur once in a thousand by chance alone ($p < 0.001$) and a log-likelihood of 15.13 refers to a one in ten thousand chance ($p < 0.0001$) of being random. The differences in keyword use that we display in Tables 8.1 and 8.2 are therefore all statistically significant which simply means that they almost certainly occurred as a result of the team-blogging experience rather than representing random changes (Dunning, 1993; Rayson and Garside, 2000).

We lemmatized the text data when comparing the post-results for the 'how' question (outlined above) with the pre-results. To lemmatize means to reduce words to their base form. For example, the verb 'to be' might appear in several different forms as 'is', 'was', 'am' or 'are' but when lemmatized all these forms are reduced to the single form 'be'. Once lemmatized the comparison of the pre-reflection and the post-reflection texts written in response to the question 'how do you feel about …' showed a clear pattern of development.

Table 8.1 shows the top twelve most significant changes in word use in the post data compared to the pre data with a word frequency greater than 10 out of a data set of 1,923 words in the post data (very similar to the size of the pre-data set which was 2,033 words). Exploring further, looking at these keywords in context and then at the full texts, it is clear that several of these key terms expressed positive affect. 'Very', for example, was collocated most often with 'interesting', 'good' and 'nice'. In the language of corpus linguistics, the use of 'very' shows positive semantic prosody. Words such as 'faith', 'culture' and 'community' reflected the content of the team-blogging exercise. What is perhaps most striking in this list is the appearance of the word 'we'. This draws attention to a shift in personal pronoun use. Personal pronoun use is often central to analyses of dialogicity and also to studies of identity change (Sanderson, 2008).

Table 8.1 Difference in the post-blog reflection for 'how' question

Frequency	Log-likelihood	Word
21	74.728	faith
18	43.085	country
40	33.939	different
19	29.138	view
35	25.581	culture
29	23.826	very
11	23.331	tradition
43	19.644	we
26	19.469	other
22	18.764	like
11	18.073	experience
18	14.763	good

Table 8.2 shows that both the use of 'we' and 'they' increase markedly between the pre- and the post-reflection while the use of 'I' declines. What is more interesting is the way in which the use of 'we' and 'they' changes.

Before the blogging experience 'we' refers most commonly to the home group as in the following typical use:

When I heard from my teacher that we were going to team blog, I was very excited.

In addition, 'we' is also sometimes used to refer to a very abstract notion of the unity of the human race:

We all made from the same mud which is God create us from.

After the team-blogging experience the way in which 'we' is used changes to refer to a much more concrete sense of shared identity:

Table 8.2 Change in pronoun use from pre- to post-reflection for 'how' question

Pronoun	Pre-frequency	As %	Post-frequency	As %
I	122	6	105	5.46
We	32	1.6	43	2.2
They	45	2.2	65	3.3

It was a wonderful experience. As i blogged and they commented on my blog, i found out that somehow we share similar beliefs and all of us wants to spend our life loving each other. Also i got to know that there are some common problems we face and its time we should find a solution to these problems and should stand up for each other.

We could easily find common ground and it was good to splash up my views and recive comments of what they think of my thoughts.

At the same time the use of 'They' to refer to the other also changed. Before the team-blogging experience 'they' were clearly simply 'other'. The following statement is typical:

I feel curious to know about the lifestyle they live, also the kind of problem they face in the society.

After the team-blogging experience the 'other' took on a much more concrete form and was seen as 'like us', perhaps even as part of an extended sense of 'us'.

After the team blogging I feel that they are also like us. they also enjoy singing, dancing, act, ect.

All of them where extremely different. Each has their own opinion and worldview. Some of them differ from me and some are quite similar.

On qualitative examination, the change in the use of pronouns to refer to self and other between the pre- and post-team-blogging reflection indicates a shift in identity from a relatively closed sense of 'us' defined against an abstract sense of 'them' towards a more dialogic identity which can best be described as identification not with 'us' against 'them' but with the dialogue that unites the two terms.

The corpus-linguistics-inspired discourse analysis of changes in the use of language in online reflections by young people both before and after team-blogging experiences of online dialogue with other schools showed clear evidence of changes in the way in which they identified themselves and others. These changes were in the direction of increased dialogic open-mindedness promoted by the GG programme. This method showed one way in which the inside perspective of reflections by individuals can be combined with the outside perspective of statistical rigour in describing a general change. The changes in each individual's attitudes towards others and otherness were reflected in changes in the use of pronouns such as 'we' and 'they' that could be picked up by a general corpus-linguistics analysis of the difference between two corpora. At the same time that general difference helped the analysis focus in on the individual utterances that led to it. This illustration shows the potential of a dynamic circular dialogic interaction between inside and outside perspectives in which neither aspect is reduced to the other and yet there is no synthesis because it is through the juxtaposition of inside and outside views that the reader is led to understand both the significance of the statistical changes (outside view) and the causal processes that led to those statistically significant changes (inside view).

Concluding remarks

The online context offers new possibilities for dialogue and new forms of dialogue. Developing a methodology for researching online dialogue pushes us to identify that which is most essential to educational dialogue. Online dialogue is often multimodal so a focus on 'talk' is no longer possible. In this chapter I argued that what is most essential to dialogic learning is the creative tension of bringing together an inside point of view with an outside point of view. Researching this dialogic phenomenon requires a dialogic methodology. This chapter presented the 'chiasm' methodology for research on dialogue that is itself a form of dialogic learning.

This methodology is about the systematic inter-animation or inter-illumination of outside perspectives with inside perspectives such that they speak to each other in dialogue without either side being reduced to the other. In practice, as shown by an illustration, the application of this methodology can show how the lived experience of participants in any educational programme feed into the development of objective and rigorous measures of the impact of the programme while these more abstract quantitative measures are used to focus in on aspects of the lived experience of participants, revealing exactly how and why the programme worked or did not work. The ideal of this approach is to lead the reader into greater understanding of any educational programme through following the dynamic iteration of views from the outside and views from the inside.

In the commentary Beatrice Ligorio makes a connection between this chiasm approach to researching online dialogues and her online research in Italy looking at how experiences online develop a more dialogic sense of self.

Expert commentary

Researching online dialogues: Introducing the 'Chiasm' Methodology – a commentary

M. Beatrice Ligorio, University of Bari, Italy

In this chapter, three interconnected and interesting questions are examined. First of all, Rupert Wegerif raises the concept of learning. Second, he points out a methodological problem. Third, he reflects on the role of technology. In this commentary, I will try to outline the main points raised in the chapter for each question and I will add a few personal comments.

One implicit question Wegerif seems to ponder is: What is learning? Surely, learning as simple accumulation of information is superseded by a more complex idea of learning, closely related to the capability of students to express themselves, to understand, recognize, and capitalize different points of view and, ultimately, to use differences as means to improve not only individual knowledge but also the concept of knowledge itself. This is very close to what Scardamalia and Bereiter (2006) define as "knowledge building" and it is related to the dialogical approach in education, of which Wegerif is an advocate. While Scardamalia and Bereiter remain mainly focused on what happens to knowledge, Wegerif and the dialogical perspective look at what happens to individuals and groups of individuals. In both cases, knowledge is not limited to what is in heads of learners, but it is within an intersubjective space, established between people while interacting. I am aware that intersubjectivity is a complex theme. Many authors attempted to study it during collaborative learning tasks, coming to slightly different definitions. For instance, Wells (1993) considers the construction of intersubjectivity as occurring while participants are converging their attention to the joint task. Matusov (2001) includes in intersubjectivity the reciprocal understanding of what the partners have in mind. Crossley (1996) points to the concept of inter-world as a symbolic space emerging during interaction, filled up by meanings not thinkable individually. Besides the differences in definitions, all these authors concur in considering learning as an intersubjective phenomenon. Receiving and offering information, ideas, no matter the means used, is a process of recognizing the other as part of our learning process. Building intersubjectivity at a distance, with partners communicating over a computer screen, allows this process to be more visible and traceable. Deeper understanding of how intersubjectivity is initiated, how it evolves and how it is maintained, is required (Ligorio, Cesareni, & Schwartz, 2008; Ligorio, Talamo & Pontecorvo, 2005). I see a strong connection between this and the inside-out problem raised in Wegerif's chapter. The way the dialogical approach is implemented by Wegerif, implies that "you" and "I" are progressively confronted, combined, and, to some extent, reciprocally appropriated. Therefore, dialogism in learning is also a matter of intersubjectivity.

So how can we study learning? The way Wegerif poses this question is much more complex than the opposition of quantitative versus qualitative, or idiographic versus nomothetic. His point is: How can we look at the same time into two different places, namely inside the students – in their minds, understanding, awareness – and outside them, considering the objects, the products, the outcomes? And how much will these latter represent what students learnt?

Wegerif describes an evolution of the Dynamic Inverted Pyramid (DIP) into the chiasm method that "describes the essence of a dialogic relation as one in which two or more perspectives mutually envelope each other and reverse about each other without merging". Chiasm promises to keep the complexity of what we study, linking together the inside-out perspective and the outside-in perspective. Very challenging. Indeed, methodology is not just a question of coherence between research questions and instruments used to collect data; nor between theory and practice. Methodological innovation does not imply just a new technique to treat data but it should allow a better understanding of what it is that we observe.

Technology is an artefact and "an artifact is an aspect of the material world that has been modified over the history of its incorporation into goal directed human action" (Cole, 1996). Therefore, artefacts contain the signs of the cultural within which they appear and are used. Current technology is changing the way we talk and discuss. Online dialogues are threaded (forum, chat), multimedia and hyperlinked (blog, personal web-pages), visual (YouTube; virtual worlds such as Second Life), networked (i.e. Facebook), multiple-layered and with nested space-time frames (Ligorio & Ritella, 2010).

According to Vygotsky ([1934] 1962), there is a close relationship between language and thought; therefore, a new way of talking should imply an innovative way of thinking. Wegerif offers an attempt to show what happened to shared thinking on the GG programme. He shows how students shift from a contraposition between 'us' and 'them' "towards a more dialogic identity which can best be described as identification not with 'us' against 'them' but with the dialogue that unites the two terms".

I have also analysed data generated from the same GG program, in particular blogs connected to the topic of food, as a way to describe family habits, local traditions, and social, religious and personal values. Three dimensions were retrieved: (a) cross-generation interaction, (b) multi-layered space of dialogue, and (c) cultural identity (Ligorio & Barzanò, 2018). These dimensions included many identity positions; I as student, teenager, friend, member of a family, part of a culture. Many "voices" were raised from the past (i.e. parents and grandparents), intertwined with those in the present and in the future; and they were located into a multi-layered space-time emerging from the blogging activity itself, where other contexts (both online and face-to-face) were re-narrated and reiterated. We also understood that the space-time offered by the blog allowed students to express feelings and opinions otherwise silent. Furthermore, students shared parts of their identity through a network – constituted by the blogosphere of the project – where they could connect, reciprocally build on one another's contributions and further discover and negotiate who they are and who they could be. This may be the added value of using technology in education: offering innovative spaces to talk and think in an innovative way.

In higher education I conducted a relevant study of a web-platform based course intended to support a progressive shift from self-positions that relate to the role of student toward more professional self-positions (Amenduni & Ligorio, 2017; Ligorio & Sansone, 2014). Digital environments here were a space where (1) links are made with companies; the course was on e-learning and companies from this field were invited to propose real professional activities to students attending the course; (2) different collaborative activities are engaged in with peers; (3) different roles are played as a simulation of the professional profiles the course aims to train and (4) the environment supports the role of 'friend of zone of proximal development (ZPD)' (Impedovo, Ligorio & McLay, 2018). Clearly inspired by Vygotsky (1978), this 'friend of ZPD' role implies that each student nominates a friend, based on personal sympathy and trust, that should monitor the performance, give suggestions and offer advice to improve performance on the course. This role implies also self-reflection; in assessing someone else's performance in order to give advice, it is unavoidable that one will have to reflect upon one's own performance.

Online dialogue is a new phenomenon, entering more and more into a range of educational contexts. This implies that methodological innovation is needed urgently. This chapter is taking up this task. Now applications of chiasm are encouraged, to exploit its limits and potentialities.

CHAPTER NINE

Dialogue, Participation and Social Relationships

Ruth Kershner

Introduction

This chapter is concerned with researching *social* and *relational* aspects of participation in educational dialogue. There are many potential lines of inquiry in this area. Projects may focus on investigating people's *social* behaviour, expectations and interactions when participating in dialogue. There may also be interest in finding out about the *relational* ties between people engaged in dialogue, raising questions about participants' experiences of friendship, empathy, intercultural understanding, respect and trust. In this chapter, the broad notion of *social relationships* is intended to refer to both of these social and relational dimensions.

It is not difficult to find reasons to investigate participation and social relationships in educational dialogue. Educational dialogue is intrinsically social and relational, in that its essence can be said to lie in the human activity of 'engaging with another (or others) as if they really matter' (Higham, 2018, p. 355). Believing that learners and teachers do indeed 'really matter' to each other underpins research in this area. The most pressing educational questions might be about how students can be supported to interact positively with each other and learn best in the social world of the classroom. There may also be concerns about meeting everyone's fundamental needs for belonging, communication and care in any educational context (Cameron & Moss, 2011; Noddings, 2012). Engaging in educational dialogue can be emotionally challenging for students and teachers, as can learning itself. So mutual trust must be embedded in classroom learning relations when dialogic inquiry is promoted. As Haynes (2018) puts it, 'Caring about another person's ideas requires respecting the other as a separate autonomous person, worthy of caring. It is an attitude of valuing and attending to another and because entering into that relation could be threatening as much as consolidating or positive, the relation presumes a mutual trust' (p. 149). In sociocultural terms, productive dialogue for learning depends on students' capability and willingness to engage with each other actively, collaboratively and responsively in discussion and knowledge-sharing. Yet this places considerable social demands on participants, especially children. Baines, Rubie-Davies and Blatchford (2009) investigated 5- to 14-year-old children as 'co-learners' in group work, in their large-scale four-year SPRinG (Social Pedagogic Research into Group Work) intervention programme. They identified four key principles for successful collaboration and high-quality discussion between students in groups (p. 97):

- a relational approach to developing students' group working skills emphasizing sensitivity, trust, inclusion and mutual respect between group members as well as communication and advanced group work skills;

- classroom and grouping arrangements (e.g. class layout, group size, composition, stability) that encourage group work;

- tasks and lessons that warrant and develop the use of group work and talk;

- adult involvement (e.g. monitoring, scaffolding) that facilitates autonomous group functioning.

Two points leap out from these findings: first, social relationships are likely to be highly relevant in developing high-quality dialogue between students and teachers, and, second, social relationships do not stand alone as they are linked, in turn, to classroom arrangements, tasks and adult involvement. The first research implication is that investigation of social relationships is important for understanding educational dialogue, while the second reminds us that social relationships are grounded in the **affordances** of the learning context as well as in the motivations, emotions, beliefs and skills of each person involved.

From a social justice perspective, it can be argued that all students have a right to be heard, to contribute to dialogue and learn from each other. Some inclusive educational approaches are grounded in beliefs about the distinctive and valuable contributions that *all* students can make to classroom learning when they have the opportunity and motivation to participate in a supportive and culturally responsive setting. Richards and Robertson (2016) point out that while much research on responsive teaching has focused on the teacher's role in attending to students' ideas, it is constructive engagement between students that holds potential for breaking traditional modes of teacher-led classroom talk. However, as Richards and Robertson say, students need courage to make their thinking visible and open to challenge from others.

So can an educational culture of 'responsiveness' be established, supporting the social relationships that enable students to participate actively? Educational activities like collaborative group work, whole-class discussion and online debate are often deliberately planned to support social interaction, dialogue and learning. Dialogue may also develop outside these contexts when people mix together more informally, such as break-time conversations, talking to visitors, discussing the news, handling interpersonal conflicts, and so on. Social relationships inevitably cut across the formal and informal boundaries of educational activities and they are affected by participants' interpersonal histories, motivations, emotions and understandings of self and others. This web of social connections and personal experiences presents practical, methodological and conceptual challenges for research:

- Practically, any single research project has to be manageable. If we focus on the social relationships of particular participants in specific dialogic activity contexts how can we not only design a feasible project but also remain open to understanding wider social influences and relational factors?

- Methodologically, the sheer pace and range of social life, together with the intrinsic 'invisibility' of social experience and relational quality, presents significant challenges for capturing and understanding what happens between people.

- Conceptual problems are likely to arise in understanding the wide-ranging social and relational conditions, processes and outcomes of dialogue that are intertwined in practice over time.

In addition, there are significant cultural and ethical considerations:

- Cultural beliefs, values and expectations about how students and teachers *should* interact with each other have to be questioned. Researchers and participants may each hold fundamental beliefs about, say, turn-taking that have to be revealed rather than assumed. This calls for critical reflection on the sociocultural context as well as personal capacities and willingness to participate.

- Ethical considerations apply at all stages of research in this area. Undertaking research will have a personal effect on all involved, because observing and asking people about their social relationships is not a neutral process. Inquiring into people's behaviour, experiences and feelings becomes an intervention in people's lives, whatever the research intention. Even the most apparently simple interview questions, for instance, can be emotionally charged if they prompt one to think about personal relationships, hopes and difficulties – not all of which will be revealed, resolved or even acknowledged at the time. The interpersonal perceptions and relationships between researchers and participants are also influential, as has long been discussed in texts on research methodology (e.g. Drew, Raymond & Weinberg, 2006). Research methods like interviews and observations are relational experiences, but not always with conscious intention or awareness.

Designing feasible investigations requires sharp focusing on particular research concerns, issues and questions, and underlying cultural, ethical and conceptual issues may not be at the forefront of every investigation of social relationships and participation in dialogue. However, critical reference to wider social and relational contexts always helps in interpreting findings and building useful knowledge cumulatively between projects.

This chapter draws on two overlapping perspectives: (1) the social and relational processes that create the conditions for productive dialogue to occur including people's beliefs, emotions and social interactions and (2) the dialogic processes that may in turn help to develop positive social relationships, social understanding and mutual effort for collaborative learning and problem-solving. Of particular interest is the use of dialogic methods for both of these research purposes, involving participants actively. The next section looks at ways of getting a foothold and deciding on the research focus. This is followed by a discussion of relevant methods for investigating social and relational aspects of educational dialogue, thinking particularly about the value of combining multiple methods in order to answer research questions. The chapter ends with some ideas about useful next steps in this field of study. The research examples throughout this chapter have been selected from a wide field of study, aiming to illustrate some of the many types of research questions and approaches that could drive investigation.

Deciding on a research focus

A vast range of factors and processes can be seen as potentially relevant to participation and social relationships in dialogue, ranging from biological interests in, say, emotional arousal, social anxiety and sensory perception when talking with others, to psychological, social and cultural ways of understanding people's experiences of friendship, emotion, group dynamics, power hierarchies and so on. Indeed, there is a growing interest in researching the relational context of any complex field of human activity, including areas in which social relationships are not commonly seen as relevant. For instance, Clark-Polner and Clark (2014) make a case for the systematic investigation of neuroscience in a relational context, suggesting six ways in which relational contexts may vary: (1) the type of relationship, (2) the character (or 'personality') of the relationship (as distinct from the personalities of individuals involved in the relationship), (3) individual differences in members' orientations towards relationships, (4) the history of the relationships, (5) the developmental stage of the relationships and (6) the broader relationship network within which a particular relationship being studied is embedded. This categorization is useful in drawing attention to the need to investigate social relationships from both the 'inside' (e.g. personal experience) and the 'outside' (e.g. observable behaviour), as well as considering what happens over time. An essential point, as emphasized throughout this book with reference to dialogue, is that social relationships lie between people and they cannot be understood entirely from the observable characteristics and responses of individual participants.

Without wanting to oversimplify things, it can be useful to identify what is informing and driving individual projects in order to make links with existing work and focus new research. Table 9.1 outlines how different beliefs, interests and concerns may provide different starting points for research efforts in this area, bearing in mind that there are inevitable overlaps in practice.

Focusing research and building knowledge: Five examples

The starting points identified in Table 9.1 can be used as a framework for positioning and linking individual research studies within the broad field of social and relational aspects of participation in educational dialogue. To illustrate this, here are brief accounts of five published international studies from Namibia, Spain, England, New Zealand and Scotland. These projects are concerned in different ways with the role of communication and dialogue in developing social cohesion, intercultural understanding, educational inclusion, friendship and group engagement. They are, variously, aiming to investigate these relational phenomena in dialogic terms, with some alternative uses of dialogic research methodology. Selected quotes from each paper are included in order to convey the authors' voices directly (see Figure 9.1).

There are connections between the starting points of each study, in that all are finding ways to generate or build on empirical evidence and theoretical understanding of democratic and socially useful dialogic practices. They differ, however, not only in their particular research focus and scale, but also in their research trajectory – that is, where they stand in relation to their own and others' previous research. For instance, in Bialostocka's (2017) paper, the author refers to her own previous empirical research as a basis for developing further theoretical understanding of intercultural dialogue and social cohesion. Her theoretical discussion is inspired by her study

Table 9.1 Starting points for developing research on social and relational aspects of educational dialogue, with possible aims and outcomes

What is informing and driving the research interest?	Possible starting points for a project	Possible aims and outcomes
Theoretical interest and understanding	Identifying key concepts and processes in social relationships (*such as communication, intercultural understanding, participation structure, ethos, belonging, attunement, trust, etc.*) and specifying their possible links to educational dialogue	Further development of theory and enriched conceptual frameworks Opening up new research questions and projects
Empirical research evidence	Responding to accumulated findings from published research, and asking about the current 'gaps', areas of consensus and points of debate about social interaction, relationships and educational dialogue	More comprehensive literature reviews and summaries of evidence about social and relational conditions and factors affecting educational dialogue Stronger evidence about relevant contextual and cultural factors, including potential supports and barriers
	Generating new data sets of educational talk (*e.g. video and audio recordings*), and/or re-analysing existing data sets, allowing close analysis of conversation, social interaction and other forms of communication	More detailed and valid understanding of different forms of interpersonal communication Adding to a shared bank of dialogic data for further analysis

	Evaluating interventions that are designed to promote active engagement in dialogue, focusing on social and emotional factors and processes	Better evidence-informed knowledge exchange between researchers and practitioners; Increased understanding of how strategies may generalize to different contexts; Formulation of intervention principles for wider application; associated development of practice and policy
	Investigating practice systematically in diverse naturalistic educational contexts	Development of robust and novel research designs and methods to generate qualitative and quantitative data with a contextual dimension
Principles of democratic and socially useful stakeholder engagement	Engaging stakeholders in dialogue and co-research focusing on their relational experiences, beliefs, preferences and emotions	Challenges to marginalization and power imbalances in knowledge creation
	Including participant 'voices'	Active participant involvement in personally relevant research and intervention
	Exploring different perspectives and conventional assumptions about 'good practice'	Greater insight into participant experience, and increased understanding of personal, social and cultural barriers to participation

New technologies	Using new methods for observation and discussion (*e.g. video-focused reflective dialogue using tablet computers allowing joint attention to focus reflective discussion; and eye-tracking technology to investigate who and what is 'noticed' in classrooms*)	Greater understanding of technological affordances for researching and participating in educational dialogue Increased visibility of rapid social interactions, eye contact, etc.
	New forms of 'ownership' of classroom space by individuals and groups (*e.g. student use of interactive whiteboards*)	Improved decision-making and guidance for technologically innovative classroom practice that supports dialogue
Problem-solving concerns	Responding to professional concerns about the dialogic participation of particular individuals and groups	More equitable participation in dialogue for identified individuals and groups
	Developing skills to participate in dialogue	Enhanced contributions and confidence to participate More informed implementation of educational programmes and professional skills training
	Resolving interpersonal and cultural conflict in and through dialogue	Establishment and maintenance of peaceful outcomes
	Programme evaluation	Increased embedding of dialogic approaches in policy and practice

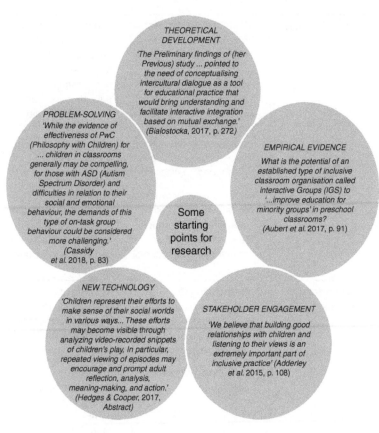

FIGURE 9.1 *Some examples of research starting points.*

of multicultural education conducted in Namibia, focusing on the African concept of Ubuntu and the corresponding teaching of the philosophers of dialogue, including reference to the work of Durkheim, Dewey, Buber, Bakhtin, Giroux, Koczanowicz, Mignolo and others. She concludes, 'Looking into the African concept of Ubuntu and the corresponding teachings of the philosophers of dialogue, this theoretical paper suggests dialogic learning as an approach to multiculturalism that can enhance tolerance among peoples and produce a society united through understanding' (Abstract). In contrast, Aubert, Molina, Schubert and Vidu (2017) report on their extension of an existing empirical evidence base for an inclusive pedagogical approach that was already grounded in a well-established dialogic paradigm and methodology. They conducted a case study in one Spanish school in three classrooms (3- to 5-year-olds), evaluating the introduction of their 'Interactive Group' approach. Three communicative research methods were used: (1) interviews with teachers, (2) life-stories with mothers and children and (3) classroom observations discussed subsequently with participants. They asked whether Interactive Groups could help to prevent vulnerable groups of children being segregated at this very early stages of schooling avoiding low expectations for educational attainment. The authors remark on the research process:

'The communicative methodology ... not only describes a reality but also analyses how the reality can be improved ... an intersubjective dialogue between researchers and the research participants is established and based on an egalitarian dialogue. During fieldwork the researcher has the responsibility to contribute with the scientific knowledge while the stakeholders bring in the context-specific knowledge' (p. 94). Adderley et al. (2015) place the democratic principles of consulting children to the fore, seeing the responsibility to listen to children's 'voices' as intrinsically part of the inclusive practice that they are concerned with. They worked with forty-eight children (six groups of eight children), aged 5, 7 and 9 years, seeking to understand children's views about the ways in which teachers promote or hinder inclusion in classroom. They were also interested methodologically in the use of various tools to facilitate an engagement with children's views. Their approach was interpretive and naturalistic, using participatory methods for group interviews and qualitative data analysis. They found that:

Even though the children were mostly happy with their school experience, it was noticeable that there were some areas for concern for some children that related to four interconnecting themes: unfairness, shouting, loneliness and seating plans. All of these themes seemed to be connected with the children's interpersonal relationships – with teachers and each other – and can be seen as crucial in terms of understanding inclusion in schools and further developing existing practices. (Abstract)

Hedges and Cooper (2017) are similarly concerned with understanding young children's classroom experiences, but their discussion is led by the emerging affordances of reflective video analysis discussions to make children's thinking about friendship 'more visible' to teachers. They conducted an interpretivist case study in an early-years setting in New Zealand. The study involved teachers and university researchers in reflective analysis and discussion of video episodes of children and teachers in everyday teaching and learning interactions. The authors were concerned not only to contribute to understandings of children's thinking (working theories) about friendships but also to highlight the value of using video footage as a method and to illustrate their belief that teachers' and researchers' engagement in dialogue can promote deeper analysis of what is viewed. One of their findings was: 'In our study the use of video footage provided opportunities to "press pause" on children's play in order to discuss, make sense of, and appreciate children's working theories about being and making friends, and to guide authentic responses and actions' (p. 402). Cassidy, Marwick, Deeney and McLean's (2018) exploratory study of philosophical discussions with children is more directly 'problem-solving'. It was driven by their concerns about the challenges of participation faced by particular children identified with additional learning needs, an area where they had found little existing research. They were concerned about helping children identified with emotional, behavioural and social communication needs to engage in 'Community of Philosophical Inquiry (CoPI)' sessions in school. They conducted an exploratory ten-week intervention study of philosophy discussions involving seventeen children (9–12 years) from two primary schools, all identified with various social, communication, behavioural and emotional difficulties. Their **qualitative** and **quantitative data analyses** were based on teachers' observations, reflective logs and interviews, aiming to find out the impact on the children's dialogic participation, self-regulation and transfer to other social and academic situations. They answered one of their questions as follows:

> In relation to social interaction. ... The teachers reported that ... [f]or one child who had a particularly difficult relationship with his sibling class-mate ... [h]e became able to listen to her input and engage with it in a more reflective manner, considering her points, dis/agreeing and providing reasons. Overall, the teachers reported that the children listened better as the CoPI sessions

progressed. They did not interrupt and made connections with what was being said. (p. 89)

These five examples have been included to illustrate some of the different ways in which researchers may succeed in completing a project with a specific purpose in mind. They build on previous research, contribute knowledge and potentially open up new avenues of inquiry. The reporting of such projects is an essential aspect of the research process, offering readers new starting points for their own research. It would be interesting, perhaps, to stop here before reading on, and reflect on what your own 'next steps' would be in building on each of the above five studies.

Combining methods: Not just helpful, but essential?

As we saw in the previous section, research projects are designed for different purposes. Approaches vary according to research trajectory (e.g. exploring new areas or applying established knowledge in new contexts) and depending on the primary interest and aims. Multiple, combined methods are often used to meet multiple aims in this and other complex areas of educational concern. As outlined earlier, social relationships extend beyond the immediate contexts of interaction, and they are woven together with dialogic participation over time. People's thoughts and feelings about each other are not directly visible, so interpretation, empathy and imagination are required. Figure 9.2 offers a simple aide-memoire for beginning to pin down and plan a feasible investigation of social relationships in dialogue. The core purposes, as outlined earlier, are commonly to describe and understand why people do or do not participate in dialogue, and/or to see how participation in dialogue may in turn promote positive social relationships.

Methodological options

The main principle for researching social relationships is that the investigative methods somehow target relational links between

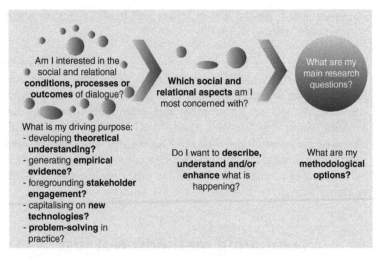

FIGURE 9.2 *Focusing a research project on social and relational aspects of educational dialogue.*

people engaged in dialogue. This could involve direct observation of people's social interactions. It could also focus on what people think or feel about their social relationships, without direct observation. Descriptions from direct observation may appear to have a relatively low level of inference, but they will be partial and dependent on where attention is focused (see Chapter 6). Attempts to understand people's thoughts and feelings inevitably have a high level of inference, not least because it is hard even to articulate one's own feelings that are often mixed and changeable. This makes research challenging but not impossible, as we have seen in the examples above.

Researchers may ask about any or all of the following:

1. social interactions and patterns of participation in dialogue
2. participants' social and relational experience of dialogue
3. wider social and relational conditions for dialogue, and possible outcomes

Research options in these broad areas are expanded in Table 9.2, with an indication of empirical methods that could be useful individually and in combination.

Table 9.2 Common empirical methods used in, and across, three core strands of research interest in social relationships and dialogue

Strand of investigation	Some possible research interests and questions	Some common research methods
Social interactions and patterns of participation in dialogue	Who speaks and responds to whom? What is the role of informal and playful conversations in dialogue? Who has opportunities to contribute to dialogue? How are contributions responded to? Is there evidence of cultural differences in social behaviour? Is participation equitable over time?	*structured and unstructured observation* *conversation analysis* *field notes* *audio/video recording* *verbal flow diagrams* *classroom maps and sketches*
Participants' social and relational experiences of dialogue	How do participants experience and exercise their agency in dialogue? How do participants develop emotional understanding and attunement to each other? How may people's beliefs, emotions and motivations help or hinder productive dialogic engagement? How are different opinions and sources of knowledge valued?	*interviews* *group discussion* *video-focused reflective dialogue* *written assignments* *reflective journals* *storytelling and drama* *arts-based activities* *self-report questionnaires*

Wider social and relational conditions for dialogue, and possible outcomes	Is social cohesion and constructive dialogue valued in educational and social discourse and policy? Are relevant cultural differences in communication fully understood and respected? Is dialogue employed to resolve bullying and other social conflicts? Are young people taught and encouraged to engage critically and respectfully with social media? Are students involved in discussing decisions intended to support social interaction and dialogue, e.g. the arrangement of physical space	*document analysis* *discourse analysis* *philosophical reading and discussion* *ethnographic approaches* *programme evaluation (employing various methods and qualitative and/or quantitative data analysis)*

Research examples in each of these areas include systematic observation of children's social behaviour and communication when they are engaged together in a collaborative activity, investigating participants' social and relational experience of dialogue, and may involve investigating wider social and relational contexts of dialogue using **ethnography**. See Boxes 9.1, 9.2 and 9.3.

Box 9.1 Observing cultural patterns of collaboration and communication

Correa-Chávez (2016) investigated cultural patterns of collaboration and communication (verbal and non-verbal) between young Mexican-heritage siblings in the United States. She wanted to find out if children from 'pueblo' families and communities with more indigenous forms of organizing learning (such as 'Learning and Pitching In') differed in their collaboration from children more experienced with the middle-class European American cultural practices familiar in many schools. She videoed sibling pairs as they constructed a puzzle together, and then coded the children's behaviour as 'jointly engaged', 'checking in', 'solo' or 'off task'. She found that the children from the pueblo families tended to engage jointly for longer stretches of collaborative interaction. They also used proportionally more non-verbal joint activity and multiple means of communication, compared to the 'high schooling' group who tended to coordinate their own joint engagement through talk. A study like this addresses questions about the social experience that children bring to formal education, which in turn may influence their participation in collaborative activities and dialogue. The methods are highly structured with quantitative data analysis, offering an additional research approach to the ethnographic methods and qualitative data analysis also used to investigate cultural variations in participation.

Box 9.2 Understanding participants' social and relational experience of dialogue

Kershner, Warwick, Mercer and Kleine Staarman (2012) investigated 8- to 10-year-old children's social relationships and co-regulation in science-focused group work around an interactive whiteboard. They used sociocultural discourse analysis of the children's classroom talk followed up by group interviews. The aim was to explore the children's experience of managing their own and each other's participation, especially at times when disputes or other problems arose between them. The sociocultural discourse analysis (Mercer, 2008) focused on what the children said about the need to 'be patient' and 'wait' when they were held up or irritated for different technical and social reasons. This involved searching through the video recordings and transcripts of the groups in action to see how these children spoke to each other. The subsequent group interviews were intended to provide a forum for the children to reflect together on their experience. The tensions sometimes experienced are evident in this interview extract with Simone and Rita, suggesting that their experiences of group work do not match what they know about the principles espoused in their class (p. 7):

Simone: We shouldn't argue all the time, you should let some people do things and if it doesn't look right you can change it.
　　Rita: Probably try and cooperate with people in different lessons and see other people's mistakes and learn from them.
...
Simone: Sometimes it's really irritating when you've got lots of people
Rita: I was going to say it's probably quite hard to get your work done because some people are a lot slower learning things than others in the lesson so you'd be staying there trying to explain it to them while you could be getting your work done.

This exchange brings out all too well how children may experience the conflicting demands of classroom life, which is why the next strand of research on conditions for productive dialogue can be vital.

Box 9.3 Investigating wider social and relational contexts of dialogue

Helgevold (2016) conducted an ethnographic study in Norway, intending to develop understanding of teaching as a relational activity in itself, with both moral and academic principles informing the daily interdependent encounters between teachers and students. She argues on philosophical grounds that '[a] constant moral challenge for teachers in diverse classrooms is to recognize the different learners as participants, not just recipients of a present academic content that is to be evaluated according to certain standards' (p. 316). Her ethnographic study of a lower secondary school classroom involved observations and interviews with teachers and students. Her discourse analysis of one science lesson focused closely on how the teacher 'creates space for participation', using tactics of 'holding back', 'passing on' and 'non-valuing' in the discussion. Here we see how a focused analysis of classroom talk, conducted in the context of a larger ethnographic study, can illuminate the wider social and relational conditions for educational dialogue. Helgevold in turn has in mind the implications of this research for teacher education, with ethical implications for teachers to learn how to attune to students and remain open to what may happen when student participation is invited and valued.

The methodological toolbox

As the various research examples have shown, individual and combined methods can form a repertoire or 'toolbox' that can be applied in different research projects for purposes that include developing theoretical understanding; adding to empirical evidence: following principles of stakeholder engagement, capitalizing on new technologies and problem-solving in practice. Before thinking about why certain combinations of methods are particularly useful for researching dialogic participation and social relationships, it is worth looking at the distinctive purposes of some of the most common methods. Table 9.3 gives some examples.

Some common approaches to combining methods

Combinations of research methods work in different ways. One approach is to combine the methods in generating data (e.g. using observations to focus reflective discussion). Another is to combine the data that is produced from different methods, using one or more forms of analysis with these different sources in a form of 'triangulation'. The next few examples provide insight into how combining methods may work in practice.

One of the most common approaches to combining methods for generating data is seen when observational data (e.g. video) is used to focus reflective dialogue about what is observed on the video. The

Table 9.3 Some distinctive purposes of common methods for researching dialogic participation and social relationships and generating data for analysis

Method	Purposes	Some options for generating data for analysis
Observation	How does interaction flow between people? What seems to prompt certain forms of social behaviour and what happens afterwards?	Narrative accounts Structured tick lists and ratings Verbal flow diagrams (e.g. Equity Maps) Audio/video recording Photographs
Conversation analysis	How do people communicate with each other? What are the norms and practices for turn-taking, etc.?	Transcripts
Field notes	What is noticed about social activity beyond the immediate focus of observation?	Jottings during activity (e.g. key words) Sticky note-taking Audio memos Classroom sketches Daily diaries
Interviews	What do people remember and feel about their interactions and conversations with others?	Structured and unstructured question schedules Video-focused reflective dialogue Photograph prompts Activity – e.g. facilitated construction of narrative timeline
Group discussion	How do people share ideas and come to mutual understandings?	Focus groups Video-focused reflective dialogue Philosophical reading and discussion Joint activity – e.g. creating mind maps

Written assignments	How do people respond to questions and reflect further on their social and relational experiences?	Reflective journals Sentence-completion activities Story writing Self-report questionnaires
Storytelling, drama and other arts-based activities	How do people engage in, and learn from, imaginative activities, individually and with others? How do they represent their ideas and feelings in different ways?	Audio and video recording of planning and performance Products (e.g. stories, poems, pictures, role plays) Discussion of experiences and products
Document analysis (including discourse analysis)	What is written about values, principles and 'ground rules' for social interaction and dialogue? What language is used in written documents?	Wall displays Meeting notes Guidance notes Written communications Policy documents Curriculum plans

reflective dialogue can then be analysed as the main data source, if the research interest lies there. Alternatively the reflective dialogue can itself become an intervention designed to enhance social interaction and classroom communication, as Brown and Kennedy (2011) explain with reference to the dialogic approach of Video Interaction Guidance (VIG) with teachers. Structured observation is followed up with video-focused reflective dialogue in order to gain insight into teacher–pupil interactions and communication (Brown & Kennedy, 2011; Fukkink & Tavecchio, 2010): 'VIG is a method used to support practitioners in reflecting positively on communication and uses principles of effective communication to guide observations of interactive behaviour. The aim is to improve the quality of interactions between those involved by supporting the teacher in activity identifying and extending the positive elements of communication observed in interactive sequences' (p. 382). The use of multiple data sources almost inevitably involves willingness to engage with the data over a period of time, moving iteratively between them to build understanding. Engin (2017) describes this process well in reporting her research on older students' motivations to talk or remain silent in dialogue at university level:

The data were analysed as an iterative process, going back to the audio recordings multiple times as I read and re-read textual data. I transcribed parts of the audio recordings verbatim (Rapley, 2008). The reason for this is that my purpose was understanding the functions of the talk within dialogic interaction. ... As well as the data set of talk, the interviews provided the students' perspective on beliefs about discussions, and the stimulated recall added another layer to interpretations of the talk analysis. ... My initial interpretations and evaluations of the dialogue (or lack of it) were confirmed and further elaborated on by getting the emic perspective of the participants. This was crucial to understanding learner experiences of dialogic teaching and the different motivations for participating. For issues of transparency and trustworthiness, and to mitigate my possible researcher bias, I shared my data with members of the Language and Literacy Research Group who gave feedback and commented on my data. (p. 81)

There may also be a need for several forms of data analysis, as Clarke, Howley, Resnick and Rosé (2016) explain with reference to their research on high school students' intentions of agency, their exercise of agency, and the social structures that may support these for participation in dialogue in science lessons:

We make use of several forms of discourse analysis to analyze observation and interview data. We used conversation analysis on the observational data to examine turn-taking patterns (Hutchby & Wooffitt, 2008). Turn-taking refers to ways in which speakers take turns in conversation, e.g., teacher asks question, followed a student's response to that question. ... In seeking an analytical approach to examining students' enactment of agency in classroom dialog, we examined particular turn-taking patterns. ... We used narrative analysis to examine the interview data for students' sense of agency. ... We examined the reasoning structures in their stories about salient moments in discussions in order to gain insight into the participation patterns we observed in the class discussions. (p. 31)

All the research examples and frameworks included in this chapter are intended to show how research can be done in this area, which can seem so complicated and sensitive. The main message is that it *can and should* be done in order to improve our understanding of the social, relational and personal experiences of educational dialogue, increasing understanding about possible barriers to participation and sources of support.

Concluding remarks

The next steps in this research field are exciting, with many possibilities for contributing valuable knowledge and understanding that will enhance participation in educational dialogue. Particularly promising areas may be the following:

1. To develop more complex multi-method studies, taking into account how social relationships and dialogic participation can be developed in real learning contexts. These can be relatively small-scale, without losing depth. For instance, Baskerville (2011) used a combination of storytelling workshops, journal entries, focus groups and individual interviews and reflective discussions to foster positive relationships and build cohesion between adolescents in one culturally diverse classroom in New Zealand.

2. To capitalize on technological advances, especially in combination with more established research methods. For instance, eye-tracking data can be used as a prompt for reflective discussion about what is 'noticed' in students' social behaviour. Our own early trials with student volunteers have revealed differences in how people look at classroom pictures, having been primed with different questions (e.g. 'what is happening here?' vs 'how are these people getting on with each other?'). Follow-up reflective discussions about these differences benefited from focusing on the eye-tracking results as a critical and joint point of reference.

3. To go further in investigating multimodal aspects of dialogue in a systematic and culturally-sensitive way. This connects with the need to make a serious effort to understand silence and listening in dialogue. Engin (2017)

used interviews, audio-recorded discussions, stimulated recall, and written assignments to investigate bilingual students' experiences of dialogic interaction in higher education, including their reasons for contributing to discussion or remaining silent. The students' willingness to speak up was influenced by a combination of factors, including confidence in their linguistic resources and in having something to say, their previous learning experiences, expectations of their roles, and the nature of the tasks.

It has long been recognized that classroom interactions are infused with often subtle emotional processes (Elfer, 2017), and positive interactions and social relationships can be difficult to sustain. It is a collective challenge and responsibility to gain deeper understanding of how participation in educational dialogue actually works and where the barriers to participation may be lifted.

Antti Rajala adds a welcome perspective on this chapter with reference to the research he is conducting with colleagues on care and compassion in early childhood education. It is interesting to see how this empirical work employs different research methods to build a full picture of children's compassionate activity within and beyond the school context. His commentary raises questions about how this approach fundamentally challenges the very aims of education.

Expert commentary

Researching care in educational dialogue and activity

Antti Rajala, University of Helsinki, Finland

In her chapter, Ruth Kershner argues for the need to examine the social and relational aspects of educational dialogue and activity. She maintains that care and empathy should be considered as essential means and ends of education. She discusses a wide range of methodological approaches that I believe are very useful for researchers working in these areas. Furthermore, the chapter helps to broaden the research on socio-emotional aspects of education from the dominant narrow focus on measurement and remediation of individual deficits towards the relational contexts of education (Hoffman, 2009).

In this commentary, I aim to further the discussion around how care can be conceptualized and researched in social and relational terms. Together with my colleagues, I am researching the related concept of compassion in early childhood education. We define compassion in terms of what people do rather than what they are. In our definition, acts of compassion involve the following aspects: (1) noticing or attending to another's suffering or distress, (2) displaying other-regarding emotions and (3) acting to alleviate the suffering or distress (Lipponen, Rajala, & Hilppö, 2018; see also Lilius, Worline, Dutton, Kanov & Maitlis, 2011).

In our empirical work, we address the three research foci suggested by Kershner: social interactions and patterns of participation, participants' social and relational experience, and wider social and relational conditions for dialogue. First, we use the methods of structured observation and video-based interaction analysis to understand how compassion is performed in naturally occurring interactions of early childhood education settings. The age of the child participants range from 1 to 6 years. The caring and compassionate actions identified in this research include acts of comforting, including, helping, and sharing. Our current research shows that acts of compassion cannot be explained by only examining the properties of individuals; the observed acts of compassion were socially determined and often the outcome of collaboration between the children and educators.

Second, to examine early childhood educators' social and relational experience of their dialogue and activity, we analysed student teachers' narratives of compassion and care in their work (Rajala & Lipponen, 2018). In the narratives, the need for compassion stemmed from concerns in the participants' personal lives or work. Compassion was manifested in both non-transformative and transformative forms in the narratives. Some compassionate acts helped others to adapt to the difficult situations without an attempt to change the circumstances that produced suffering. Other acts questioned existing practices and sought to transform the situation.

Our research points to the importance of attending to the organizational culture to understand how care and compassion are practiced in educational institutions. In the narratives we collected, compassion or its denial was not described merely as individual isolated instances but as a recurrent feature of how the social practices were organized in kindergartens (Rajala & Lipponen, 2018). Our observational research indicates the relevance of the division of labor (Rajala, Lipponen, Kontiola & Hilppö, in press) as well as the implicit and explicit rules and norms for acts of compassion and caring (Lipponen et al., 2018). However, we feel that these methods are not sufficient to generate in-depth understanding of the wider social and relational conditions of compassionate activity. Therefore, we are currently engaging in an educational ethnography to better understand what is at stake in the children's lives as well as in the collective response of a kindergarten community to distress of its members.

Furthermore, I propose that the focus on social relations of care should not be confined only within the school or kindergarten community. Educational institutions are increasingly shifting their attention to the surrounding society, creating collaborations with other cultural, neighborhood and professional organizations. Such collaborations could be used in school projects to engage students to develop caring relations with people outside the school community. One example is a project in which upper secondary school students cooperated with cycling activists and city authorities to influence the decision-making of the city concerning cycling (Rajala et al., 2013). The project was motivated by an environmental concern, and the students were held accountable for their contributions not only to their teachers but also to the citizens and cyclists living in the area. This project illuminates how education can foster not only care for one's immediate community but also solidarity for less familiar people. Another example is the research of Wegerif et al. (2019) on a project in which students from different countries engaged in dialogue with each other through videos and blogs.

Ultimately, the focus on care in education can potentially challenge the foundations of how educational activity and its outcomes are usually conceived. Is the most important task of educators and educational policymakers to optimize conditions for individual achievement or should more attention be paid to how education can foster care and compassion in children?

CHAPTER TEN

Researching Dialogue in Educational Decision-Making

Ruth Kershner

Introduction

This chapter is concerned with research into educational decision-making in which dialogue is central. Students, staff and other adults are often involved in debating issues and problems that are significant in their personal and social lives. This may occur within the planned curriculum in areas like citizenship and health education as well as subjects in the sciences, arts, humanities and sports. Dialogue may be woven into school practices and responsibilities, such as deciding on how to allocate limited resources to meet students'· additional educational needs. The learning process itself involves decision-making when choices are made about what, and how, to study or teach. Those who are involved in all of these practices may need to learn how to 'speak up' for themselves or, alternatively, to listen carefully and fairly to others.

Questions arise about whether educational decision-making is actually dialogic, in the sense that different views are taken into account and discussed critically in coming to a collective conclusion about what to do. Who is participating in these dialogues and how are everyone's contributions included and valued, even if full consensus is not gained? Certain stakeholder 'voices' may remain marginal without explicit steps to encourage everyone's active participation and mutual understanding. Methodological choices in this area therefore call for attention to ethical and cultural considerations of equitable participation and power relations in the complex arenas of educational practice. Of central interest is how understanding is built collectively and how different participants – including students – are respected as legitimate sources of knowledge.

Let us begin with three research examples, all in some way to do with student involvement in decision-making, see Boxes 10.1, 10.2 and 10.3.

Box 10.1   Example 1: From didactic to dialogue: Assessing the use of an innovative classroom resource to support decision-making about cannabis use

Moffat, Haines-Saah and Johnson's (2017) study in Canada was driven by previous findings that young people would welcome more opportunities to engage in discussion about their own and others' cannabis use. The authors note that young people's views are not systematically represented in Canadian drug education programmes, which are themselves fragmented. They set up a 'knowledge translation' study which included an innovative set of lesson materials incorporating a film, lesson plans and suggestions for group activities. These were designed as a resource for facilitators to help them in engaging students in critical thinking and dialogue about cannabis use. The resource was distributed widely and used 122 times in fifty-five different sites with more than 2,500 students in grades 7–12. The researchers' thematic coding of the facilitators' evaluations (from surveys and telephone interviews) indicated how facilitators used or modified the resource materials with their students. The authors gained insight into factors affecting the uptake of the resource in different settings and the conditions that supported its use in classroom discussion.

They concluded from the facilitators' feedback that '[s]haring different points of view was an opportunity to learn from peers and consider unexplored consequences of the film characters' decisions which added depth to the discussion ... many young people were drawn to exploring the nuances reinforcing how young people *do* have the ability to contemplate decisions in the midst of ambiguity' (p. 91).

Box 10.2 Example 2: Students' views of factors affecting their bystander behaviours in response to school bullying: A cross-collaborative conceptual qualitative analysis

Forsberg et al. (2018) were concerned to find out more about why students may decide, or not, to defend victims when witnessing bullying. Noting that bullying is prevalent in all countries, although to different degrees, the authors aimed to investigate why student bystanders may or may not act in accordance with how they interpreted the situation. The authors conducted eighty-nine individual interviews with students aged 9–14 in Sweden and the United States. The research approach was collaborative between the Swedish and US research teams, who jointly constructed the interview protocol and then compared their initial coding of each data set in order to merge their results into one model of 'bystander motivation, decision making and behaviour in bullying' (p. 130). They identified five factors articulated by the students, including informed awareness, behavioural seriousness, personal feelings, bystander expectations and a sense of responsibility, with just a small number of cross-cultural differences in the factors mentioned by each group. The authors comment that the interviews gave the students 'a space, time and human connection to reflect on events and personal conceptions' (p. 139). Furthermore '(s)chools and teachers need to listen carefully to students ... since previous research has suggested that students and teachers might have different perspectives on bullying' (p. 140).

Box 10.3 Example 3: Authenticity and the relevance of discourse and figured worlds in secondary students' discussions of socioscientific issues

Åkerblom and Lindahl (2017) based their research on the long-held belief that students learn best when they can see how education is relevant to their lives. They located their investigation in the context of a research tradition involving the introduction of authentic socioscientific issues (SSI) into the classroom, pointing out that the definition of an 'authentic task' will not necessarily be the same for teachers and students. They conducted a case study of one class in Sweden, with twenty-eight students aged 15–16 years. The task was for students to discuss how to deal with the genuine problem of inbreeding in Swedish wolves. Newspaper articles with different views were provided for students to discuss in groups. Two forms of 'authenticity' were introduced in the programme: first, students were asked to produce individual written assignments presenting their personal views on the issue (to be assessed by the teacher); second, they were asked to write a letter about the wolf issue to the minister of the environment, who was responsible for making a decision. Students' classroom discussions were recorded and analysed for their use of language and apparent communication of meaning. The authors found that the students' use of language and argument differed between the two tasks. In the letter to the minister, which was extensively discussed by the students, they dropped certain ideas from their earlier classroom discussions and gave greater privilege to the use of specialist scientific terms and existing policy documents. The authors say that this represented a transition from students' 'everyday' thinking to the use of formal 'school knowledge' in communicating with a different stakeholder (i.e. the minister). Associated gains in rational precision, as expressed in the letter, were accompanied by the removal of relevant emotional reasoning that occurred in their earlier arguments. This led the authors to suggest that teachers need to be aware of the potential impact of different forms of task 'authenticity' on students' discussions, decision-making and learning.

These three research examples help to pinpoint questions about decision-making on issues that may be more or less directly personal and 'authentic'. The three studies are all concerned in some way with solving existing problems in education, in this case relating to young people's motivations for drug use, their responses to bullying, and their understanding of SSI. All three studies take account of the different knowledge and opinions that are brought to the issue in question, but there are some differences between their research approaches. In Example 1, it is the researchers and lesson facilitators who are in direct communication with each other, working with a teaching resource that was explicitly designed to engage students in discussion about cannabis use. In Example 2, the students are themselves directly involved in expressing their views about bullying, although this is in the context of individual interviews rather than group discussions. In this case, we also see that the two research teams in Sweden and the United States were collaborating and deciding together about the interview method and data analysis.

Examples 1 and 2 are both concerned with personal experiences that students are likely to have to decide about at some point in their lives. Example 3 is different in that students will not themselves make a decision about the Swedish wolf population. Yet this is presented to them as an important debate in their country and they are invited to attempt to influence the minister responsible by writing a letter to her. The students also collaborate on what to write to the minister, giving them a direct decision-making experience in the classroom.

In addition to these differences in research topic and design, we can also see methodological contrasts in the level of analysis of each study: Research Example 3 is the only one that focuses in detail on analysing the students' dialogue at a linguistic level, that is, what they say to each other and write in their letter to the minister. In doing this they employ Gee's (2011) model of **discourse analysis**, focusing on the students' uses of language and their 'figured worlds' of taken-for-granted concepts and meanings. In Example 2, the researchers organized the students' ideas into themes. The interview discussions are not presented in the article, but the authors included some illustrative interview quotes. In Example 1, it is the facilitators' voices that are heard in illustrative quotes, while the students' talk is reported indirectly via the facilitators.

In weighing up these different approaches we see that decisions always have to be made about methods that are 'fit for purpose' in answering research questions. In the three examples above, the authors point out several strengths and limitations in their own work. For instance, Moffat et al. (2017) recognize that their findings are based on the optional reports of a diverse group of 'end-user' facilitators, who may themselves have been particularly receptive to the innovation. No direct field observations were made so there was no way for the authors to compare facilitators' different styles of delivery or to gauge student response for themselves. Forsberg et al. (2018) comment positively on the value of their large sample of participants from two countries, but they also note limitations in the lack of direct observations or peer reports about what actually happened in bullying situations. Åkerblom and Lindahl's (2017) research did involve direct observation of students in action, but they do not report what the students said about their experiences and choices in these lessons.

This brief comparison of three relevant studies helps to demonstrate the key themes of this chapter, several of which occur throughout this book:

- *Stakeholders may be both present and absent.*

    Research on educational decision-making may focus directly on key stakeholders, such as students, teachers and researchers in the three examples above, but what about the roles of others who are concerned directly or indirectly with the issues in question, such as peers and politicians? The point is that the decision-making discussion cannot be fully analysed and understood without a wider perspective on the 'absent' stakeholders who may be present in the research participants' thinking (as seen in the different forms of authenticity in Example 3).

- *Activities and materials affect participation and dialogue.*

    People generally bring different beliefs and opinions to any complex issue, yet those with a personal stake may not always have the opportunity to participate in dialogue about what to do. In these cases, designing activities to spark discussion and offering resources with alternative views can inform and provoke critical thinking (as seen in

Examples 1 and 3). The task and materials set the scene for the development of dialogue, and potentially influence the course of discussion, so they are highly relevant to the analysis of dialogic data.

- *Language and communication occur at different levels.*

  The language and communication of decision-making, both spoken and written, may be analysed at different levels, sometimes focusing directly on the linguistic form and content of the talk and writing (as in Example 3) and sometimes focusing on the researchers' interpretations of what is meant in talk and writing (as in Examples 1 and 2). It is also worth bearing in mind that non-verbal communication, emotions and social relationships could be relevant levels of analysis, depending on the core research purposes and questions (as discussed in Chapter 9).

- *Researchers need to invest time in understanding the research context.*

  Researchers or members of the research team may already be practitioners in the given site, or the investigation may itself involve seeking their views as in Example 1. In Example 2, the collaboration between research teams in different countries is central to the project. In Example 3, the study depends on the active involvement of the class teacher. So, time needs to be invested in building relationships with participants, institutional leaders, 'gatekeepers' and so on, as well as finding out about the research context (as discussed below in terms of 'grasping the issues').

- *Research may have unintended and unpredictable consequences for the participants.*

  Whether intended or not, it is possible that the research will itself act as a sort of intervention, so things may happen in the decision-making process that would not have happened without the research activity. The idea of **observer effects** is well known in research, whether it is caused by the nature of the measuring instruments in physics or an apparent alteration of participants' behaviour in response to being observed. These reactions present ethical concerns about research accuracy and unintended consequences, but these are not insuperable. In the area of health education research, Paradis and Sutkin (2017) offer recommendations to take account of 'participant reactivity', suggesting that researchers need to invest in interpersonal relationships with participants, and that researchers should use theory to make sense of participants' altered behaviour and use it as a window into the social world. In more dialogic terms we would recognize research as a human social process. Research effects are therefore mitigated, and may even become irrelevant, when participants' interpretations and agency are actively acknowledged.

These themes are threaded through rest of this chapter, raising questions about how to focus investigations and what data to bring to the foreground for analysis. Further research examples are given to illustrate how research may focus on different aspects of decision-making discussions, such as how individuals may learn to participate, how communications may be facilitated by digital methods, and the importance of considering wider institutional values and practices. A final research example emphasizes the value of looking closely at the actual talk involved in decision-making. This can lead to unexpected (and sometimes unwelcome) results about an apparent lack of dialogicality in situations where participants might be assumed to have the potential to share their knowledge and expertise very productively. So a skeptical view is important in researching dialogue and decision-making in often difficult and contested areas, and careful choice of methods should support this.

Methodological perspectives: The real world of research on dialogue in educational decision-making

All research on educational dialogue is in the 'real world' in the sense that participants are, ideally, involved in productive interaction and authentically valuable conversation with others. Research on dialogue and decision-making really highlights this real-world context, especially in the way it may involve stepping beyond classroom learning to bring in wider interests, knowledge and experience. Methodological principles for analysing educational dialogue are commonly based on **sociocultural discourse analysis** (Mercer, 2004) and **linguistic ethnography** (e.g. Copland & Creese, 2015), as mentioned earlier in Chapters 2, 4 and 6. The associated approaches to data analysis can be multimodal, multilevel and multi-method. For instance, a study may involve the analysis of social interaction and non-verbal communication as well as spoken dialogue, or the same episodes of dialogue may be analysed at different levels (such as conversational tactics in conjunction with joint construction of meaning). Studies may look closely at the immediate and wider context of the dialogic interaction, in addition to analysing the dialogue itself. It is also common to supplement dialogue analysis with reference to other data sources, such as participant interviews, **focus groups**, relevant documents, and features of the physical and social environment.

Flexible methods that attend to the passage of time are central to tracing what happens in decision-making. Dialogue continues over time, sometimes crossing boundaries between different contexts of discussion. In Moffat et al.'s (2017) research outlined in Example 1 above, some facilitators remarked that students had followed up lessons by initiating private conversations afterwards. Data may therefore be somewhat 'messy' and incomplete if the dialogue and decision-making continue in ways that are not open to a researcher's eyes. Indeed it is, of course, never possible to produce a full picture: research data is inevitably selective. Research designs are also likely to be flexible rather than fixed from the start, not least to respond to the unexpected and, perhaps, follow-up gaps that become evident and important.

Many of the principles of **real-world research** are worth exploring in this context. Robson and McCartan (2016, p. 149) identify the general skills needed by flexible design investigators as

- question asking
- good listening
- adaptiveness and flexibility
- grasp of the issues
- lack of bias

Table 10.1 Self-audit for identifying an initial 'grasp of the issues' (Robson & McCartan, 2016) when researching dialogue and decision-making

What do I know about the following areas that might be relevant to my research?	Sample questions to ask oneself	Are there also some harder questions to answer?
Theory	What theories are relevant to my research topic? How have researchers in this field referred to theory? Does there seem to be a consensual theoretical approach? Is my research concerned with new theory-building? How can a theoretical perspective inform my methods and data analysis?	What are my own theoretical assumptions and how are these affecting my research planning? Do I need to read more and discuss theory with others? Are there contradictions in the theoretical field (e.g. between different definitions of 'dialogue')? Can my preferred theory apply universally – i.e. to all people, of all ages, in all activities and settings?
Policy	What policy exists in this area of decision-making? Has policy development been stable over recent years? What is the policy discourse and rhetoric?	How does policy match practice in my field of interest? Are there significant international policy differences that could affect how I draw conclusions from my research? To what extent does local and national policy discourse infuse people's thinking?

| Environment | What seems to be important in the physical, social and cultural setting of my research? Are there certain ways of speaking and particular terms in use (e.g. to describe 'ground rules' for talk)? Do participants mix freely or tend to stay in the same groups? Are there any barriers to the participation of particular groups and individuals? What do I experience as the social and emotional tone of the research setting? | Do my perceptions of important environmental features match what is significant to others involved? Should I include environmental features in my research questions? Should I conduct an initial environmental audit to set the scene? If so, should I ask participants to do the same (e.g. a map or a photobook indicating where participants perceive that communication is supported or hindered)? Are barriers to participation systematic and visible (e.g. students not admitted to school staffrooms) or hidden and sometimes unconscious (e.g. gender differences in how ideas are taken up in meetings)? |

In presenting these principles, Robson and McCartan highlight the need for researchers to enquire constantly about events, taking in information as neutrally as possible, using all the senses and appreciating the tone and context of what is observed, heard or read. They say that this needs to be accompanied by a willingness to change procedures or plans, balancing adaptiveness and rigour, based on a sound grasp of relevant theory and policy. The aim is to interpret information in an informed way, remaining open to contrary findings and explanations. Robson and McCartan do not emphasize the idea of dialogue in research, but they seem to reflect some core dialogic principles in their thinking. Table 10.1 offers a 'self-audit' tool for taking up one of their recommended skills: 'grasp of the issues'. This could be helpful in designing a project and in returning to it later to check on whether more information is needed to interpret findings confidently.

Box 10.4 Example 4: A sociocultural understanding of children's 'voice'

Maybin (2013) employed Bakhtinian theory with linguistic ethnography to investigate how 10- to 11-year-old English children constructed knowledge and identity within the informal language practices of their school. She recorded and observed the children in the classroom and playground, followed by interviews with them in pairs or trios. One of her main findings was about how classroom dialogues were 'constructed through the echoing, borrowing and appropriation of voices between teachers and pupils' (p. 386). This was particularly evident in relation to evaluations of attainment within the formal school curriculum, leading to the unfortunately familiar shorthand expression by children of themselves in English national 'assessment level' terms such as 'I'm a 4b'. Children's informal talk was also infused by other reference points, such as popular songs and shows, as well as the people in their own wider social world of family and friends. Maybin concludes that this sociocultural understanding of children's actively negotiated 'voice' differs fundamentally from the idea that listening to students necessarily gives empowering access to what might be assumed to be individual students' core identities.

Participants in educational dialogue and decision-making: Who has a 'voice'?

Recent decades have seen a great deal of research into **student voice** and it is almost taken for granted that students may reasonably be consulted about matters that affect them (e.g. Flutter & Rudduck 2004; Mager & Nowak, 2012; and see Chapter 4). Yet this process is not necessarily dialogic, and students cannot always see visible results for their efforts. Listening to students can become formulaic, especially when a few students are presumed to speak for all. In addition, the influence of the wider school environment is not always taken into account, including students' own ways of making sense of the worlds in which they live. See Box 10.4.

The key methodological point here is that what people say cannot easily be separated from what they hear and respond to in their social activities and relationships. This is not to say that students (or other potentially marginalized groups) do not have valuable knowledge to contribute to decision-making. People's thinking is not entirely determined by the immediate context, but more by the process of learning and moving between contexts (Salomon & Perkins, 1998). Yet knowledge offered by the child is not always heard by the adult listener. Murris (2013) discusses this in terms of Fricker's (2007) notion of 'epistemic injustice', meaning that the implicit and explicit assumptions and prejudices are held about the child's capacity as a knower. A child may lack credibility in the listener's prejudiced view (*testimonial injustice*) or, more fundamentally, a child may lack faith in their own ability to make sense of their experiences in a world which does not even have an authentic concept of 'student voice' (*hermeneutical injustice*). Ethical questions therefore arise about the research intent and the potentially contradictory lack of genuine attention to the views of children or other marginalized groups of participants. Cultural gaps and inconsistencies may compound hermeneutical injustice if the social and educational world lacks the very concepts that allow students to be heard. Paris (2012) points out that beliefs about cultural deficits have marginalized students of colour for decades in the United States and many other countries. While culturally relevant and responsive pedagogies have flourished in attempting to counter assumptions of deficit and difference, Paris questions whether these have gone far enough. He suggests a new construct: *culturally sustaining pedagogy* which 'seeks to perpetuate and foster – to sustain – linguistic, literature and cultural pluralism as part of the democratic process of schooling' (p. 95).

These discussions of sociocultural processes, epistemic injustice and cultural devaluation could suggest that research on student involvement in educational decision-making is difficult to do well. As seen in Table 10.1, a 'grasp of the issues' is essential, as is continuing to ask hard questions.

Moving on to consider further research approaches, Example 5 focuses on the development of individual skills and dispositions through experiential learning; Example 6 on the particular affordances of digital means of communication and Example 7 on the importance of institutional structures, values and commitments over time. Research methods are italicized in the following summaries, in order to draw attention to the options and potential combinations. See Boxes 10.5, 10.6 and 10.7.

Box 10.5 Example 5: Experiential learning to develop voice

Oliver, Jones, Rayner, Penner and Jamieson (2017) carried out a small-scale pilot study in Canada with twelve adult social work students, who are expected to learn how to engage in 'difficult conversations' with clients. The authors note that it is not just the students who need moral courage to take on professional responsibility and defend one's values and boundaries in the face of potential personal and emotional risk. It is also the students' supervisors who need to support students in their practical placements and seminar discussions. The authors developed a 'difficult conversations' learning module, with three core aims: (1) creating a safe space for students to talk about difficult conversations, (2) orienting students towards the concept of difficult conversations and introducing a model for navigating these conversations and (3) prompting applications of the model to real-life difficult conversations. The research methods included *an online evaluation survey together with a sample focus group or interview* with six students. The findings highlighted the students' views about the value of particular elements of the course, and the authors reported student views about the theoretical model, the authenticity and support of the learning activity, and questions of power in the profession and the seminar itself. In all, this is an interesting example of research employing experiential learning and dialogue, which is itself directed towards helping participants develop skills for their future professional decision-making.

Box 10.6 Example 6: Use of digital media to amplify voice

The idea of 'amplifying' voice is taken up by Cook-Sather (2017) in the United States. She gives examples of this in a consortium linking students in high school, teacher preparation and academic development for faculty, graduate and undergraduate students. It involved high school students and teachers in weekly email exchanges, and it included undergraduate students' use of *visual mapping technology for classroom observation* as well as the use of an online platform by staff and students to publish *reflective essays* on their collaborative work. Cook-Sather used *narrative analysis* of participants' reflections on these experiences, to 'offer glimpses into how the virtual forms created by the digital media of email, visual mapping technologies, and online journals have actual effects' (p. 1145). She concluded that the key affordances include the possibility of exchanges in which others can be imagined without physical presence, thus avoiding the social encounters in which power differentials can become all too apparent. The digital records were seen to allow engagement in dialogue and reflective practice both in real time and with later reference. Cook-Sather argues that the virtual forms of dialogue support the development of pedagogical partnerships in which exchanges are based on respect for different voices, sharing of power and reciprocity.

Box 10.7 Example 7: Institutional structures, values and commitments

Baroutsis, Mills, McGregor, te Riele and Hayes (2016) were concerned about students' potential disconnection from learning and lack of belonging in school. They saw this as a cultural issue: 'Opportunities from students to speak and to be heard are important elements of democratic school processes but research into student voice has shown that a culture of silence is a more common feature of schooling' (p. 438). They conducted research over eighteen months in an alternative Community College context in Australia, involving students in Years 10–12 identified with a range of complex social and learning needs. One practice was the 'community forum', held each morning in which young people and staff sat together in a circle arrangement. The meetings included reflection and discussion about current issues leading to decisions about operational matters. There were also opportunities for students and staff to listen to each other and consult about plans for the day. They aimed to identify how these and other school practices represented forms of social justice that could be applied more widely to all schools. They generated data *from interviews, observations, photography, and the collection of artefacts such as school documents.* They reflect on underlying principles seen in this whole-school commitment to engaging students in authentic dialogue, bearing in mind that 'adult power was also a presence' and student voice in decision-making is limited (p. 447). They suggest that '(m)aintaining the balance between individual agency and community welfare is an ongoing project' (p. 451).

These three research examples show how research studies may converge on the broad topic of participation in dialogue and decision making from different directions, focusing in these cases on individual learning, digitally facilitated means of communication, and wider institutional values and practices. In Example 5, the authors report on students' views about their learning experiences with a view to their further development of professional learning. Example 6 is also based on participants' reflections about their communications with others, but Cook-Sather's reflections on different experiences of digital communication focus her argument on the dialogic affordances of digital technology itself (see Chapter 8) Example 7 includes direct observation of school meetings as well as a range of other methods, leading to a broader discussion about socially just practices in schools. None of these studies offers uncritical success stories, but all allow some insights into the ways in which course materials, learning activities, means of communication and institutional structures may support (or hinder) dialogue for decision-making.

There could be many other avenues to explore in this field with international perspectives, such as the use of **reflective dialogue** in participatory evaluation by youth workers in England (Cooper, 2014), the involvement of Dutch researchers and student teachers in **participatory action research** on classroom communications and relations in inclusive elementary school settings (Montesano Montessori & Ponte, 2012) and the use of dialogic conferences for bringing together research with traditional ways of mutual problem solving in Tanzania (Ahmad, Gjøtterud & Krogh, 2016). But these are just four more single examples from a rapidly growing field of study.

What becomes evident in this particular field is how common it is for researchers to report that productive dialogue happened and decisions were made. Illustrative quotes are often incorporated, which can be vivid and interesting, but readers cannot always see how these were selected from the actual talk that took place between people. The final example in this chapter therefore returns to this conversational level of analysis to show what might be gained in this way. See Box 10.8.

Box 10.8 Example 8: Sharing expertise in interprofessional collaboration

Hjörne and Säljö (2014) were concerned with how specialist knowledge has to be shared in order for schools to provide required services. Multidisciplinary collaboration is common in education, often involving teachers, psychologists, health professionals and so on. As the authors say, interprofessional collaboration is assumed to improve the quality of decision-making and problem-solving, but there is not a great deal of research demonstrating this. They followed pupil health team meetings in four schools in Sweden. Data were generated using a **micro-ethnographic approach**, which involved documenting and audio recording the meetings, resulting in about hundred hours of recordings. *They used discourse analysis to see how school difficulties were discussed and how decisions were made, focusing particularly on the role of multidisciplinarity.* They first looked into the school contexts to find out how the problems came to be presented at team meetings, noting that the person who initiated this process (e.g. the class teacher) was not generally present in the meeting. In analysing the meeting conversations, they then found a global pattern of phases: 'presentation' of the problem, 'elaboration' with comments invited from team members and 'conclusion' where a decision is taken about how to respond. *The micro-level analysis of talk is presented in transcribed excerpts, with a line-by-line commentary on what was said.* Somewhat dishearteningly, they found that the multidisciplinary discussions did not actually add much new knowledge to the perceived problem. Little tended to be added beyond the initial presentation of the 'case'. A high level of consensus tended to support the view of individual deficit within the child, so the discussions could be seen as collegial but not critically dialogic. Furthermore, they comment that little attention was paid to previous decision-making, so knowledge was not built cumulatively and systematically over time.

This finding about apparent *lack of dialogue* in Example 8 brings out the potential benefits of looking closely at the talk that occurs in decision-making. In this way it is possible to see precisely what each person contributed to the conversation and how ideas were taken up or dropped over time. When accompanied by other sources of data it is also possible to explore the extent to which the decision-making occurred within the discussion itself and the ways in which other knowledge is incorporated. For instance, how does a spoken contribution to a discussion match a previously written document or the subsequent meeting minutes? This sort of detailed and multilevel approach to analysis is not always necessary in every project, and sometimes researchers will report different aspects of their full data analysis in different papers. The key point is that direct attention to what people actually say to each other can help to establish a critical perspective on 'real-life' discussions and decision-making that may not actually be fundamentally dialogic.

Concluding remarks

This chapter has included several examples in the broad field of researching dialogue and educational decision-making. Researchers may inquire into various aspects of educational practice, both in schools and more widely in public life. Questions inevitably arise about whether educational decision-making is actually dialogic. A skeptical perspective is therefore essential in investigating how people may 'speak up' for themselves and listen carefully and respectfully to others. One of the main conclusions is that when trying to find out how different participants are included as legitimate contributors to decision-making, it is extremely useful to attend closely to what people actually say to each other. This may involve analysing recordings and transcriptions of conversations as well as live observations. Other sources of data include observations, interviews, focus groups, survey questionnaires, written assignments, document analysis, photography and so on. Use may also be made of systematic participatory methods that are designed to tackle complex educational problems by enabling non-specialist stakeholders to engage with 'experts' in order to weigh up evidence to reach a joint decision, such as 'Deliberative Mapping'[1] and **dialogue mapping**.[2]

It can be important in this area to take deliberate steps to inquire beyond one's usual ways of thinking, including the influence of existing research conventions. As one early reviewer of this chapter helpfully pointed out, there are some national differences in research traditions, such as those that focus on culture (as is common in the United States) or on social class, or both, or neither. As Brown (2010, pp. 61–2) puts it in her discussion of transdisciplinary inquiry into 'wicked' issues that are unusually resistant to resolution through existing modes of problem-solving, 'in times of change, in any serious decision making everyone becomes their own researcher. The need to make sense of a complex and changing world is part of the human condition.' There is therefore a need to 'grasp the issues' in referring to relevant theory, policy and environmental factors in order to keep alert to gaps and contradictions in the data analysis. Thinking about challenging concepts like 'epistemic injustice' (Fricker, 2007) can really help to open one's eyes to understanding the bigger moral picture of dialogue and decision-making. Ethical considerations are very much to the fore in this area, not least in asking whether the research processes and reporting may interfere with the primary educational purpose. For instance, analysing multi-professional decision-making about a student's future school placement may be of research interest, but the primary educational purpose is to protect the student's interests. Balancing different concerns in an ethical way is central to research on dialogue and educational decision-making.

---

[1]http://www.participatorymethods.org/authors/deliberative-mapping.
[2]http://cognexus.org/id41.htm.

In her commentary, Sherice Clarke adds further clarity on this topic. Drawing on her own and others' research, she explains how the analysis of conversational turns can provide ways of tracing the processes that result in decisions. Her examples bring out the need to attend to the coordinated processes that result in decisions, including whose voices are represented or excluded.

Expert commentary

Affordances of dialogue for researching educational decision-making and dialogism

Sherice Clarke, University of California San Diego, United States

This chapter takes as its focus methodological concerns when researching educational decision-making in which dialogue is central. In this commentary, I focus my attention on three methodological questions that arise when endeavouring to research educational decision-making in and through dialogue.

Educational decisions occur at various levels of the educational system: macro-, meso- and micro-levels. For example, a 'macro-level' educational decision may be a school district's adoption of an educational policy. A 'meso-level' educational decision may be a classroom's consensus on the solution to a subject-matter problem (such as Example 3, this chapter). A 'micro-level' decision may be a teacher's decision of what question to ask next in the flow of a dialogic class discussions. A researcher of educational decision-making must take into account the level at which a decision is made, the sites in which decision-making might be observed and the stakeholders involved (implicitly or explicitly) in the decision-making process. These levels of analysis have direct implications for the data sources one might select and the population(s) one might investigate to gain insight into educational decision-making.

Dialogue, most simply defined, is discussion between voices. These voices may be historical (Bakhtin, 1981), embodied by a social other/interlocutor (i.e. Vygotsky, 1978), collocated or otherwise. In my own work, I have been interested in conversational interaction in which interlocutors work together to achieve joint understanding and meaning around problems. What makes dialogue particularly useful for the study of educational decision-making is that interactionally each conversational turn provides an opportunity to trace the ideational space and its evolution. In this sense, each conversational turn serves as an observation of how interlocutors expand, elaborate, contract or maintain the ideational space. If the outcome of a classroom dialogue is consensus, then each conversational turn in that dialogue can afford the analyst a means through which to observe how verbal participation helped to achieve consensus.

One particular example helps to highlight the affordances of dialogue for researching educational decision-making. In Popp and Goldman's (2016) study of teacher professional learning communities, they applied Scardamalia and Bereiter's (2006) 'knowledge building' analytic schema to examine dialogue in these meetings. The educational decisions that teachers were making in these meetings related to instruction and assessment practices. The means through which these decisions were made were discussions in team meetings. In this case, the analyst has both the decision (outcome) and the decision-making processes (discourse) to trace how outcomes were achieved. In their analysis of knowledge building, Popp and Goldman were able to determine which meetings afforded more collaborative knowledge building in which teachers were building on one another's ideas as opposed to simply advancing one's own position or thinking. This study provides an example of how dialogue can afford the examination of how collaborative decision-making in teacher teams may be. Other examples of the affordances of dialogue for researching decision-making include Clarke (2015) and Clarke, Howley, Resnick and Rosé (2016) which examine students' participation in whole-class discussions and intersubjective dynamics that shape their participation.

As Kershner (this chapter) highlights, the question of who has 'voice' in educational decision-making arises when researching educational decisions and educational dialogue. Another way to formulate this question is that researching educational decision-making (specifically through dialogue) affords the researcher a means to examine how dialogic decision-making may be. By examining whose voices are represented in educational decision-making, it becomes possible to problematize why certain voices might be more or less salient and/or visible.

Two examples help to illustrate this question of voice. The first comes from another data set on teacher-professional learning communities (Resnick, 2014). The decision-making the teachers were engaged in was co-planning dialogic class discussions in algebra, with the aid of a coach. The data consisted of the discussions in these co-planning meetings. Numbers and dates were ubiquitous in these discussions (e.g. 2.5, 2.6, 2.7, 8 March, 15 March, etc.). As teachers coordinated the work of co-planning they used these numbers as a shorthand to refer to places within the planned curriculum, and corresponding dates at which they ought to be covering that respective content. What is interesting, analytically, is that in these conversational exchanges, the teachers never referred to the algebra content by name or concept, but rather their interactions referred only to the numbers and dates that corresponded to the coverage of that content. This coordinated way of talking about practice may reflect familiar routines in the teachers' co-planning. However, in terms of voice, they bring to the fore a kind of omnipresent 'voice' involved in their decision-making process: district leadership's expectations about pacing. It therefore becomes possible to problematize their decision-making through the lens of an interlocutor who is 'heard' but physically absent.

The second example (Clarke, 2015) is a study of whole-class discussions during a single unit of instruction in biology. Over the course of an instructional unit, the teacher led students in discussions about core concepts of genetic inheritance. These discussions were collaborative sense-making discussions about the scientific concepts. Analysis of turns in talk, and who those turns were attributed to, revealed that over a six-week period of discussions, there were four primary participants, the remainder of which either rarely or never participated in discussions. In terms of educational decisions, students were engaging in a process of joint meaning-making and understanding of the concepts. In terms of voice, only a few students verbally participated in that process. This example, like the previous ones, allows the researcher to not only trace the ideational space and its development, but also whose voices were reflected in that development and problematize why.

Researching educational decision-making through dialogue provides ways of tracing the processes that result in decisions. Research designs must therefore attend to (1) the education decision, (2) the level of the decision and (3) the stakeholders involved in these decisions. Analyses can uncover the coordinated processes that result in decisions.

CHAPTER ELEVEN

Conclusion

Rupert Wegerif, Ruth Kershner, Sara Hennessy and Ayesha Ahmed

Bakhtin (1986), a major source for the dialogic theory we are applying to educational research in this book, famously wrote that 'there are no first or last words'. In one way his point is very simple and obvious. This book, like any other book, is not a final statement. It will stimulate answering words in the minds of readers who take the dialogue further. But if we think it through, the implication of Bakhtin's claim has profound implications for how we conduct educational research. If we know really that it is not possible to do research that offers the final truth on things – the 'last word' – then we ought to acknowledge that in the way that we conduct and communicate research. This book is a long attempt to answer the question: how can we conduct research on educational dialogues that is itself dialogic or, in other words, is itself reflectively part of an ongoing educational dialogue?

Too much research in education appears to offer final words that will close down all the other voices. In 2018, the Education Endowment Foundation (EEF) published a guide for schools on the implementation of evidence-based practices, entitled 'Putting Evidence to Work',[1] but that guide touches only briefly on the

---

[1] educationendowmentfoundation.org.uk/tools/guidance-reports/a-schools-guide-to-implementation.

notion of dialogue: namely a dialogic approach to enabling implementation to succeed. In education it is not just a question of applying research findings in different contexts. This is because educational contexts are really complex and practitioners' active engagement is a key part of whether or not the apparent findings of research will succeed in different contexts of practice. Teachers and other practitioner colleagues are professionals who must make decisions that involve choosing between relevant and meaningful alternatives.

The outcomes of research in one setting – including materials designed for teachers – can form a springboard for adaptation in other settings, and can be laid open to further scrutiny and critique through that dialogic process. That there are no final words means that there are always other voices or multiple possible interpretations of educational research findings. This view challenges conventional views of reporting *from* research *to* practice. In contrast, it suggests that the practical 'impact' of research can best be seen as a dynamic process in which knowledge is shared and developed in response to investigations of what happens in different contexts, without losing awareness of crucial contextual factors. Wrigley (2018) highlights the dangers of aggregating results across studies to produce an 'average'. This is a critical point for educational research. In particular, adding together the results of multiple small-scale studies carried out in different classrooms does not equal a large data set that can inform practice in any classroom. At the most extreme, what works in one context may not work in *any other*. Wrigley argues that statistical evidence can offer a seductive illusion of objectivity that can blind us to the importance of context and interpretation and meaning in the real world.

Another major challenge for dialogic forms of research engagement and reporting is the navigation of online platforms. In particular, dissemination by social media can spiral out of the control of the researcher. Whatever the positive power of such methods for widespread communication, the meaning of the research is immediately removed from the researcher's hands. We have to recognize that opening up genuine dialogue is risky and demanding and dialogue may ultimately break down as the loudest voices dominate.

Some commentators might question the value of listening to multiple voices and claim, reasonably enough, that scientific research should be about finding the truth rather than participating in endless talk about the truth. Bakhtin (1984) answered this challenge through his idea of 'polyphonic truth' – that truth is found in dialogues and not in single utterances. To grasp his point it might be useful to think in terms of understanding. A formula on its own, or a yes/no answer to an education question is not a useful truth: to become useful it needs to be understood and understanding statements always implies relating them to contexts of use in which there are multiple factors and usually multiple voices in play. Understanding is demonstrated by being able to engage in dialogues and explain decisions to others.

In this book we have outlined and illustrated a number of useful approaches to researching educational dialogue that are reflectively self-consistent in being themselves dialogic. All of these examples can fit under the broad umbrella of the 'chiasm' approach introduced in Chapter 2 as a way of thinking about the kind of understanding we are striving for in educational research on dialogue. Chiasm, from rhetoric, means the reversal of the order of the subject and the object in a sentence to create an effect such as 'I speak the truth: the truth speaks me'. In research it is the claim that understanding always implies the co-presence in dialogue together of outside perspectives with inside perspectives. To understand an educational dialogue it is never enough simply to count the words or other signs exchanged, we also need to relate such a count to the meaning of the dialogue which we can only access as participants or vicarious participants. On the other hand, interpreting the meaning of an educational dialogue is not, on its own, research. This is because it does not transfer beyond the context of interpretation to help guide teachers in different contexts and build further knowledge. Research always requires an 'outside' voice as well as an inside voice, a voice able to compare and contrast in order to discern which elements of the complexity of a real dialogue might be of particular value to achieving educational ends.

We believe that this book is not only distinctive in opening up questions about methods for researching educational dialogue across a wide range of contexts, but is also very timely. There is a now an established research base in this diverse field, so attention can be given to moving forward. Research collaborations with practitioners are discussed, and emerging approaches such as design-based research are adding new horizons to existing models of reflective inquiry and action research. Another key theme is the role of technology, offering new affordances both for supporting dialogue and for analysing large data sets. We have moved beyond purely cognitive approaches to reflect also on social and relational aspects of dialogue, highlighting the need to examine both dialogic conditions and outcomes in these terms. We have also pointed to the need to develop new research designs for investigating complex contexts like classrooms, using combinations of methods to understand different levels and processes of dialogic engagement. Our expert commentators from around the world have helpfully provided unique insights and further examples to extend the scope and the thinking. A common thread is the theoretical challenge. As noted in Chapter 3, 'to advance the research on educational dialogue and its relevance to learning we need a clearer theory of thinking and learning. … Empirical research interested in classroom dialogue should pay careful attention to theoretical constructs and assumptions that orient its practice.' We hope that the consequence of this book will be that you, dear reader, are inspired to take up and try out some of these ideas in order to challenge them, develop them and, above all, to engage with them in order to take them forward into the future and into the ongoing dialogue that is educational research.

GLOSSARY OF RESEARCH METHODS AND TERMINOLOGY

This glossary comprises a selection of key methods and methodological terminology appearing in different chapters of this book. These terms appear in **bold** on their first occasion of use in each chapter. Other methodological terms that are explained in individual chapters are not included here.

Abductive/Abduction: Abduction is the creative formation of theory to make sense of observations. It is relevant to the analysis of data that moves iteratively between observation and theory, also bringing in wider knowledge. Conclusions are commonly understood and conveyed in terms of their likelihood rather than certainty, remaining open to further reflection and inquiry.

Action research: An approach often used by practitioners to understand and improve their own practice, focusing on their own actions and their reflections on evidence about the effects of those actions. It involves the construction of further knowledge and understanding through cycles of planning, implementing, recording and analysing changes in practice.

Affordance: The opportunities (and constraints) that are perceived in a situation, including uses of technology and other available resources, to engage in productive activity that leads to achieving a desired goal.

Analytical mark scheme: A response-scoring scheme containing multiple criteria, usually represented as a grid with criteria as column labels and levels of achievement as row labels. Sometimes the criteria are explicitly weighted.

Case study: In-depth, intensive analysis of a single case within its naturalistic context, valuing its particularity, complexity and relationships with the context. This approach uses multiple methods and perspectives to look at the case (or several cases) holistically.

Chiasm: Research methodology combining together an insider perspective (emic) with an outsider perspective (etic) or perspectives in a systematic way such that these are in dialogue with each other. It also refers to the dialogic tension between figure and ground in interpretation of texts such that the meaning of a word or short utterance in the text is in dialogue with an (often quantitative) analysis of the structure of the text as a whole.

Close-to-practice research: Research that focuses on issues defined by practitioners as relevant to their practice, and that involves collaboration between people whose main expertise is research, practice or both.

Coding/coding scheme: A system of labels and symbols used to represent themes and concepts in the analysis of spoken, written and visual texts.

Community of inquiry/enquiry: An approach grounded in Dewey's work on reflective inquiry as a social activity, incorporating elements of cognitive and social 'presence' in learning, teaching and research interactions.

Conceptual framework: A representation of the central theoretical ideas and **constructs**, or the key elements of activity in the research site, that serves to focus and guide study design.

Concordance/concordancers: A concordancer is a computer program that automatically constructs a concordance: an alphabetical list of all the words used in a text. Concordance software enables rapid access to where words appear in a text, calculation of their frequencies and exploration of links.

Confounding variables/confounds: Factors and processes that are not accounted for in the research design and data analysis, and that may have a 'hidden' influence that could limit or bias the research conclusions.

Construct: The factors, attributes and characteristics that we want to investigate, and sometimes measure. Constructs may be complex and require clear definition: for example, 'achievement', 'proficiency', 'attitude', 'motivation' and so on.

Construct under-representation: Critical aspects of the construct that are not sampled in the assessment

Conversation/al analysis: An approach for studying in detail audio-/video-recorded social interaction and conversation, paying particular attention to how the conversation works in terms of turn taking, sequences and communicative functions in the given context.

Correlational design: A research design that seeks to discover the relationship or correspondence between two variables, factors or processes, without inferring any causal direction. Statistical data analysis may indicate a positive correlation, negative correlation or no correlation.

Critical event/incident analysis: A method to focus the researcher on a critical incident or turning point (defined using specific criteria), exploring people's behaviour and experience before, during and after the incident to analyse its meaning for those involved.

Data mining: An automated computer process of exploring patterns, trends and relationships in large data sets.

Deductive/deduction: Relating to the 'top-down' analysis of data that are based on theoretical understanding and existing concepts.

Descriptive statistics: The use of numerical strategies to count phenomena of interest (e.g. length of utterance) and represent these data in terms of their frequencies, proportions, averages and so on, often using charts and similar visual devices.

Design-based research: In education this is the systematic study of designing, implementing and evaluating educational interventions with a view not only to solving a problem but also to advancing knowledge about the characteristics of the interventions and how to improve them.

Dialogue mapping: Providing a visual representation of a conversation, using a diagram to show who speaks to whom as the conversation unfolds.

Discourse analysis: A term given to various approaches to the analysis of texts (spoken, verbal or written), which communicate something of what is taken for granted in the social situation. Different models of discourse analysis may represent different understanding of language in use in different contexts.

Emic: An approach to understanding particular and local ways of thinking, knowledge and culture, often associated with an 'insider' research orientation.

Episode: A defined period of dialogue (substantial sequence of exchanges) identified for analysis.

Epistemic network analysis (ENA): An approach that offers tools for exploring the sequential patterns in classroom dialogue, or other texts, using the open-source tool nCoder.[1] See also **quantitative ethnography.**

Epistemology/epistemological stance: Relating to the theory of knowledge, including beliefs about the nature, formation and justification of knowledge.

Ethnographic/ethnography: A research approach aimed at understanding an insider perspective on a particular community, practice or setting by focusing on the meaning of social action from the point of view of the participants. Methods of progressively focused observation, interview and diary are typically used by the researcher who is immersed in the situation, generating complex, detailed data to enable deep descriptions and theorization of the cultural context.

Etic: An approach to understanding general ways of thinking, knowledge and culture, often associated with the outsider perspective of an external researcher.

Fidelity: The extent to which an intervention is delivered as designed and intended by researchers and practitioners.

Focus group: A group interview method in which participants are invited to explore a given topic in a group discussion. Participants respond to each other, to activities or stimuli rather than just to the researcher's questions; they co-construct their responses. The researcher facilitates rather than directs.

Granularity: The size of a unit of analysis or level of description of a **coding** scheme.

Holistic judgement: An assessment of the overall level of quality of a piece of evidence, for example, an essay or a performance.

Inductive/Induction: Relating to the 'bottom-up' analysis of data, based initially on the open-ended identification of patterns in the data.

Inference: A conclusion reached on the basis of evidence and reasoning.

---

[1] The nCoder web tool is available at www.epistemicanalytics.org.

Inferential statistics: The use of numerical strategies both to describe data (descriptive statistics) and to go beyond these data in order to make inferences about the probability that the findings apply to a wider population. This commonly involves calculating the likelihood that differences could have occurred by chance.

Interpretative narrative: Integrating the outcomes from, and across, different analyses through an analytic commentary that offers an account of what happened and why.

Keyword analysis: Counting the relative frequencies of occurrence of particular words or patterns of language use across a data set or in data subsets (see also concordance).

Linguistic ethnography: A research approach to studying language, culture and identity that combines linguistic and ethnographic approaches in order to investigate how people communicate and act in particular situations in relation to wider social and cultural contexts and structures. It has connections to 'linguistic anthropology' developed in the United States.

Log-likelihood: A statistical measure of probability used in analysing patterns in texts. The higher the log-likelihood is, the less likely it is that the result is random.

Machine learning: A computer software programme that has the ability to automatically 'learn' and improve from experience (e.g. to code questions or dialogue) without being explicitly programmed.

Macro-analytic approach: Focusing analysis on the main event and context of interest (e.g. a lesson or lesson sequence).

Meso-analytic approach: Focusing analysis on the level at which ideas are exchanged, sequences of talk developed and/or topics are considered with a given episode.

Micro-analytic approach: Focusing analysis at the level of conversational utterances and turns, or grammatical features like clauses and sentences.

Micro-ethnographic approach: An approach to understanding a particular community, practice or setting (see ethnography) that gives particular attention to detailed observation and analysis of communicative behaviour and interactions in the given context.

Mixed methods approach: An approach to research design that combines methods and data to answer single or multiple research questions. This commonly involves the combination of qualitative and quantitative data generated from methods used in parallel or sequentially.

Multi-voice analysis/multi-voiced analysis: A set of approaches, based on dialogic theory, used to identify and analyse the ways in which the self and others are constituted as multiple voices in dialogue.

Multilevel modelling: Statistical **regression** modelling of parameters that have several, hierarchical levels; for example, students are nested within classrooms in schools.

Multiple regression analysis: An approach to modelling the relationship between two or more explanatory variables and a response variable by fitting a linear equation to observed data. Every value of the independent variable x is associated with a value of the dependent variable y.

Observer effects: Processes by which the act of observing may change what is being observed, either through the effects of using certain observation instruments (e.g. in physics) or by people's reactions to being observed in educational and social settings.

Ontological: Relating to the nature of being – that is, what sort of 'thing' or process is being discussed and the degree to which reality is 'out there' or constructed.

Participatory action research: A research process that actively involves those being researched or implicated in the research in the decision-making and conduct of the research itself. This is often seen as a means towards social action and improvement.

Pre- and post-test design: A design measuring change (e.g. development of practice or learning gains) by testing the same participants before and after an intervention using similar or the same measures.

Qualitative data analysis: The processes and procedures for identifying and interpreting patterns in qualitative (non-numerical) data and moving towards some form of account, understanding and possible explanation of the phenomena being researched.

Quantitative data analysis: The descriptive calculation of frequencies, or use of **inferential statistical** tests to analyse numerical data, aiming to understand relationships or differences between variables.

Quantitative ethnography: An approach that integrates in-depth, qualitative analysis with statistical tools to handle large data sets.

Specifically, it models the connections made by each participant between ideas (Shaffer, 2017). See also **epistemic network analysis.**

Quasi-experimental trials: Research that compares **pre- and post-test** results for interventions with different groups of participants, or the same group over time, usually taking place in 'real-life' settings where the random allocation of participants is not possible or appropriate. Close attention must therefore be given to potentially **confounding variables.**

Rating scale: A framework for recording the occurrence of patterns of observable behaviour and talk, based on a set of pre-existing categories that usually indicate 'how much' or 'how well' something is happening.

Raven's progressive matrices test: An extensively used standardized test that involves the completion of visual matrix patterns. This was originally designed as a non-verbal test of intelligence, with claims to be 'culture-fair' (although this has since been critically debated).

Real-world research: Applied research that focuses on personal experience in the context of social life and systems. It aims to understand the 'lived-in reality' of people in society and its consequences, often with a view to changing the situation (Robson & McCartan, 2016).

Reflective dialogue: Reflection on practice and pedagogical strategies through dialogic discussion with colleagues and/or others.

Regression analyses: Statistical processes for modelling and estimating relationships between variables and understanding which among the pre-existing and often uncontrollable independent variables (e.g. age) are related to the dependent variable, namely the target variable being measured (e.g. learning outcomes).

Relevance: The extent to which research focuses on investigating clearly defined, important and representative aspects of educational practice.

Reliability (inter-coder): The degree of match between coders working independently on the same data; usually measured using a statistical technique such as Cohen's kappa or Krippendorf's alpha.

Reliability (test): The accuracy and dependency of scores or judgements.

Segmentation: Division of data into defined **units of analysis** using consistent criteria such as number of turns or change of activity.

Sequential analysis: Focusing analysis on chains of interaction moves, commonly using a computer programme. 'Lag sequential analysis' calculates the probabilities of certain moves following other moves.

Social network analysis: Production of an adjacency matrix of turns connecting speakers (sociogram), showing frequency and sequence of communication, individual roles and team cohesion.

Sociocultural discourse analysis (SDA): An approach that combines qualitative and quantitative data to investigate the content and function of spoken language as shared understanding is developed in social context over time, supported by the use of new technologies to analyse large quantities of data.

Stimulated recall interview: In which participants are asked to revisit and articulate their thinking and actions from an earlier activity, using selected stimuli such as a video clip or written work.

Student voice: A perspective in research that gives weight to eliciting students' views on different aspects of education, using a range of methods based on talk, writing, visual expression and so on.

Systematic observation: A method of recording behavioural events, typically in classrooms, from direct observations using a predetermined set of categories and generating quantitative data.

Thematic analysis: Systematic exploration of patterns or "themes" within qualitative data (typically from interviews or observations) in order to describe or understand a phenomenon. Analysis may be **inductive, deductive, abductive** or a mixture.

Think-aloud protocols/methods: A range of methods and procedures developed in order to learn more about the thinking that underlies observable verbal and non-verbal interaction, thus enabling researchers (and participants) to access participants' introspective mental processes.

Time sampling: Observations made at specific time intervals during the interactions of interest, for example, recording all instances of a behaviour within a 1-minute window out of every 5 minutes.

Unit of analysis: The individual or combined focus and level at which data are generated and analysed in order to investigate and understand the phenomenon in question, for example, a turn in the dialogue, a short sequence of turns or a longer episode.

Validation: The process of determining the quality of a research or assessment process.

Validity (research): The extent to which the design and methodology of a piece of research allows us to make claims about what is being researched.

Validity (measurement): The extent to which an assessment measures the construct that it is intended to measure and appropriate inferences can be made from the results.

BIBLIOGRAPHY

Adderley, R. J., Hope, M. A., Hughes, G. C., Jones, L., Messiou, K., & Shaw, P. A. (2015). Exploring inclusive practices in primary schools: Focusing on children's voices. *European Journal of Special Needs Education*, *30*(1), 106–21.

Ahmad, A. K., Gjøtterud, S., & Krogh, E. (2016). Dialogue conferences and empowerment: Transforming primary education in Tanzania through cooperation. *Educational Action Research*, *24*(2), 300–16.

Ahmed, A., & Johnson, R. (in preparation). *Developing a Dialogue-based Assessment of Students' Collaborative Problem Solving Skills*.

Ahmed, A., & Pollitt, A. (2010). The support model for interactive assessment. *Assessment in Education: Principles, Policy and Practice*, *17*(2), 133–67.

Åkerblom, D., & Lindahl, M. (2017). Authenticity and the relevance of discourse and figured worlds in secondary students' discussions of socioscientific issues. *Teaching and Teacher Education*, *65*, 205–14.

Alexander, R. J. (2008). *Towards Dialogic Teaching. Rethinking Classroom Talk* (4th edn). Cambridge: Dialogos UK, http://www.robinalexander.org.uk/dialogos.htm.

Amenduni, F., & Ligorio, M. B. (2017). Becoming at the borders: The role of positioning in boundary-crossing between university and workplaces. *Cultural-Historical Psychology*, *13*(1), 89–104.

Anderson, T., Liam, R., Garrison, D. R., & Archer, W. (2001). Assessing teaching presence in a computer conferencing context. *Journal of Asynchronous Learning Networks*, *5*(2), 1–17.

Aubert, A., Molina, S., Schubert, T., & Vidu, A. (2017). Learning and inclusivity via Interactive Groups in early childhood education and care in the Hope school, Spain. *Learning, Culture and Social Interaction*, *13*, 90–103.

Aveling, E-L., Gillespie. A., & Cornish, F. (2015). A qualitative method for analysing multivoicedness. *Qualitative Research*, *15*(6), 670–87.

Axelrod, R. (1997). *The Complexity of Cooperation: Agent-based Models of Competition and Collaboration*. Princeton, NJ: Princeton University Press.

Azmitia, M., & Montgomery, R. (1993). Friendship, transactive dialogues, and the development of scientific reasoning. *Social Development*, 2(3), 202–21.

Baines, E., Rubie-Davies, C., & Blatchford, P. (2009). Improving pupil group work interaction and dialogue in primary classrooms: Results from a year-long intervention study. *Cambridge Journal of Education*, 39(1), 95–117.

Baird, J-A., Andrich, D., Hopfenbeck, T. N., & Stobart, G. (2017). Assessment and learning: Fields apart? *Assessment in Education: Principles, Policy and Practice*, 24(3), 317–50.

Bakhtin, M. M. (1981). *The Dialogic Imagination*. Austin: University of Texas Press.

Bakhtin, M. M. (1984). *Problems of Dostoevsky's Poetics* (C. Emerson, Ed. and Trans.). Minneapolis: University of Minnesota Press.

Bakhtin, M. M. (1986). *Speech Genres and Other Late Essays*. Austin: University of Texas Press.

Bakker, A. (2018). *Design Research in Education: A Practical Guide for Early Career Researchers*. London: Routledge.

Bakker, A., Smit, J., & Wegerif, R. (2015). Scaffolding and dialogic teaching in mathematics education: Introduction and review. *ZDM*, 47(7), 1047–65.

Barnes, D. (1976). *From Communication to Curriculum*. Portsmouth: Boynton/Cook-Heinemann.

Barnett-Page, E., & Thomas, J. (2009). Methods for the synthesis of qualitative research: A critical review. *BMC Medical Research Methodology*, 9(59). doi:10.1186/1471-2288-9-59.

Baroutsis, A., Mills, M., McGregor, G., te Riele, K., & Hayes, D. (2016). Student voice and the community forum: Finding ways of 'being heard' at an alternative school for disenfranchised young people. *British Educational Research Journal*, 42(3), 438–53.

Baskerville, D. (2011). Developing cohesion and building positive relationships through storytelling in a culturally diverse New Zealand classroom. *Teaching and Teacher Education*, 27, 107–15.

Bayard, P. (2007). *How to Talk about Books You Haven't Read* (J. Mehlman, Trans.). London: Bloomsbury.

Beauchamp, G., Joyce-Gibbons, A., McNaughton, J., Young, N., & Crick, T. (2019). Exploring synchronous, remote collaborative interaction between learners using multi-touch tables in UK primary schools. *British Journal of Educational Technology* (published online). https://doi.org/10.1111/bjet.12728.

Becker, H. S. (2007). *Writing for Social Scientists: How to Start and Finish Your Thesis, Book, or Article* (2nd edn). Chicago, IL: University of Chicago Press.

Berkowitz, M. W., & Gibbs, J. C. (1983). Measuring the developmental features of moral discussion. *Merrill-Palmer Quarterly, 29*(4), 399–410.

Bertau, M.-C. (2011). Language for the other: Constructing cultural–historical psycholinguistics. *Tätigkeitstheorie: E-Journal for Activity Theoretical Research in Germany, 5*, 13–44.

Besley, T., & Peters, M. A. (2012). Introduction: Interculturalism, education and dialogue. In T. Besley & M. A. Peters (Eds), *Interculturalism, Education and Dialogue* (pp. 1–25). New York: Peter Lang.

Bialostocka, O. (2017). Dialogic education as an approach to multiculturalism for social cohesion in Namibia. *Globalisation, Societies and Education, 15*(2), 271–81.

Bilmes, J. (1993). Ethnomethodology, culture, and implicature. *Pragmatics. Quarterly Publication of the International Pragmatics Association, 3*(4), 387–409.

Black, P. (2015). Formative assessment – an optimistic but incomplete vision. *Assessment in Education: Principles, Policy and Practice, 22*(1), 161–77.

Boyd, M. P., & Markarian, W. C. (2015). Dialogic teaching and dialogic stance: moving beyond interactional form. *Research in the Teaching of English, 49*(3), 272–96.

British Educational Research Association [BERA] (2018a). Ethical Guidelines for Educational Research, (4th edn). London. Retrieved from https://www.bera.ac.uk/researchers-resources/publications/ethical-guidelines-for-educational-research-2018.

British Educational Research Association [BERA] (2018b). BERA Statement on close-to-practice research. Retrieved from https://www.bera.ac.uk/researchers-resources/publications/bera-statement-on-close-to-practice-research.

Brophy, J. E., & Good, T. L. (1970). Teachers' communication of differential expectations for children's classroom performance: Some behavioral data. *Journal of Educational Psychology, 61*(5), 365–74.

Brown, K., & Kennedy, H. (2011). Learning through conversation: Exploring and extending teacher and children's involvement in classroom talk. *School Psychology International, 32*(4), 377–96.

Brown, V. A. (2010). Collective inquiry and its wicked problems. In V. A. Brown, J. A. Harris & J. Y. Russell (Eds), *Tackling Wicked Problems: Through the Transdisciplinary Imagination* (pp. 61–83). London: Earthscan Publications.

Buber, M. (1958). *I and Thou* (R. Gregory Smith, Trans.). Edinburgh: T & T Clark. (Original work published in 1923.)

Burbules, N. (1993). *Dialogue and Teaching: Theory and Practice.* New York: Teachers College Press.

Cain, T., & Allan, D. (2017). The invisible impact of educational research. *Oxford Review of Education, 43*(6), 718–32.

Caldwell, H., & Heaton, R. (2016). The interdisciplinary use of blogs and online communities in teacher education. *The International Journal of Information and Learning Technology. 33*(3), 142–58.

Cameron, C., & Moss, P. (Eds) (2011). *Social Pedagogy and Working with Young People: Where Care and Education Meet.* London: Jessica Kingsley.

Carter, R. (1999). Common language: corpus, creativity and cognition. *Language and Literature, 8*(3), 195–216.

Carter, R. (2015). *Language and Creativity: The Art of Common Talk.* Abingdon: Routledge.

Cassidy, C., Marwick, H., Deeney, L., & McLean, G. (2018). Philosophy with children, self-regulation and engaged participation for children with emotional-behavioural and social communication needs. *Emotional and Behavioural Difficulties, 23*(1), 81–96.

Cassidy, C., Conrad S.-J., & José de Figueiroa-Rego, M. (2019). Research with children: A philosophical, rights-based approach. *International Journal of Research & Method in Education,* doi: 10.1080/1743727X.2018.1563063.

Casti, J. (1997). *Would Be Worlds.* New York: Wiley.

CEDiR Group (2018). *A dialogue about educational dialogue: Reflections on the field and the work of the Cambridge Educational Dialogue Research (CEDiR) group.* Faculty of Education Working Paper 2018/4, University of Cambridge. Retrieved from http://bit.ly/cedirWP.

Chapin, S. O'Connor, C., & Anderson, N. (2009). *Classroom Discussions: Using Math Talk to Help Students Learn, Grades 1–6.* Sausalito, CA: Math Solutions.

Clark-Polner, E., & Clark, M. S. (2014). Understanding and accounting for relational context is critical for social neuroscience. *Frontiers in Human Neuroscience, 8,* 127.

Clarke, D., & Hollingsworth, H. (2002). Elaborating a model of teacher professional growth. *Teaching and Teacher Education, 18,* 947–67.

Clarke, S. N. (2015). The right to speak. In L. B. Resnick, C. S. C. Asterhan & S. N. Clarke (Eds), *Socializing Intelligence through Academic Talk and Dialogue* (pp. 167–80). Washington, DC: American Educational Research Association.

Clarke, S. N., Howley, I., Resnick, L. B., & Rosé, C. P. (2016). Student agency to participate in dialogic science discussions. *Learning, Culture and Social Interaction, 10,* 27–39.

Clarke, S. N., Resnick, L. B., & Rosé, C. P. (2016). Dialogic instruction: A new frontier. In L. Corno & E. Anderman (Eds), *Third Handbook of Educational Psychology*. New York: Routledge.

Cole, M. (1996). *Cultural Psychology: A Once and Future Discipline*. Cambridge: Harvard University Press.

Cole, M. A. (1994). A conception of culture for a communication theory of mind. In D. R. Vocate (Ed.), *Intrapersonal Communication: Different Voices, different minds*. Hillsdale, NJ: Erlbaum.

Cook-Sather, A. (2017). Virtual forms, actual effects: How amplifying student voice through digital media promotes reflective practice and positions students as pedagogical partners to prospective high school and practicing college teachers. *British Journal of Educational Technology, 48*(5), 1143–52.

Cooper, S. (2014). Putting collective reflective dialogue at the heart of the evaluation process. *Reflective Practice, 15*(5), 563–78.

Copland, F., & Creese, A. (2015). *Linguistic Ethnography: Collecting, Analysing and Presenting Data*. London: Sage.

Cornelissen, F., McLellan, R. W., & Schofield, J. (2017). Fostering research engagement in partnership schools: networking and value creation. *Oxford Review of Education, 43*(6), 695–717.

Correa-Chávez, M. (2016). Cultural patterns of collaboration and communication while working together among U.S. Mexican heritage children. *Learning, Culture and Social Interaction, 11*, 130–41.

Correnti, R., Stein, M. K., Smith, M., Scherrer, J., McKeown, M., Greeno, J., & Ashley, K. (2015). Improving teaching at scale: Design for the scientific measurement and learning of discourse practice. In L. B. Resnick, C. S. C. Asterhan & S. N. Clarke (Eds), *Socializing Intelligence through Academic Talk and Dialogue* (pp. 315–32). Washington, DC: American Educational Research Association.

Council of Europe. (2001). *Common European Framework of Reference for Languages: Learning, Teaching, Assessment*. Cambridge, UK: Press Syndicate of the University of Cambridge.

Cowan, K. (2014). Multimodal transcription of video: Examining interaction in Early Years classrooms. *Classroom Discourse, 5*(1), 6–21.

Cremin, H., & Bevington, T. (2017). *Positive Peace in Schools: Tackling Conflict and Creating a Culture of Peace in the Classroom*. London: Routledge.

Crook, C. (1994). *Computers and the Collaborative Experience of Learning*. London: Routledge.

Crossley, N. (1996). *Intersubjectivity: The Fabric of Social Becoming*. London: Sage.

Csanadi, A., Eagan, B., Kollar, I., Shaffer, D. W., & Fisher, F. (2018). When coding-and-counting is not enough: Using epistemic network analysis (ENA) to analyze verbal data in CSCL research. *International Journal of Computer-Supported Collaborative Learning, 13*(4), 419–38.

Dann, R. (2014). Assessment as learning: Blurring the boundaries of assessment and learning for theory, policy and practice. *Assessment in Education: Principles, Policy and Practice, 21*(2), 149–66.

Dann, R. (2017). *Developing Feedback for Pupil Learning: Teaching, Learning and Assessment in Schools.* London: Routledge.

Dawes, L. (2011). *Talking Points: Discussion Activities in the Primary Classroom.* London: Routledge.

Dawes, L., Mercer, N., & Wegerif, R. (2000). *Thinking Together: A Programme of Activities for Developing Thinking Skills at KS2.* Questions Publishing Company.

Delahunty, J., Verenikina, I., & Jones, P. (2014). Socio-emotional connections: Identity, belonging and learning in online interactions. A literature review. *Technology, Pedagogy and Education, 23*(2), 243–65.

Derrida, J. (1982). *Margins of Philosophy.* Chicago, IL: University of Chicago Press.

Djohari, N., & Higham, R. (submitted) *Peer-led Focus Groups as 'Dialogic Spaces' for Exploring Young People's Evolving Values.* Manuscript submitted for publication.

Drew, P., Raymond, G., & Weinberg, D. (2006). *Talk and Interaction in Social Research Methods.* London: Sage.

Dudley, P. (2013). Teacher learning in Lesson Study: What interaction-level discourse analysis revealed about how teachers utilised imagination, tacit knowledge of teaching and fresh evidence of pupils learning, to develop practice knowledge and so enhance their pupils' learning. *Teaching and Teacher Education, 34*, 107–21.

Dunbar, K. (1997). How scientists think: On-line creativity and conceptual change in science. In T. B. Ward, S. M. Smith & J. Vaid (Eds), *Creative Thought: An Investigation of Conceptual Structures and Processes* (pp. 461–93). Washington, DC: American Psychological Association.

Dunning, T. (1993). Accurate methods for the statistics of surprise and coincidence. *Computational Linguistics, 19*(1), 61–74.

Durrant, P., & Schmitt, N. (2010). Adult learners' retention of collocations from exposure. *Second Language Research, 26*(2), 163–88.

Eagan, B. R., Rogers, R., Serlin, R., Ruis, A. R., Irgens, G. A., & Shaffer, D. W. (2017). *Can we rely on IRR? Testing the assumptions of inter-rater reliability.* Paper presented at International Conference on Computer Supported Collaborative Learning, Philadelphia.

Edmonds, B., & Meyer, R. (2015). *Simulating Social Complexity.* Berlin: Springer-Verlag.

Elfer, P. (2017). Subtle emotional processes in early childhood pedagogy: Evaluating the contribution of the Tavistock Observation Method. *Pedagogy, Culture and Society, 25*(3), 431–45.

Engin, M. (2017). Contributions and silence in academic talk: Exploring learner experiences of dialogic interaction. *Learning, Culture and Social Interaction, 12*, 78–86.

Erduran, S., Ozdem, Y., & Park, J.-Y. (2015). Research trends on argumentation in science education: A journal content analysis from 1998–2014. *International Journal of STEM Education, 2*(5), 1–12.

Ericsson, K., & Simon, H. (1993). *Protocol Analysis: Verbal Reports as Data* (2nd edn). Cambridge, MA: MIT Press.

Espasa, A., Guasch, T., Mayordomo, R. M., Martinez-Melo, M., & Carless, D. (2018). A Dialogic Feedback Index measuring key aspects of feedback processes in online learning environments. *Higher Education Research and Development, 37*(3), 499–513.

Fayette, R., & Bond, C. (2018). A systematic literature review of qualitative research methods for eliciting the views of young people with ASD about their educational experiences. *European Journal of Special Needs Education, 33*(3), 349–65.

Ferguson, R. (2012). Learning analytics: Drivers, developments and challenges. *International Journal of Technology Enhanced Learning, 4*(5/6), 304–17.

Fernández-Cárdenas, J. M., & Silveyra-De La Garza, M. L. (2010). Disciplinary knowledge and gesturing in communicative events: A comparative study between lessons using interactive whiteboards and traditional whiteboards in Mexican schools. *Technology, Pedagogy and Education, 19*(2), 173–93.

Fernández, M., Wegerif, R., Mercer, N., & Rojas-Drummond, S. (2001). Re-conceptualizing 'scaffolding' and the zone of proximal development in the context of symmetrical collaborative learning. *Journal of Classroom Interaction, 36/37* (2/1), 40–54.

Fernyhough, C. (1996). The dialogic mind: A dialogic approach to the higher mental functions. *New Ideas in Psychology, 14*, 47–62.

Fisher, E. (1993). Distinctive features of pupil-pupil classroom talk and their relationship to learning: How discursive exploration might be encouraged. *Language and Education, 7*(4), 239–57.

Fishman, E. J., Borko, H., Osborne, J., Gomez, F., Rafanelli, S., Reigh, E., Tseng, A., Million, S., & Berson, E. (2017). A practice-based professional development program to support scientific argumentation from evidence in the elementary classroom. *Journal of Science Teacher Education, 28*(3), 222–49.

Flecha, R. (2000). *Sharing Words: Theory and Practice of Dialogic Learning.* Lanham, MD: Rowman & Littlefield.

Flecha, R., & Soler, M. (2013). Turning difficulties into possibilities: Engaging Roma families and students in school through dialogic learning. *Cambridge Journal of Education, 43*(4), 451–65.

Floriani, A. (1993). Negotiating what counts: Roles and relationships, texts and contexts, content and meaning. *Linguistics and Education, 5*(3/4), 241–74.

Flutter, J., & Rudduck, J. (2004). *Consulting Pupils: What's in It for Schools?* London: RoutledgeFalmer.

Forsberg, C., Wood, L., Smith, J., Varjas, K., Meyers, J., Jungert, T., & Thornberg, R. (2018). Students' views of factors affecting their bystander behaviors in response to school bullying: A cross-collaborative conceptual qualitative analysis. *Research Papers in Education, 33*(1), 127–42.

Foucault, M. (1972). *The Archaeology of Knowledge* (A. M. Sheridan Smith, Trans.). London: Tavistock.

Freire, P. (1971). *Pedagogy of the Oppressed.* New York: Seabury Press.

Fricker, M. (2007). *Epistemic Injustice: Power and the Ethics of Knowing.* Oxford: Oxford University Press.

Friedman, M. (2001). Martin Buber and Mikhail Bakhtin: The dialogue of voices and the word that is spoken. *Religion & Literature, 33*(3), 25–36.

Fukkink, R. G., & Tavecchio, L. W. C. (2010). Effects of Video Interaction Guidance on early childhood teachers. *Teaching and Teacher Education 26,* 1652–9.

Fukuyama, F. (1995). *Trust: The Social Virtues and the Creation of Prosperity.* New York: Free Press.

Galaczi, E. (2008). Peer–peer interaction in a speaking test: The case of the First Certificate in English examination. *Language Assessment Quarterly, 5*(2), 89–119.

Galaczi, E. (2013). Interactional competence across proficiency levels: How do learners manage interaction in paired speaking tests? *Applied Linguistics, 35*(5), 553–74.

Gay, G. (2010). *Culturally Responsive Teaching: Theory, Research and Practice.* New York: Teachers College Press.

Gee, J. P. (2011). *An Introduction to Discourse Analysis – Theory and Method* (3rd edn). New York: Routledge.

Gee, J. P., & Green, J. (1998). Discourse analysis, learning and social practice. *Review of Research in Education, 23,* 119–69.

Gibson, E. J. (1982). The concept of affordances in development: The renascence of functionalism. In W. A. Collins (Ed.), *The Concept of Development: The Minnesota Symposia on Child Psychology*, volume 15 (pp. 55–81). Hillsdale, NJ: Lawrence Erlbaum.

Gibson, J. J. (1979). *The Ecological Approach to Visual Perception*. Boston, MA: Houghton Mifflin.

Gill, S., & Niens, U. (2014). Education as humanisation: A theoretical review on the role of dialogic pedagogy in peacebuilding education. *Compare: A Journal of Comparative and International Education*, *44*(1), 10–31.

GL Assessment (2013). *PASS: Pupil Attitudes to Self and School*. London: GL Assessment.

Glaser, B. G., & Strauss, L. L. (1967). *The Discovery of Grounded Theory: Strategies for Qualitative Research*. Chicago, IL: Aldine.

Gobbo, F. (2012). Intercultural dialogue and ethnography: On learning about diversity in Italian multicultural classrooms. In T. Besley & M. A. Peters (Eds), *Interculturalism, Education and Dialogue* (pp. 224–36). Oxford: Peter Lang.

Goodwin, C. (2007). Environmentally coupled gestures. In S. D. Duncan, J. Cassell & E. T. Levy (Eds), *Gesture and the Dynamic Dimension of Language* (pp. 195–212). Amsterdam: John Benjamins.

Goody, J., & Goody, J. R. (1977). *The Domestication of the Savage Mind*. Cambridge: Cambridge University Press.

Goos, M., Galbraith, P., & Renshaw, P. (2002). Socially mediated metacognition: Creating collaborative zones of proximal development in small group problem solving. *Educational Studies in Mathematics*, *49*, 193–223.

Gough, D., Thomas, J., & Oliver, S. (2012). Clarifying differences between review designs and methods. *Systematic Reviews*, *1*, 28.

Graesser, A., Dowell, N., & Clewley, D. (2017). Assessing collaborative problem solving through conversational agents. In A. A. Von Davier, M. Zhu & P. C. Kyllonen (Eds), *Innovative Assessment of Collaboration*. New York: Springer.

Greeno, J. G. (2016). Classroom talk sequences and learning. In L. B. Resnick, C. S. C. Asterhan & S. N. Clarke (Eds), *Socializing Intelligence through Academic Talk and Dialogue* (pp. 255–62). Washington, DC: American Educational Research Association.

Grice, H. P. (1975). Logic and conversation. In P. Cole & J. Morgan (Eds), *Speech Acts [Syntax and Semantics 3]*. New York: Academic Press.

Gröschner, A., Seidel, T., Kiemer, K., & Pehmer, A.-K. (2015). Through the lens of teacher professional development components: The 'Dialogic Video Cycle' as an innovative program to foster classroom dialogue. *Professional Development in Education*, *41*(4), 729–56.

Gröschner, A., Seidel, T., Pehmer, A. K., & Kiemer, K. (2014). Facilitating collaborative teacher learning: The role of 'mindfulness' in video-based teacher professional development programs. *Gruppendynamik und Organisationsberatung, 45*(3), 273–90.

Gunawardena, C. N., Flor, N. V., Gómez, D., & Sánchez, D. (2016). Analyzing social construction of knowledge online by employing interaction analysis, learning analytics, and social network analysis. *Quarterly Review of Distance Education, 17*(3), 35.

Gweon, G., Jain, M., Mc Donough, J., Raj, B., & Rosé, C. P. (2013). Measuring prevalence of other-oriented transactive contributions using an automated measure of speech style accommodation. *International Journal of Computer Supported Collaborative Learning, 8*(2), 245–65.

Habermas, J. (1979). What is universal pragmatics? In J. Habermas, *Communication and the Evolution of Society* (T. McCarthy, Trans.). Cambridge: Polity.

Habermas, J. (1984). *The Theory of Communicative Action, Volume 1: Reason and the Rationalization of Society* (T. McCarthy, Trans.). Cambridge: Polity.

Hakkarainen, K., & Paavola, S. (2007). *From Monological and Dialogical to Trialogical Approaches to Learning*. Paper presented at the international workshop 'Guided Construction of Knowledge in Classrooms'. Retrieved from http://escalate.org.il/construction_knowledge/papers/hakkarainen.pdf.

Hammersley, M. (1992). *What's Wrong with Ethnography*. London: Routledge.

Harlen, W. (2006). The relationship between assessment for formative and summative purposes. In J. Gardner (Ed.), *Assessment and Learning*. London: Sage.

Harsch, C., & Martin, G. (2013). Comparing holistic and analytic scoring methods: Issues of validity and reliability. *Assessment in Education: Principles, Policy and Practice, 20*(3), 281–307.

Harvey, L. (2015). Beyond member-checking: A dialogic approach to the research interview. *International Journal of Research & Method in Education, 38*(1), 23–38.

Hattie, J. (2012). *Visible Learning for Teachers: Maximizing Impact on Learning*. London: Routledge.

Havnes, A. (2009). Talk, planning and decision-making in interdisciplinary teacher teams: A case study. *Teachers and Teaching: Theory and Practice, 15*(1), 155–76.

Haynes, F. (2018). Trust and the community of inquiry. *Educational Philosophy and Theory, 50*(2), 144–51.

Hedges, H., & Cooper, M. (2017). Collaborative meaning-making using video footage: Teachers and researchers analyse children's working theories about friendship. *European Early Childhood Education Research Journal, 25*(3), 398–411.

Helgevold, N. (2016). Teaching as creating space for participation – establishing a learning community in diverse classrooms. *Teachers and Teaching, 22*(3), 315–28.

Hennessy, S. (2011). The role of digital artefacts on the interactive whiteboard in mediating dialogic teaching and learning. *Journal of Computer Assisted Learning, 27*(6), 463–586.

Hennessy, S. (2014). *Bridging between Research and Practice: Supporting Professional Development through Collaborative Studies of Classroom Teaching with Interactive Whiteboard Technology.* Rotterdam: Sense.

Hennessy, S., & Deaney, R. (2009). 'Intermediate theory' building: Integrating multiple teacher and researcher perspectives through in-depth video analysis of pedagogic strategies. *Teachers College Record, 111*(7), 1753–95.

Hennessy, S., Dragovic, T., & Warwick, P. (2018). A research-informed, school-based professional development workshop programme to promote dialogic teaching with interactive technologies. *Professional Development in Education, 44*(2), 145–68.

Hennessy, S., Rojas-Drummond, S., Higham, R., Márquez, A. M., Maine, F., Ríos, R. M., (...) Barrera, M. J. (2016). Developing a coding scheme for analysing classroom dialogue across educational contexts. *Learning, Culture and Social Interaction, 9*, 16–44.

Hennessy, S., Warwick, P., & Mercer, N. (2011). A dialogic inquiry approach to working with teachers in developing classroom dialogue. *Teachers College Record, 113*(9), 1906–59.

Hewitt, A. (2008). Children's creative collaboration during a computer-based music task. *International Journal of Educational Research, 47*(1), 11–26.

Higham R. (2018). 'To be is to respond': Realising a dialogic ontology for Deweyan pragmatism. *Journal of Philosophy of Education, 52*, 2.

Hilliard, D. (2013). Exploring the links between dialogic interaction and written argumentation in A level History (16–19 years old): A design-based PhD research study. In T. Plomp & N. Nieveen (Eds), *Educational Design Research – Part B: Illustrative Cases* (pp. 555–79). Enschede, the Netherlands: SLO.

Hine, C. (2000). *Virtual Ethnography.* London: Sage.

Hjörne, E., & Säljö, R. (2014). Analysing and preventing school failure: Exploring the role of multi-professionality in pupil health team meetings. *International Journal of Educational Research, 63*, 5–14.

Holbraad, M., & Pedersen, M. A. (2017). *The Ontological Turn: An Anthropological Exposition.* Cambridge: Cambridge University Press.

Hoffman, D. (2009). Reflecting on social emotional learning: A critical perspective on trends in the United States. *Review of Educational Research, 79,* 533–56.

Hofmann, R., & Ruthven, K. (2018). Operational, interpersonal, discussional and ideational dimensions of classroom norms for dialogic practice in school mathematics. *British Educational Research Journal, 44*(3), 496–514.

Horkheimer, M., & Adorno, T. W. (2002). *Dialectic of Enlightenment.* Stanford, CA: Stanford University Press.

Howe, A. (1991). *Making Talk Work.* NATE Papers in Education. London: National Association for the Teaching of English.

Howe, C. (2009). Collaborative group work in middle childhood. *Human Development, 52*(4), 215–39.

Howe, C., & Abedin, M. (2013) Classroom dialogue: A systematic review across four decades of research. *Cambridge Journal of Education, 43*(3), 325–56.

Howe, C., Hennessy, S., Mercer, N. Vrikki, M., & Wheatley, L. (2019). Teacher-student dialogue during classroom teaching: Does it really impact upon student outcomes? *Journal for the Learning Sciences.* https://doi.org/10.1080/10508406.2019.1573730.

Howe, C., & Mercer, N. (2016). Commentary on the papers. *Language and Education, 31*(1), 83–92.

Howe, C., Tolmie, A., & Rodgers, C. (1992). The acquisition of conceptual knowledge in science by primary school children: Group interaction and the understanding of motion down an incline. *British Journal of Developmental Psychology, 10*(2), 113–30.

Hutchby, I., & Wooffitt, R. (2008). *Conversation Analysis* (2nd edn). Cambridge, MA: Polity.

Hymes, D. (1972). Models of interaction in language and social life. In J. J. Gumperz & D. Hymes (Eds), *Directions in Sociolinguistics: The Ethnography of Communication* (pp. 35–71). London: Basil Blackwell.

Impedovo, M. A., Ligorio, M. B., & McLay, K. F. (2018). The 'friend of zone of proximal development' role: Empowering ePortfolios as boundary objects from student to-work I-position transaction. *Journal of Assisted Computer Learning, 34*(6), 753–61.

Ingram, J., & Elliott, V. (2019). *Research Methods for Classroom Discourse.* London: Bloomsbury.

Ingulfsen, L., Furberg, A., & Strømme, T. A. (2018). Students' engagement with real-time graphs in CSCL: Scrutinizing the role of teacher support. *International Journal of Computer-Supported Collaborative Learning, 13,* 365–90.

Jefferson, G. (1984). Transcription notation. In J. Atkinson & J. Heritage (Eds), *Structures of Social Interaction*. Cambridge: Cambridge University Press.

Jewitt, C. (2006). *Technology, Literacy and Learning: A Multimodal Approach*. London: Routledge.

Jordan, B., & Henderson, A. (1995). Interaction analysis: Foundations and practice. *The Journal of the Learning Sciences, 4*(1), 39–103.

Junker, B., Weisberg, Y., Matsumura, L. C., Crosson, A., Wolf, M. K., Levison, A., & Resnick, L. (2006). *Overview of the Instructional Quality Assessment. CSE Technical Report 671*. Los Angeles: CRESST.

Kahn, P., Wareham, T., Young, R., Willis, I., & Pilkington, R. (2008). Exploring a practitioner-based interpretive approach to reviewing research literature. *International Journal of Research & Method in Education, 31*(2), 169–80.

Kamler, B., & Thomson, P. (2014). *Helping Doctoral Students Write: Pedagogies for Supervision* (2nd edn). Abingdon: Routledge.

Kane, M. (2001). Current concerns in validity theory. *Journal of Educational Measurement, 38*(4), 319–42.

Kazak, S., Wegerif, R., & Fujita, T. (2015). Combining scaffolding for content and scaffolding for dialogue to support conceptual breakthroughs in understanding probability. *ZDM, 47*(7), 1269–83.

Kelly, S., Olney, A. M., Donnelly, P. J., Nystrand, M., & D'Mello, S. K. (2018). Automatically measuring question authenticity in real-world classrooms. *Educational Researcher, 47* (7), 451–64.

Kennedy, D. (2014). Neoteny, dialogic education and an emergent psychoculture: Notes on theory and practice. *Journal of Philosophy of Education, 48*(1), 100–17.

Kennewell, S., & Beauchamp, G. (2007). The features of interactive whiteboards and their influence on learning. *Learning, Media and Technology, 32*(3), 227–41.

Kershner, R. (2016). Including psychology in inclusive pedagogy: Enriching the dialogue? *International Journal of Educational Psychology, 5*(2), 112–39.

Kershner, R., Mercer, N., Warwick, P., & Kleine Staarman, J. (2010). Can the interactive whiteboard support young children's collaborative communication and thinking in classroom science activities? *International Journal of Computer-Supported Collaborative Learning, 5*(4), 359–83.

Kershner, R., Warwick, P., Mercer, N., & Kleine Staarman, J. (2014) Primary children's management of themselves and others in collaborative group work: 'Sometimes it takes patience …'. *Education 3–13: International Journal of Primary, Elementary and Early Years Education, 42*(2) 201–16.

Knight, S., & Littleton, K. (2017). Socialising epistemic cognition. *Educational Research Review*, *21*, 17–32.

Kruger, A. C. (1993). Peer collaboration: conflict, cooperation or both? *Social Development*, *2*, 165–82.

Kuhn, T. S. (2012). *The Structure of Scientific Revolutions*. Chicago, IL: University of Chicago press.

Kumpulainen, K., & Wray, D. (Eds) (2002). *Classroom Interaction and Social Learning: From Theory to Practice*. London: RoutledgeFalmer.

Kutnick, P., & Blatchford, P. (2013). *Effective Group Work in Primary Classrooms*. Dordrecht: Springer.

Lambirth, A. (2009). Ground rules for talk: The acceptable face of prescription. *The Curriculum Journal*, *20*(4), 423–35.

Larrain, A. (2017). Argumentation and concept development: The role of imagination. *European Journal of Psychology of Education*, *32*(4), 521–36.

Larry, F. A. (2018). *Discursive assessment practices in a special school for girls identified with a disability in one Arabic-speaking Gulf-Arabian country* [PhD thesis]. University of Cambridge.

Larsen, M. (2012). Beyond binaries: A way forward for comparative education. *Revista Española de Educación Comparada*, *20*, 146–66.

Laux, K. (2018). A theoretical understanding of the literature on student voice in the science classroom. *Research in Science & Technological Education*, *36*(1), 111–29.

Lefstein, A., & Snell, J. (2014). *Better than Best Practice: Developing Teaching and Learning through Dialogue*. Abingdon: Routledge.

Lefstein, A., Snell, J., & Israeli, M. (2015). From moves to sequences: Expanding the unit of analysis in the study of classroom discourse. *British Educational Research Journal*, *41*(5), 866–85.

Ligorio, M. B., & Barzanò, G. (2018). 'Food for thought': Blogging about food as dialogical strategy for self-disclosure and otherness. *Learning, Culture and Social Interaction*, *18*, 124–32.

Ligorio, M. B., Cesareni, D., & Schwartz, N. (2008). Collaborative virtual environments as means to increase the level of intersubjectivity in a distributed cognition system. *Journal of Research on Technology in Education*, *40*(3), 339–58.

Ligorio, M. B., & Ritella, G. (2010). The collaborative construction of chronotopes during computer-supported collaborative professional tasks. *International Journal of Computer Supported Collaborative Learning*, *5*(4), 433–52.

Ligorio, M. B., & Sansone N. (2014). An Italian model: Blended collaborative and constructive participation. *European Lifelong Learning Magazine*, *4*. Retrieved from https://www.elmmagazine.eu/articles/an-italian-model-blended-collaborative-and-constructive-participation/.

Ligorio, M. B., Talamo, A., & Pontecorvo, C. (2005). Building intersubjectivity at a distance during the collaborative writing of fairytales. *Computers & Education*, 45(3), 357–74.

Lilius J., Worline, M., Dutton, J., Kanov, J., & Maitlis, S. (2011). Understanding compassion capability. *Human Relations*, 64, 873–99.

Linden, I. (2016). From Freire to religious pluralism: Exploring dialogue in the classroom. *International Studies in Catholic Education*, 8(2), 231–40.

Linell, P. (2001). *Approaching Dialogue: Talk, Interaction and Contexts in Dialogical Perspectives*. Amsterdam: John Benjamins.

Linell, P. (2009). *Rethinking Language, Mind and World Dialogically: Interactional and Contextual Theories of Human Sense-making*. Charlotte, NC: Information Age.

Lipman, M. (2003). *Thinking in Education*. Cambridge: Cambridge University Press.

Lipponen, L. (2000). Towards knowledge building: From facts to explanations in primary students' computer mediated discourse. *Learning Environments Research*, 3(2), 179–99.

Lipponen, L., Rajala, A., & Hilppö, J. (2018). Compassion and emotional worlds in early childhood education. In C. Pascal, A. Bertram & M. Veisson (Eds), *Early Childhood Education and Change in Diverse Cultural Contexts* (pp. 168–78). New York: Routledge.

Littleton, K., & Mercer, N. (2013). *Interthinking: Putting Talk to Work*. Abingdon: Routledge.

Locke, J. (1689). An essay concerning human understanding. In R. Maynard Hutchins (Ed.). *Great books of the western world*, volume 35 (pp. 85–402). Chicago, IL: William Benton.

Louw, B., & Milojkovic, M. (2016). *Corpus Stylistics as Contextual Prosodic Theory and Subtext*. Amsterdam: John Benjamins.

Luka, I. (2012). Fostering intercultural dialogue in tourism studies: The case of Latvia. In T. Besley & M. A. Peters (Eds), *Interculturalism, Education and Dialogue* (pp. 257–79). New York: Peter Lang.

Lyle, J. (2003). Stimulated recall: A report on its use in naturalistic research. *British Educational Research Journal*, 29(6), 861–78.

Madsen, M., & O'Mullan, C. (2018). Power, participation and partnerships: Reflections on the co-creation of knowledge. *Reflective Practice*, 19(1), 26–34.

Mager, U., & Nowak, P. (2012). Effects of student participation in decision making at school: A systematic review and synthesis of empirical research. *Educational Research Review*, 7, 38–61.

Maher, C., & Martino, A. (1996). The development of the idea of mathematical proof: a 5-year case study. *Journal for Research in Mathematics Education*, 27(2), 194–214.

Major, L., & Warwick, P. (in press). 'Affordances for dialogue': The role of digital technology in supporting productive classroom talk. In N. Mercer, R. Wegerif & L. Major (Eds), *The Routledge International Handbook of Research on Dialogic Education*. London: Routledge.

Major, L., Warwick, P., Rasmussen, I., Ludvigsen, S., & Cook, V. (2018). Classroom dialogue and digital technologies: A scoping review. *Education and Information Technologies*, 23(5), 1995–2028.

Mameli, C., Mazzoni, E., & Molinari, L. (2015). Patterns of discursive interactions in primary classrooms: An application of social network analysis. *Research Papers in Education*, 30(5), 546–66.

Matusov, E. (2001). Intersubjectivity as a way of informing teaching design for a community of learners classroom. *Teaching and Teacher Education*, 17(4), 383–402.

Matusov, E. (2009). *Journey into Dialogic Pedagogy*. Hauppauge, NY: Nova.

Maybin, J. (2013). Towards a sociocultural understanding of children's voice. *Language and Education*, 27(5), 383–97.

McNamara, T. F. (1997). 'Interaction' in second language performance assessment: Whose performance? *Applied Linguistics*, 16(2), 159–79.

Mehan, H., & Cazden, C. (2015). The study of classroom discourse: Early history and current developments. In L. B. Resnick, C. S. C. Asterhan & S. N. Clarke (Eds), *Socializing Intelligence through Academic Talk and Dialogue* (pp. 13–34). Washington, DC: American Educational Research Association.

Mercer, N. (1994). The quality of talk in children's joint activity at the computer. *Journal of Computer Assisted Learning*, 10(1), 24–32.

Mercer, N. (1995). *The Guided Construction of Knowledge: Talk amongst Teachers and Learners*. Bristol: Multilingual Matters.

Mercer, N. (2002). *Words and Minds: How We Use Language to Think Together*. London: Routledge.

Mercer, N. (2004). Sociocultural discourse analysis: Analysing classroom talk as a social mode of thinking. *Journal of Applied Linguistics*, 1(2), 137–68.

Mercer, N. (2008). The seeds of time: Why classroom dialogue needs a temporal analysis. *Journal of the Learning Sciences*, 17(1), 33–59.

Mercer, N. (2010). The analysis of classroom talk: Methods and methodologies. *British Journal of Educational Psychology*, 80(1), 1–14.

Mercer, N. (2013). The social brain, language, and goal-directed collective thinking: A social conception of cognition and its implications for understanding how we think, teach, and learn. *Educational Psychologist*, 48(3), 148–68.

Mercer, N., Dawes, L., Wegerif, R., & Sams, C. (2004). Reasoning as a scientist: Ways of helping children to use language to learn science. *British Educational Research Journal, 30*(3), 367–85.

Mercer, N., Hennessy, S., & Warwick, P. (2010). Using interactive whiteboards to orchestrate classroom dialogue. *Technology, Pedagogy and Education on Interactive Whole Class Technologies, 19*(2), 195–209.

Mercer, N., & Littleton, K. (2007). *Dialogue and the Development of Children's Thinking: A Sociocultural Approach.* London: Routledge

Mercer, N., & Sams, C. (2006). Teaching children how to use language to solve maths problems. *Language and Education, 20*(6), 507–28.

Mercer, N., Warwick, P., & Ahmed, A. (2017). An oracy assessment toolkit: Linking research and development in the assessment of students' spoken language skills at age 11–12. *Learning and Instruction, 48*, 51–60.

Mercer, N., Warwick, P., Kershner, R., & Kleine Staarman, J. (2010). Can the interactive whiteboard help to provide 'dialogic space' for children's collaborative activity? *Language and Education, 24*(5), 367–84.

Mercer, N., & Wegerif, R. (1999). Is 'exploratory talk' productive talk? In K. Littleton & P. Light (Eds), *Learning with Computers: Analyzing Productive Interaction* (pp. 79–115). Florence, KY: Routledge.

Mercer, N., & Wegerif, R. (2004). Is 'exploratory talk' productive talk? In Daniels, H., & Edwards, A. (Eds), *The RoutledgeFalmer Reader in Psychology of Education* (pp. 67–86). London. RoutledgeFalmer.

Mercer, N., Wegerif, R., & Major, L. (Eds) (in press). *International Handbook on Dialogic Education.* London: Routledge.

Merleau-Ponty, M. (1968). *The Visible and the Invisible (Studies in Phenomenology and Existential Philosophy)* (Claude Lefort, Ed. and Alphonso Lingis, Trans.). Evanston, IL: Northwestern University Press.

Messick, S. (1989). Meaning and values in test validation: The science and ethics of assessment. *Educational Researcher, 18*(2), 5–11.

Michaels, S., & O'Connor M. C. (2011). *Coding Guide for Teacher Talk Moves. [Coding Manual].* Unpublished Instrument. Pittsburgh Science of Learning Center, PA.

Michaels, S., & O'Connor, M. C. (2015). Conceptualizing talk moves as tools. Professional development approaches for academically productive discussions. In L. B. Resnick, C. S. C. Asterhan & S. N. Clarke (Eds), *Socializing Intelligence through Academic Talk and Dialogue* (pp. 347–62). Washington, DC: American Educational Research Association.

Michaels, S., O'Connor, C., & Resnick, L. B. (2008). Deliberative discourse idealized and realized: Accountable talk in the classroom and in civic life. *Studies in Philosophy and Education*, 27(4), 283–97.

Moffat, B. M., Haines-Saah, R. J., & Johnson, J. L. (2017). From didactic to dialogue: Assessing the use of an innovative classroom resource to support decision-making about cannabis use. *Drugs: Education, Prevention and Policy*, 24(1), 85–95.

Molinari, L., Mameli, C., & Gnisci, A. (2013). A sequential analysis of classroom discourse in Italian primary schools: The many faces of the IRF pattern. *British Journal of Educational Psychology*, 83(3), 414–30.

Monaghan, F. (2005). 'Don't think in your head, think aloud': ICT and exploratory talk in the primary school mathematics classroom. *Research in Mathematics Education*, 7(1), 83–100.

Montesano Montessori, N. & Ponte, P. (2012). Researching classroom communications and relations in the light of social justice. *Educational Action Research* 20(2) 251–66.

Murris, K. (2013). The epistemic challenge of hearing child's voice. *Studies in Philosophy of Education*, 32, 245–59.

Myhill, D. (2006). Talk, talk, talk: Teaching and learning in whole class discourse. *Research Papers in Education*, 21(1), 19–41.

Nassaji, H., & Wells, G. (2000). What's the use of triadic dialogue? An investigation of teacher student interaction. *Applied Linguistics*, 27, 333–63.

Nind, M., Hall, K., & Curtin, A. (2016). *Research Methods for Pedagogy*. London: Bloomsbury.

Nind, M., Kilburn, D., & Wiles, R. (2015). Using video and dialogue to generate pedagogic knowledge: Teachers, learners and researchers reflecting together on the pedagogy of social research methods. *International Journal of Social Research Methodology*, 18(5), 561–76.

Noddings, N. (2012). The caring relation in teaching. *Oxford Review of Education*, 38(6), 771–81.

Norris, S. (2004). *Analyzing Multimodal Interaction: A Methodological Framework*. New York: Routledge.

Nystrand, M., Gamoran, A., Kachur, R., & Prendergast, C. (1997). *Opening Dialogue: Understanding the Dynamics of Language and Learning in the English Classroom*. New York: Teachers College Press.

Nystrand, M., Wu, L. L., Gamoran, A., Zeiser, S., & Long, D. A. (2003). Questions in time: Investigating the structure and dynamics of unfolding classroom discourse. *Discourse Processes*, 35(2), 135–98.

Oliver, C., Jones, E., Rayner, A., Penner, J., & Jamieson, A. (2017). Teaching social work students to speak up. *Social Work Education*, 36(6), 702–14.

Ong, W. J. (2013). *Orality and Literacy*. London: Routledge.

Onwuegbuzie, A. J., & Frels, R. K. (2016). *Seven Steps to a Comprehensive Literature Review: A Multimodal & Cultural Approach*. Los Angeles, CA: Sage.

Padilla, R. V. (1992). Using dialogical research methods to study Chicano college students. *The Urban Review*, 24(3), 175–83.

Paradis, E., & Sutkin, G. (2017). Beyond a good story: From Hawthorne Effect to reactivity in health professions education research. *Medical Education 51*, 31–9.

Paris, D. (2012). Culturally sustaining pedagogy: A needed change in stance, terminology and practice. *Educational Researcher*, 41(3), 93–7.

Park, J. Y., Michaels, S., Affolter, R., & O'Connor, M. C. (2017). Traditions, research and practice supporting academically productive classroom discourse. *Oxford Research Encyclopaedia of Education*. Oxford: Oxford University Press.

Patakorpi, E. (2009). What could abductive reasoning contribute to human computer interaction? A technology domestication view. *PsychNology Journal*, 7(1), 113–31.

Peirce, C. S. (1955). The scientific attitude and fallibilism. In J. Buchler (Ed.), *Philosophical Writings of Peirce* (pp. 42–59). New York: Dover.

Peirce, C. S. (1974). *Collected Papers of Charles Sanders Peirce*, volume 5. Cambridge, MA: Harvard University Press.

Pelto, P. J., & Pelto, G. H. (1978). *Anthropological Research: The Structure of Inquiry*. Cambridge: Cambridge University Press.

Pérez-Paredes, P. (2017). A keyword analysis of the 2015 UK Higher Education Green Paper and the twitter debate. In M. A. Orts, R. Breeze & M. Gotti (Eds), *Power, Persuasion and Manipulation in Specialised Genres: Providing Keys to the Rhetoric of Professional Communities* (pp. 161–94). Bern: Peter Lang.

Phillipson, N., & Wegerif, R. (2017). *Dialogic Education: Mastering Core Concepts through Thinking Together*. Abingdon: Routledge.

Piazza, S. V., Rao, S., & Protacio, M. S. (2015). Converging recommendations for culturally responsive literacy practices: Students with learning disabilities, English language learners, and socioculturally diverse learners. *International Journal of Multicultural Education*, 17(3), 1–20.

Pifarré, M., & Li, L. (2018). Characterizing and unpacking learning to learn together skills in a wiki project in primary education. *Thinking Skills and Creativity*, 29, 45–58.

Poehner, M. E., & Lantolf, J. P. (2005). Dynamic assessment in the language classroom. *Language Teaching Research*, 9(3), 233–65.

Pollitt, A. (2012). Comparative judgement for assessment. *Journal of Technology and Design Assessment*, 22(2), 157–70.

Popp, J. S., & Goldman, S. R. (2016). Knowledge building in teacher professional learning communities: Focus of meeting matters. *Teaching and Teacher Education, 59*, 347–59.

Preiser, R., Biggs, R., De Vos, A., & Folke, C. (2018). Social-ecological systems as complex adaptive systems: Organizing principles for advancing research methods and approaches. *Ecology and Society, 23*(4).

Rajala, A., Hilppö, J., Lipponen, L., & Kumpulainen, K. (2013). Expanding the chronotopes of schooling for the promotion of students' agency. In O. Erstad & J. Sefton-Green (Eds), *Identity, Community, and Learning Lives in the Digital Age* (pp. 107–25). Cambridge: Cambridge University Press.

Rajala, A., Kontiola, H., Hilppö, J., & Lipponen L. (In press). *Lohdutustilanteet ja myötätuntokulttuuri alle kolmivuotiaiden päiväkotiryhmässä. Kasvatus. [Soothing situations and culture of compassion in a kindergarten group of below three years olds].*

Rajala, A., & Lipponen, L. (2018). Compassion in narrations of early childhood education student teachers in Finland. In S. Garvis, S. Phillipson, & S. Harju Luukkainen (Eds), *International Perspectives on Early Childhood Education and Care. Early Childhood Education in the 21st Century*, volume 1. New York: Routledge.

Rapley, T. (2008). *Doing Conversation, Discourse and Document Analysis*. London: Sage.

Raven, J., Raven, J. C., & Court, J. H. (2003, updated 2004). *Manual for Raven's Progressive Matrices and Vocabulary Scales.* Oxford: Psychology Press.

Ravenscroft, A. (2007). Promoting thinking and conceptual change with digital dialogue games: Thinking and dialogue games. *Journal of Computer Assisted Learning, 23*(6), 453–65.

Rayson, P., & Garside, R. (2000). Comparing corpora using frequency profiling. In *Proceedings of the Workshop on Comparing Corpora*, volume 9 (pp. 1–6). Stroudsburg, PA: Association for Computational Linguistics.

Resnick, L. B. (2014). *Supporting Teachers' Development of Accountable Talk in Science and Mathematics.* Unpublished data file and code book.

Resnick, L. B., Asterhan, C. S. C., & Clarke, S. N. (Eds) (2015). *Socializing Intelligence through Academic Talk and Dialogue.* Washington, DC: American Educational Research Association.

Resnick, L. B., Michaels, S., & O'Connor, M. C. (2010). How (well structured) talk builds the mind. In D. Preiss & R. Sternberg (Eds), *Innovations in Educational Psychology* (pp. 163–94). New York: Springer.

Richards, J., & Robertson, A. D. (2016). A review of the research on responsive teaching in science and mathematics. In A. D. Robertson, R. E. Scherr & D. Hammer (Eds), *Responsive Teaching in Science and Mathematics*. New York: Routledge.

Robson, C., & McCartan, K. (2016). *Real World Research* (4th edn). Chichester: Wiley.

Rojas-Drummond, S., Perez, V., Velez, M., Gomez, L., & Mendoza, A. (2003). Talking for reasoning among Mexican primary school children. *Learning and Instruction*, 13(6), 653–70.

Rojas-Drummond, S., Mazón, N., Fernández, M., & Wegerif, R. (2006). Explicit reasoning, creativity and co-construction in primary school children's collaborative activities. *Thinking Skills and Creativity*, 1(2), 84–94.

Rojas-Drummond, S., Torreblanca, O., Pedraza, H., Vélez, M., & Guzmán, K. (2013). Dialogic scaffolding: Enhancing learning and understanding in collaborative contexts. *Learning, Culture and Social Interaction*, 1, 11–21.

Rommetveit, R. (1992). Outlines of a dialogically based social-cognitive approach to human cognition and communication. In A. Wold (Ed.), *The Dialogical Alternative: Towards a Theory of Language and Mind* (pp. 19–45). Oslo: Scandinavian Press.

Rosé, C. P., & Tovares, A. (2015). What sociolinguistics and machine learning have to say to each other about interaction analysis. In L. B. Resnick, C. S. C. Asterhan & S. N. Clarke (Eds), *Socializing Intelligence through Academic Talk and Dialogue*. Washington, DC: American Educational Research Association.

Rule, P. (2012). Intercultural dialogue, education and transformation. In T. Besley & M. A. Peters (Eds), *Interculturalism, Education and Dialogue* (pp. 330–44). Oxford: Peter Lang.

Ruthven, K., Hennessy, S., & Deaney, R. (2008). Constructions of dynamic geometry: A study of the interpretative flexibility of educational software in classroom practice. *Computers and Education*, 51(1), 297–317.

Sacks, H., Schegloff, E. A., & Jefferson, G. (1974). A simplest systematics for the organization of turn-taking for conversation. *Language*, 50, 696–735.

Sakr, M. (2018). Multimodal participation frameworks during young children's collaborative drawing on paper and on the iPad. *Thinking Skills and Creativity*, 29, 1–11.

Säljö, R. (1995). Mental and physical artefacts in cognitive practices. In P. Reimann & H. Spada (Eds), *Learning in Humans and Machines: Towards an Interdisciplinary Learning Science* (pp. 83–96). Oxford: Pergamon.

Salomon, G., & Perkins, D. N. (1998). Individual and social aspects of learning. *Review of Research in Education, 23*(1), 1–24.

Sanderson, T. (2008). Interaction, identity and culture in academic writing: The case of German, British and American academics in the humanities. In A. Adel & R. Reppen (Eds), *Corpora and Discourse: The Challenges of Different Settings* (pp. 57–94). Amsterdam, Philadelphia: John Benjamins.

Savin-Baden, M., & Tombs, G. (2017). *Research Methods for Education in the Digital Age.* London: Bloomsbury.

Scardamalia, M., & Bereiter, C. (2006). Knowledge building: Theory, pedagogy, and technology. In R. K. Sawyer (Ed.), *The Cambridge Handbook of the Learning Sciences* (pp. 97–118). Cambridge: Cambridge University Press.

Schultz, K. (2009). *Rethinking Classroom Participation: Listening to Silent Voices.* New York: Teachers College Press.

Schwarz, B. B., & Baker, M. J. (2017). *Dialogue, Argumentation and Education: History, Theory and Practice.* Cambridge: Cambridge University Press.

Schwimmer, M. (2017). Beyond theory and practice: Towards an ethics of translation. *Ethics and Education, 12*(1), 51–61.

Scribner, S., & Cole, M. (1978). Literacy without schooling: Testing for intellectual effects. *Harvard Educational Review, 48*(4), 448–61.

Searle, J. R. & Vandervecken, D. (1985). *Foundations of Illocutionary Logic.* Cambridge: Cambridge University Press.

Sedova, K., Sedlacek, M., & Svaricek, R. (2016). Teacher professional development as a means of transforming student classroom talk. *Teaching and Teacher Education, 57,* 14–25.

Sedlacek, M., & Sedova, K. (2017). How many are talking? The role of collectivity in dialogic teaching. *International Journal of Educational Research, 85,* 99–108.

Segal, A., & Lefstein, A. (2016). Exuberant, voiceless participation: An unintended consequence of dialogic sensibilities? [Special issue] *L1 - Educational Studies in Languages and Literature, 16,* 1–19.

Sfard, A. (2015). Why all this talk about talking classrooms? Theorizing the relation between talking and learning. In L. Resnick, C. S. C. Asterhan & S. N. Clarke (Eds), *Socializing Intelligence through Academic Talk and Dialogue* (pp. 245–53). Washington, DC: American Educational Research Association.

Shaffer, D. W. (2017). *Quantitative Ethnography.* Madison, WI: Cathcart.

Siddiq, F., & Scherer, R. (2017). Revealing the processes of students' interaction with a novel collaborative problem solving task: An in-depth analysis of think-aloud protocols. *Computers in Human Behavior, 76,* 509–25.

Sidorkin, A. M. (1999). *Beyond Discourse: Education, the Self, and Dialogue.* Albany: State University of New York Press.

Simon, M. K., & Goes, J. (2013). *Using LOOP learning and critical dialogue in developing innovative literature reviews.* Paper presented at the International Association for Development of the Information Society International Conference on Cognition and Exploratory Learning in the Digital Age (CELDA), Fort Worth, TX.

Sinclair, J., & Coulthard, M. (1975). *Towards an Analysis of Discourse: The English Used by Teachers and Pupils.* Oxford: Oxford University Press.

Skidmore, D., & Murakami, K. (Eds) (2016). *Dialogic Pedagogy: The Importance of Dialogue in Teaching and Learning.* Bristol: Multilingual Matters.

Sternberg, R. J., & Grigorenko, E. L. (2002). *Dynamic Testing: The Nature of Measurement of Learning Potential.* Cambridge: Cambridge University Press.

Stobart, G. (2014). *The Expert Learner: Challenging the Myth of Ability.* Maidenhead: McGraw-Hill Education.

Stubbs, M. (1994). Grammar, text and ideology: Computer-assisted methods in the linguistics of representation. *Applied Linguistics, 15*(2), 202–23.

Taylor, S. V., & Sobel, D. M. (2011). *Culturally Responsive Pedagogy: Teaching like Our Students' Lives Matter.* Bingley: Emerald Books.

Thurstone, L. L. (1927). The law of comparative judgment. *Psychological Review, 34*(4), 273–86.

Vangrieken, K., Dochy, F., Raes, E., & Kyndt, E. (2015). Teacher collaboration: A systematic review. *Educational Research Review, 15,* 17–40.

Varis, P. (2016). Digital ethnography. In A. Georgakopolou & T. Spilioti (Eds), *The Routledge Handbook of Language and Digital Communication* (pp. 55–68). New York: Routledge.

Vico, G. (1948). *The New Science* (T. G. Bergin & M. H. Fisch, Trans.). Ithaca, NY: Cornell University Press. (Original work published in 1744.)

Voloshinov, V. N. (1973). *Marxism and the Philosophy of Language,* volume 1 (L. Matejka & I. R. Titunik, Trans.). New York: Seminar Press.

Von Davier, A. A., Zhu, M., & Kyllonen, P. C. (Eds) (2017). *Innovative Assessment of Collaboration.* New York: Springer.

Vrikki, M., Kershner, R., Calcagni, E., Hennessy, S., Lee, L., Estrada, N., Hernández, F., & Ahmed, F. (2018). The Teacher Scheme for Educational Dialogue Analysis (T-SEDA): Developing a research-based observation tool for supporting teacher inquiry into pupils' participation in classroom dialogue. *International Journal of Research and Methods in Education.* https://doi.org/10.1080/17437 27X.2018.1467890.

Vrikki, M., Wheatley, L., Howe, C., Hennessy, S., & Mercer, N. (2018). Dialogic practices in primary school classrooms. *Language and Education.* https://doi.org/10.1080/09500782.2018.1509988.

Vygotsky, L. S. (1962). *Thought and Language.* Cambridge, MA: MIT Press. (Original work published in 1934.)

Vygotsky, L. S. (1978). *Mind in Society: The Development of Higher Psychological Processes.* Cambridge, MA: Harvard University Press.

Vygotsky, L. S. (1987). Thinking and speech (N. Minick, Trans.). In R. W. Rieber, A. S. Carton (Eds), *The Collected Works of L. S. Vygotsky,* volume 1 (pp. 39–285). New York: Plenum Press. (Original work published in 1934.)

Vygotsky, L. S. (1997). On psychological systems (N. Minick, Trans.). In R. W. Rieber, A. S. Carton (Eds), *The Collected Works of L. S. Vygotsky,* volume 1 (pp. 21–107). New York: Plenum. (Original work published in 1930.)

Vygotsky, L. S. (2004). Imagination and creativity in childhood. *Journal of Russian & East European Psychology, 42*(1), 7–97. (Original work published in 1930.)

Wagner, C. J., & González-Howard, M. (2018). Studying discourse as social interaction: The potential of social network analysis for discourse studies. *Educational Researcher, 47*(6), 375–83.

Waldrop, M. (1992). *Complexity: The Emerging Science at the Edge of Order and Chaos.* London: Penguin.

Warwick, P., Mercer, N., Kershner, R., & Kleine Staarman, J. (2010). In the mind and in the technology: The vicarious presence of the teacher in pupils' learning of science in collaborative group activity at the interactive whiteboard. *Computers and Education, 55*(1), 350–62.

Watson, R. A., & Szathmáry, E. (2016). How can evolution learn? *Trends in Ecology & Evolution, 31*(2), 147–57.

Webb, N. M., Franke, M. L., Ing, M., Turrou, A. C., Johnson, N. C., & Zimmerman, J. (2017). Teacher practices that promote productive dialogue and learning in mathematics classrooms. *International Journal of Educational Research.* https://doi.org/10.1016/j.ijer.2017.07.009.

Wegerif, R. (1998). The social dimension of asynchronous learning networks. *Journal of Asynchronous Learning Networks, 2*(1), 34–49.

Wegerif, R. (2001). Applying a dialogical model of reason in the classroom. In R. Joiner (Ed.), *Rethinking Collaborative Learning* (pp. 119–39). London: Free Association Books.

Wegerif, R. (2002). Walking or dancing? Images of thinking and learning to think in the classroom. *Journal of Interactive Learning Research*, *13*(1), 51–70.

Wegerif, R. (2005). Reason and creativity in classroom dialogues. *Language and Education*, *19*(3), 223–37.

Wegerif, R. (2007). *Dialogic Education and Technology: Expanding the Space of Learning*. London: Springer.

Wegerif, R. (2008). Dialogic or dialectic? The significance of ontological assumptions in research on educational dialogue. *British Educational Research Journal*, *34*(3), 347–61.

Wegerif, R. (2010). *Mind Expanding: Teaching for Thinking and Creativity in Primary Education*. Buckingham: McGraw-Hill.

Wegerif, R. (2013). *Dialogic: Education for the Internet Age*. New York: Routledge.

Wegerif, R., Doney, J., Richards, A., Mansour, N., Larkin, S., & Jamison, I. (2019). Exploring the ontological dimension of dialogic education through an evaluation of the impact of Internet mediated dialogue across cultural difference. *Learning, Culture and Social Interaction*, *20*, 80–9.

Wegerif, R., Fujita, T., Doney, J., Linares, J. P., Richards, A., & Van Rhyn, C. (2017). Developing and trialing a measure of group thinking. *Learning and Instruction*, *48*, 40–50.

Wegerif, R., Littleton, K., Dawes, L., Mercer, N., & Rowe, D. (2004). Widening access to educational opportunities through teaching children how to reason together. *Westminster Studies in Education*, *27*(2), 143–56.

Wegerif, R., McLaren, B. M., Chamrada, M., Scheuer, O., Mansour, N., Mikšátko, J., & Williams, M. (2010). Exploring creative thinking in graphically mediated synchronous dialogues. *Computers & Education*, *54*(3), 613–21.

Wegerif, R., & Mercer, N. (1997a). A dialogical framework for investigating talk. In R. Wegerif & P. Scrimshaw (Eds), *Computers and Talk in the Primary Classroom* (pp. 49–65). Bristol: Multilingual Matters.

Wegerif, R., & Mercer, N. (1997b). Using computer-based text analysis to integrate qualitative and quantitative methods in research on collaborative learning. *Language and Education*, *11*(4), 271–86.

Wegerif, R., Mercer, N., & Dawes, L. (1999). From social interaction to individual reasoning: An empirical investigation of a possible socio-cultural model of cognitive development. *Learning and Instruction*, *9*(6), 493–516.

Wegerif, R., Mercer, N., & Rojas-Drummond, S. (1999). Language for the social construction of knowledge: Comparing classroom talk in Mexican preschools. *Language and Education*, *13*(2), 133–50.

Wegerif, R., & Scrimshaw, P. (Eds) (1997). *Computers and Talk in the Primary Classroom*, volume 12. Bristol: Multilingual Matters.

Weinreich, M. (1946). *Hitler's Professors: The Part of Scholarship in Germany's Crimes against the Jewish People.* New Haven, CT: Yale University Press.

Wells, G. (1993). Intersubjectivity and the construction of knowledge. In C. Pontecorvo (Ed.), *La condivisione della conoscenza* [Knowledge sharing] (pp. 353–80). Rome: La Nuova Italia.

Wells, G. (1999). *Dialogic Inquiry: Toward a Sociocultural Practice and Theory of Education.* Cambridge: Cambridge University Press.

Wells, G., with DICEP. (2001). *Coding Scheme for the Analysis of Classroom Discourse.* Retrieved from https://people.ucsc.edu/~gwells/Files/Courses_Folder/documents/CodingManual.pdf.

Wells, G. (2009). *The Meaning Makers: Learning to Talk and Talking to Learn* (2nd edn). Bristol: Multilingual Matters.

Wells, G., & Arauz, R. M. (2006). Dialogue in the classroom. *Journal of the Learning Sciences*, *15*(3), 379–428.

Wertsch, J. V. (1998). Mediated action. In W. Bechtel & G. Graham (Eds), *A Companion to Cognitive Science* (pp. 518–25). Oxford: Blackwell.

Wertsch, J. V. (2013). The role of abstract rationality in Vygotsky's image of mind. In A. Tryphon & J. Voneche (Eds), *Piaget-Vygotsky: The Social Genesis of Thought* (pp. 33–52). London: Psychology Press.

Wheadon, C., Christodoulou, D., Barmby, P., & Henderson, B. (submitted). *A Comparative Judgement Approach to the Large-scale Assessment of Primary Writing in England.* Manuscript submitted for publication.

Wiliam, D., & Thompson, M. (2007). Integrating assessment with learning: What will it take to make it work? In C. A. Dwyer (Ed.), *The Future of Assessment: Shaping Teaching and Learning* (pp. 53–84). Mahwah, NJ: LEA.

Wilson, M. (2009). Measuring progressions: Assessment structures underlying a learning progression. *Journal of Research in Science Teaching*, *46*(6), 716–30.

Witt, P. L. (2017). Making tough choices to continue instructional communication research. *Communication Education*, *66*(4), 494–6.

Wittgenstein, L. (2009). *Philosophical Investigations* (4th edn) (P. M. S. Hacker & J. Schulte, Trans.). Chichester: Wiley-Blackwell.

Wood, D., Bruner, J. S., & Ross, G. (1976). The role of tutoring in problem solving. *Journal of Child Psychology and Psychiatry*, *17*(2), 89–100.

Wrigley, T. (2018). The power of "evidence": Reliable science or a set of blunt tools? *British Educational Research Journal, 44*(3), 359–76.

Yang, Y., van Aalst, J., Chan, C. K. K., & Tian, W. (2016). Reflective assessment in knowledge building by students with low academic achievement. *International Journal of Computer-Supported Collaborative Learning, 11*(3), 281–311.

Yang, Y., Wegerif, R., & Pifarre, M. (2013). *Final report on the role of technology in supporting individuals and group 'Learning to learn together'.* WP2 Supporting theory and the development of visual languages. Unpublished appendix D2.4 to final report to sponsor of Metafora project. Retrieved from https://cordis.europa.eu/project/rcn/95596_en.html.

Zehra, S. (2012). Intercultural understanding and social activism initiative in the western suburbs of Chicago. In T. Besley & M. A. Peters (Eds), *Interculturalism, Education and Dialogue* (pp. 345–55). New York: Peter Lang.

INDEX

abductive/abduction 50, 251, 258
accountable talk 10, 97, 102, 106, 119, 133
achievement 58, 93, 100, 175, 222, 251, 252
action research 21, 57, 62, 70, 93, 238, 250, 251, 256
affect 35, 188
affordance 21, 22, 65, 67, 137–9, 151, 158–60, 163, 168, 199, 205, 208, 235, 237, 238, 243, 250, 251
affording 151
agency 151, 211, 218, 230, 238
Alexander 9, 10, 83, 172
analytical mark scheme 88, 251
annotation 133, 138, 140, 144, 148, 151, 153–5, 162, 181
appropriation 15, 234
argumentation 4, 21, 77, 84
assessment for learning 6, 89
assessment of dialogue 76, 77, 90, 91
assessment toolkit 78, 82
asynchronous 178
authenticity 24, 226, 228, 236, 238
autonomy 60, 64

backchannelling 88, 131
Bakhtin 9, 10, 22, 26, 46, 140, 174, 184, 206, 242, 247, 249

bias 37, 98, 149, 178, 218, 231, 252
blogging 25, 47–9, 68, 176, 186, 187, 189, 190, 194, 195, 222
bracketing 165
Buber 12, 17, 18, 24, 36, 40, 184, 185, 206

case study 48, 63, 145, 187, 207, 208, 226, 252
causation 5, 15, 19, 42, 59, 84, 93, 94, 177, 186, 191, 229, 253
chiasm 5, 6, 22, 24–6, 173, 176, 182–6, 191, 192, 194, 195, 249, 252
close-to-practice 21, 49, 252
clustering 101, 106, 108, 120, 124–7, 129, 130
co-construction 15, 88, 160, 161, 170, 254
coding and counting 42, 178
coding dialogue 83, 98, 103, 109, 130, 133, 139, 162
coding schemes 6, 29, 50, 83, 89, 93, 95–7, 99, 108, 109, 129–31, 133, 134, 141, 158, 162, 165, 171, 177, 179, 252
cognition 14, 20, 45, 55
cognitive 21, 22, 50, 55, 59, 78, 102, 105, 121, 123, 132, 139, 150, 170, 250, 252
collocations 100, 181, 188, 242

community of inquiry/enquiry 10, 46, 62, 208, 252
compassion 7, 220–2
complexity 19, 20, 77, 84, 94, 102, 131, 138, 158, 168, 170, 182, 194, 249, 252
computer-supported 28, 56
conceptual framework 69, 78, 92, 96, 203, 252
concordance/concordancer 56, 66, 100, 179–81, 252, 255
confounding variables/confounds 55, 65, 84, 85, 93, 252, 257
conscientization 12
constructivism 30, 57
construct under-representation 84, 253
constructs 46, 78, 96, 250, 252
conversational implicature 16
conversational turns 6, 54, 242, 243
conversation analysis 3, 56, 88, 93, 211, 216, 218
co-researching 62, 67, 204
correlational design 55, 253
creative tension 175, 185, 191
creative thinking 5, 31, 38, 40, 41, 45, 46
creativity 38, 40, 94
critical event/incident analysis 25
cross-cultural 54, 225
cultural diversity 62, 64, 186, 194, 203, 211, 212, 219, 225, 235
cumulative talk 28, 30, 31, 41, 44
curriculum 52, 57, 78, 79, 82, 83, 146, 217, 223, 234, 244

databases 52, 56, 69
data mining 139, 253
datasets 96–100, 108, 109, 129, 153

deductive/deduction 49, 96, 106, 159, 253, 258
democratic 62, 149, 202, 204, 207, 235, 237
descriptive statistics 99, 253, 255
design-based research 5, 19, 21, 43, 61, 67, 78, 177, 249, 253
dialogic
  dialogic classroom 78, 85, 89, 107, 242, 244
  dialogic education 1, 9, 11–13, 15, 28, 172, 178
  dialogic engagement 51, 62, 64, 66, 67, 71–3, 211, 250
  dialogic inquiry 139, 198
  dialogic interactions 7, 52, 67, 77, 102, 103, 136, 138, 150, 159, 166, 170, 171, 191, 218, 220, 231
  dialogic learning 50, 61, 63, 191, 206
  dialogic pedagogy 119, 131, 151, 172
  dialogic principles 6, 48, 58, 64, 66, 68, 69, 233
  dialogic research 5, 7, 25, 51, 65, 72, 145, 182, 191, 202
  dialogic space 5, 12, 13, 17, 18, 65, 77, 95, 132, 139, 141, 151, 169, 170
  dialogic talk 19, 21, 43, 179
  dialogic teaching 9, 10, 78, 218
dialogical 20, 21, 193
dialogicality 20, 83, 97, 124, 162, 230
dialogically 23, 25
dialogicity 22, 188
dialogism 10, 11, 14, 25, 193, 242
dialogue mapping 241, 253
diary 155, 157–9, 216, 254
digital technology 110, 129, 135, 136, 138–40, 148, 160, 162, 166, 171

discourse
  discourse analysis 15, 54, 56, 95,
    102, 178, 187, 191, 212–14,
    217, 218, 227, 231, 239,
    253, 258
  discourse features 2, 28, 53,
    102, 106
disposition 9, 70, 235
disputational talk 5, 28, 29, 33,
  35, 41, 43
Dynamic-Inverted-Pyramid 179,
  180, 182

ecological 146
egalitarian 63, 207
elaboration 28, 31, 51, 76, 85,
  111–18, 120, 121, 124–6, 129,
  140, 239
e-learning 195
embodied 18, 139, 140, 166, 169,
  175, 242
emergence 20, 149, 172
emic 23, 184, 185, 218, 252, 253
emotional 46, 78, 98, 165, 170,
  201, 204, 206, 208, 211, 220,
  226, 233, 236
emotions 62, 199, 201, 204, 211,
  221, 229
empathy 18, 24, 46, 197, 209,
  220
empirical 20, 22, 43–6, 50–2, 56,
  57, 59, 69, 71, 77, 78, 83, 84,
  88, 170, 185, 202, 203, 206,
  210, 211, 215, 220, 221, 250
enlightenment 40
enquiry 10, 252
episode 33, 46, 104, 107, 109, 123,
  127, 131, 133, 152, 153, 180,
  182, 254, 255, 258
epistemic 55, 56, 100, 101, 235,
  241, 254, 257
Epistemic Network Analysis (ENA)
  56, 100, 101, 254, 257

epistemology/epistemological
  stance 10, 11, 13, 71, 131, 254
equitable 7, 13, 54, 62, 64, 88, 97,
  152, 205, 211, 216, 224
ethnographic/ethnography 6, 23,
  24, 62, 64, 95, 100, 131, 146,
  176, 178, 212–15, 222, 231,
  254–6
etic 23, 184, 185, 252, 254
evaluation 4, 6, 54, 56, 59, 66, 71,
  75, 77, 86, 91, 106, 119, 120,
  177, 179, 186, 187, 205, 212,
  218, 224, 234, 236, 238
evidence-based 247
evidence-informed 204
experiential learning 62, 174,
  235, 236
experimental 21, 39, 144, 151, 170
exploratory 5, 10, 14, 15, 21, 28–
  31, 33–43, 61, 178, 180, 208
eye-tracking 205, 219

feedback 20, 82, 84, 86, 89, 90,
  110, 121, 152, 177, 218, 225
fidelity 254
focus group 58, 63, 78, 149, 216,
  219, 231, 236, 241, 254
Freire 12, 102

generalization 25, 44, 98, 101,
  103, 108, 109, 151, 168, 178,
  179, 204
gesture 58, 70, 96, 132, 136, 140,
  156, 165, 170, 171
granularity 6, 104, 106, 109,
  129, 254
graphs 101, 141, 165, 170

Habermas 18, 35, 40, 41, 63
hermeneutic 45, 235
holistic 79, 83, 85, 88, 107, 128,
  133, 166, 170, 171, 252, 254
holistic judgement 79, 85, 254

Howe 52, 55, 83, 85, 95–7, 100, 102, 107, 119, 175
Hymes 104, 105
hypotheses 28, 31, 179

identity 4, 50, 62, 64, 70, 133, 159, 188–91, 194, 195, 234, 255
ideographic 185, 193
images 23, 38, 41, 50, 70, 138, 139, 141, 144, 146, 147, 151, 153–5, 157–60, 166, 170, 174, 175
implicature 16
inductive/induction 50, 59, 96, 145, 159, 254, 258
inference 77, 84, 85, 88, 91, 94, 108, 125, 149, 160, 210, 254, 255, 259
inferential statistics 53, 255, 256
initiation-response-feedback 53, 66
interactive whiteboard 113, 115, 127, 137, 145, 213
inter-animation 10, 24, 25, 192
intercultural 3, 4, 48, 52, 61–4, 197, 202, 203, 206
inter-illumination 25, 192
interpretative narrative 139, 166, 172, 255
interpretive 24, 71, 139, 166, 172, 186, 207, 208, 255
inter-rater reliability 105, 108, 257
intersubjectivity 20, 35, 37, 38, 40, 42, 193, 207, 243
interthinking 12
interventions 3, 55, 61, 204, 253, 257

keyword analysis 56, 69, 97, 99, 100, 110, 183, 188, 255
knowledge building/construction 4, 11, 13, 44, 49, 55, 138, 149, 151, 169, 193, 204, 243
knowledge exchange 61, 198, 204

knowledge objects 152
KWIC 181, 182, 188

learning analytics 176, 177
learning community 60, 87, 186, 243, 244
learning environments 119, 151, 160, 170, 199, 219
learning networks 178
learning outcomes 19, 37, 54, 59, 65, 66, 76, 83–5, 92, 256, 257
learning processes 21, 121, 137, 170, 172, 193, 223
learning sciences 50
learning to learn 160, 172
lemmatize 188
linguistic ethnography 6, 16, 64, 95, 131, 231, 234, 255
literacy 4, 22, 218
log-likelihood 188, 189, 255

machine learning 56, 168, 255
mathematics 14, 15, 19, 20, 42, 83, 101, 108, 109, 145, 150, 151
mediation 6, 11, 14, 21–3, 90, 139, 141, 145, 145, 150, 165, 166, 172
Mercer 1, 4, 5, 10, 12, 14–16, 28–31, 33, 36, 37, 40, 54–6, 59, 65, 77, 78, 83, 95, 97, 98, 100, 119, 137, 141, 170, 178, 180, 182, 213, 231
Merleau-Ponty 12, 17, 24, 184
meso-analytic approach 24, 104, 106, 107, 152, 184, 242, 255
meta-discourse 55, 148, 149
metaphor 38–41, 68, 69, 153, 176
micro-analytic approach 67, 95, 99, 104–7, 129, 152, 180, 239, 242, 255
micro-ethnographic 239, 255
mixed-methods 54, 162

monologic 11, 17–20, 22–6, 28, 51, 99
multiculturalism 206
multidisciplinarity 239, 240
multimedia 141, 146, 147, 174, 185, 194
multimodal 4, 6, 66, 70, 77, 89, 102, 129, 136, 138–40, 142, 151, 152, 154, 158, 162, 165–72, 191, 219, 231
multiple regression analysis 85, 256
multi-voice/multi-voiced analysis 6, 169, 170, 256

narrative accounts 99, 146, 216
narrative analysis 99, 218, 237
network analysis 56, 100, 101, 254, 257, 258
neuroscience 201
nonverbal 171
noticing 67, 69, 221
Nystrand 104, 105, 124, 133, 168, 179

objectifying 17, 26, 35, 185
observation method 53, 78, 82, 85, 146, 158, 237, 256
observer effects 229, 256
online dialogue 2, 6, 23, 51, 62, 65, 91, 149, 155, 157, 159, 168, 173, 174, 176, 191, 192, 194, 195
online ethnography 176, 178
ontological 11–13, 23, 31–3, 256
opening 13, 94, 203, 248, 249
open-source 99, 101, 153, 254
oracy 4, 22, 78, 79, 82, 83, 92, 94
orientations 2, 17, 18, 20, 27, 31, 34, 35, 37, 38, 40–2, 53, 71, 104, 123, 126, 128, 140, 201, 253

paradigms 23, 207
participatory action research 62, 207, 238, 241, 256
partnerships 49, 237
phenomenology 145, 185
philosophy for children 2, 10, 36, 38, 40, 154, 155, 206, 208, 212, 214, 216
positivism 26
pre- and post-test design 39, 55, 84, 256, 257
problem-solving 15, 57, 86, 121, 123, 140, 150, 179, 201, 205, 206, 208, 210, 215, 239, 241
prosody 55, 56, 165, 188
provisionality 152, 155, 160

qualitative data analysis 24, 53, 56, 60, 63, 99, 100, 102, 128, 133, 138, 139, 146, 162, 165, 170, 176, 178, 179, 181, 190, 193, 204, 207, 208, 212, 213, 225, 255, 256, 258
quantitative data analysis 19, 24, 53, 56, 60, 63, 100, 138, 170, 179, 181, 187, 192, 193, 204, 208, 212, 213, 252, 254, 256, 258
quantitative ethnography 24, 100, 254, 256
quasi-experimental trials 55, 179, 257
questioning 5, 12, 39, 43, 51, 53, 76, 93, 128
questionnaires 55, 58, 63, 83, 84, 93, 211, 217, 241

rating scale 79, 82, 83, 85–7, 99, 106, 107, 216, 257
Raven's progressive matrices test 34, 59, 257
real-world research 230, 231, 257

reasoning 14, 15, 29–31, 34, 36–41, 44, 45, 49, 50, 54, 76, 83, 86, 102, 105, 106, 108, 119–21, 123, 125, 127–9, 131, 136, 141, 150, 160, 162, 182, 218, 226, 254
reasoning talk 36, 38, 40, 41, 106, 128, 141, 182
reasoning test 34, 39, 83, 182
reciprocity 101, 237
reflection 11, 49, 53, 56, 60, 121, 138, 149, 178, 189, 190, 200, 206, 237, 247, 249, 251, 257
reflective 43, 49, 53, 61, 71, 72, 149, 150, 154, 155, 205, 208, 211, 215–17, 219, 237, 250, 252, 257
reflective dialogue 43, 61, 149, 205, 211, 215–17, 219, 250, 252, 257
reflexive 70
regression analyses 85, 97, 119, 256, 257
relevance 3, 16, 26, 46, 109, 222, 226, 250, 257
reliability 6, 77, 84, 90, 91, 105, 106, 108, 109, 127, 131, 257
reliable 86, 106, 108, 131, 134
resonance 6, 31, 38–41, 61
reversibility 24
rigour 49, 84, 99, 149, 191, 233
Rojas-Drummond 15, 38–40, 53, 103, 162, 179, 180

Säljö 139, 239
segmentation 105, 109, 152, 258
small-group 169, 171, 175
social cohesion 202, 212
social network analysis 101, 258
sociocultural 12, 14, 15, 53, 54, 56, 83, 95, 135, 198, 200, 213, 231, 234, 235, 258

sociocultural discourse analysis (SDA) 15, 54, 56, 95, 213, 231, 258
stance 19, 23, 24, 51, 70, 99, 131, 145, 176, 185, 254
standardized test 63, 257
statistical 24, 25, 53, 56, 93, 97, 99, 100, 108, 119, 163, 168, 176, 181, 182, 185–8, 191, 248, 253, 255–7
stimulated recall analysis 24, 139, 148–50, 171, 185, 218, 220, 258
student voice 4, 57, 58, 134, 234, 235, 237, 238, 258
symbols 58, 107, 166, 252
synchronous 96, 138, 171
systematic observation 53, 55, 96, 212, 258

tablets 140, 151
Teacher-SEDA 89, 119
team-blogging 187–91
technology-enhanced learning 119, 135, 148, 170, 172
technology-mediated dialogue 3, 4, 65, 67, 119, 135, 137, 138, 148, 163, 169–72
Tech-SEDA 119, 163, 165
temporal 55, 66, 98–101, 178
thematic analysis 106, 139, 145, 224, 258
think-aloud protocols 55, 139, 150, 171, 258
Thinking Together 36–9
time sampling 119, 150, 258
T-MEDIA 145–7, 153, 169
transactive 97, 100, 111, 121, 123–8
transcription 56, 96, 97, 153, 165, 166, 168, 181, 241
transdisciplinary 241

triangulation 215
types of talk 5, 28–31, 33, 35–8,
    40–3, 48, 54, 61
typology 121, 160

unit of analysis 64, 104, 109, 153,
    254, 258
utterance/utterances 6, 10, 11, 16,
    31, 32, 37, 42, 46, 76, 83, 95,
    96, 98, 103–5, 108, 110, 111,
    115, 125, 173–7, 179, 180,
    191, 249, 252, 253, 255

validation 77, 85, 88, 93, 259
validity (measurement) 92,
    109, 259
validity (research) 13, 77, 79, 91,
    92, 149, 203, 259
values 55, 58, 62, 131, 194, 198,
    200, 217, 230, 235–8, 252
vicarious participation 18, 34, 173,
    174, 179, 249

video 24, 34, 53, 58, 61, 67, 77–9,
    96, 97, 100, 110, 124, 139,
    144–8, 150, 153, 166, 167,
    169, 171, 174, 177, 181–3,
    203, 206, 208, 211, 213,
    215–17, 222, 253, 258
videoconferencing 186, 187
virtuality 20, 51, 52, 127, 128,
    194, 237
visual representations 70, 96, 101,
    140, 160, 166, 168, 194, 237,
    252, 253, 257, 258
vocalization 21, 153
Vygotsky 14, 15, 44, 45, 183, 184,
    194, 195, 242

Wells 10, 55, 98, 102–4, 138,
    140, 193

zone of proximal development
    (ZPD) 15, 195